This book
was placed in
your library
by
The Commission
on the
Bicentennial
of the
United States
Constitution

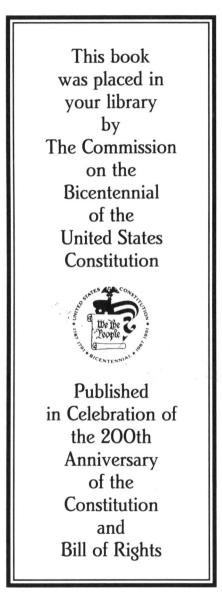

Published
in Celebration of
the 200th
Anniversary
of the
Constitution
and
Bill of Rights

Books by Jeffrey St. John

Countdown to Chaos
Noble Metals
Day of the Cobra
Constitutional Journal
Landmarks 1765–1990
A Child of Fortune

FORGE OF UNION
ANVIL OF LIBERTY

FORGE OF UNION
ANVIL OF LIBERTY

*A Correspondent's Report on
the First Federal Elections,
the First Federal Congress,
and the Bill of Rights*

Jeffrey St. John

Foreword by
Warren E. Burger

Jameson Books, Inc.
Ottawa, Illinois

Jameson Books are available at special discounts for bulk purchases for sales promotions, premiums, fundraising or educational use. Special condensed or excerpted editions can also be created to customer specification.

For information and catalog requests write:

Jameson Books, Inc.
P.O. Box 738
Ottawa, IL 61350

815-434-7905

8 7 6 5 4 3 2 1 95 94 93 92

Printed in the United States of America

Distributed to the book trade by National Book Network, Lanham, MD.

ISBN: 0-915463-62-8

Library of Congress Cataloging-in-Publication Data

St. John, Jeffrey.
      Forge of union, anvil of liberty: a correspondent's report on the first federal elections, the first federal Congress, and the Bill of Rights/ Jeffrey St. John; foreword by Warren E. Burger.
         p. cm.
      Includes bibliographical references and index.
      ISBN 0-915463-62-8: $24.95
      1. United States—Politics and government—1783–1789. 2. United States—Politics and government—1789–1797. 3. United States—Constitution—Amendments—1st–10th. 4. United States—Constitutional history. I. Title.
      E303.S79 1992   92–6343
      973.4'1—dc20   CIP

To Kathryn,
who would be
liberated
in any age

In our progress towards political happiness
my station is new; and, if I may use the
expression, I walk on untrodden ground.
There is scarcely any part of my conduct
wch. may not hereafter be drawn into precedent.

President George Washington
January 9, 1790

*To a friend eight months after being sworn in
as the first President of the United States*

CONTENTS

FOREWORD

★

This volume completes Jeffrey St. John's trilogy on the origins of our national government, from the first day of the Constitutional Convention in 1787 through the formation of the first federal government in 1789. In these three volumes, Mr. St. John has condensed an enormous amount of history in a concise and easy-to-read format. The Commission on the Bicentennial of the United States Constitution gave its support to the publication of these books and has placed them in schools, colleges, and public libraries throughout the United States and abroad.

In this, the third and final volume in the series, the author traces the formation of the first federal government. Using the narrative technique of a newspaper correspondent, he takes us from July 1788, shortly after the adoption of the Constitution had been secured in the New Hampshire Ratification Convention, through the death of Benjamin Franklin in April 1790, when, with the fledgling federal government in place, the nation embarked on a journey that has continued to the present day.

In 1789 President-elect Washington's own journey by coach from Mount Vernon to New York for his inauguration aroused widespread public attention and did much to develop a national spirit in support of the Constitution. Following his inauguration on April 30, 1789, Washington faced the important task of assembling the executive branch and making appointments to the judiciary. In many ways, the federal government still had to be invented. Although the Constitution set forth the basic framework of government, there were various ways in which that framework might have been implemented and, unlike his successors, Washington had no set pattern to follow.

By virtue of his vast experience, including his leadership during the Revolutionary War and his prominent role as President of the Constitutional Convention, Washington was familiar with many of the leading figures of the day. He drew on this knowledge in forming the first Cabinet, and appointed Thomas Jefferson Secretary of State, Alexander Hamilton Secretary of the Treasury, Henry Knox Secretary of War, and Edmund Randolph Attorney General. In modern terms, Washington's first cabinet might be viewed as a "coalition cabinet." While Jefferson and Randolph were somewhat skeptical of the new federal government and, in particular, the shift in power from the state to the national level, Hamilton and Knox were firmly behind the enterprise. The opposing points of view held by these men and others like them had not yet given rise to political parties, but soon would with the emergence of the Jeffersonian Republicans in the 1790s.

The respective roles of the executive and legislative branches were also not fully understood at the outset. The experiences of various state governments provided some insight into the difficulties that could potentially arise, but Washington sought to avoid tensions wherever possible by keeping the legislative branch at arm's length. Rather than embroil himself in the affairs of the Congress, he left the business of legislation largely up to the legislators, and focused on matters that were clearly within his sphere of authority. During this formative period, the most significant accomplishment of the Congress was the approval of the Bill of Rights on September 25, 1789, and its subsequent submission to the States for ratification. The author's narrative shows how important the adoption of the first ten amendments was to popular acceptance of the new government and it also makes clear James Madison's central role in that adoption.

Finally, Washington faced the difficult task of appointing qualified individuals to the federal judiciary and, in particular, the Supreme Court. Under the Judiciary Act of 1789, Justices of the Supreme Court were required to "ride circuit" twice a year—making vast journeys around different parts of the country to serve as trial and appellate judges. Moreover, the judicial branch had no clear antecedent, since there had been no national judiciary at all under the Articles of Confederation, and even informed observers were uncertain how important—or unimportant—a role the federal courts would ultimately play in the new national government.

Although it was not easy to persuade some individuals to accept the heavy burdens that Supreme Court work entailed, Washington was quite successful in his recruiting efforts, and the Supreme Court was established under the firm stewardship of Chief Justice John Jay, who served as President of the Continental Congress and had been a contributor to *The Federalist Papers*.

It is our sincere hope that this volume, in conjunction with the two volumes that preceded it, will be widely read, especially by students. In retelling the important and colorful history of our nation's founding, these books will help to ensure that the central goal of the Bicentennial Commission—"a history and civics lesson for all of us"—is fulfilled for generations to come.

Warren E. Burger

Washington, D.C.
January 1992

PREFACE

★

A Republic in the Wilderness

In 1789 the American population of 3.9 million lived in or on the fringes of a vast forest wilderness. A French traveler observed that "the entire country is one vast wood." Not only was America rudely rural; it was also rustic. Almost everything required for survival was by necessity homemade, except in the heart of the large towns and the few cities spread out along the Atlantic coastline and on the shores of a few rivers.

The vast American wilderness and the great geographical distances within the thirteen Colonies proved to be one of the principal reasons that the British failed to defeat the inferior military forces of General George Washington before France became the colonists' military ally. British forces during the eight-year War of Independence held only the port cities of New York and Charleston, lacking the resources and manpower to control the other cities and towns spread from New England to the southern Colonies.

It was also the great distances and bad roads (or, more accurately, rutted wagon and horse trails) between Boston, New York, Philadelphia, Baltimore, and Charleston in the 1780s that contributed to the failure of the Articles of Confederation, the first constitution of the newly independent States. Chronic absenteeism by members of the Confederation (or Continental) Congress, which sat in New York City, was due to poor traveling conditions and inclement weather, which resulted in delay in calling quorums and in deadlocks over vital issues since the Confederation Congress was the sole governing body for the confederated States. This record of inaction gave powerful impetus to creating the U.S. Constitution and a new form of government.

Critics of the new Constitution maintained that the great distances and the slow if not impossible communications between the seat of the national government and the governed would mean that freedoms would be sacrificed to tyranny in order to command obedience to the laws of the land. Initially, the critics seemed to have been proved correct when the First Congress was a month late in convening with a quorum because of bad weather and poor traveling conditions.

The New Beginning

Geography was only one of a number of formidable obstacles faced in 1789 by the men who created, ratified, and implemented the U.S. Constitution. In a real sense, the document was born in the caldron of the American Revolution and went on to serve as the forge of the American Union, with the Bill of Rights becoming the anvil for individual liberties.

The American Revolution came to a successful conclusion when the confederated States joined to become a Union of States with ratification of the new Constitution and when the first Federal elections were held in the fall of 1788 and the winter of 1789, as mandated by the newly ratified Constitution. Phenomenally, just thirteen years after the Colonies had issued their Declaration of Independence from Great Britain, there took place the elections of George Washington as President, John Adams as Vice President, and members of the First Congress.

The era of the Federal American Republic commenced when the new Congress met in New York in April 1789 for its first legislative deliberations and remained in session through September. During these six months, the foundation for the American system of government was formed.

History provided no examples and no political theory existed in the 1780s that offered any hope that a republican form of government, based on the new concept of consent of the governed, could succeed on a wilderness continent larger than any European state except Russia, which was governed in 1789 by the autocratic Empress Catherine the Great.

Act Three of the Constitutional Drama

The making and ratification of the U.S. Constitution were the first two acts of an epic political drama. The author has told this story in two previously published volumes, written in a news story style as though he were a journalist at the 1787 Philadelphia Constitutional Convention and later at the twelve State Ratifying Conventions held between fall 1787 and summer 1788 (Rhode Island held no ratifying convention).

This third and final volume describes the crucial third act of the American constitutional drama: the translation of the document from words on parchment to institutional form and structure. Besides contributing concrete form to the new national government, the First Congress debated and approved in September 1789 a bill of rights and sent it to the States for ratification. Those ten amendments became part of the Constitution on December 15, 1791.

The Bill of Rights was the culmination of a fierce political struggle that had been waged by critics of the Constitution from the time it emerged from the secret Philadelphia Convention held during the summer of 1787. A majority of delegates at the convention, many of them lawyers, refused to consider a bill of rights because they believed it was unnecessary. The Constitution limited the powers of the new national government, they believed, to those specifically stated in the document and individual freedoms were adequately protected by the States' constitutions. Federalists like James Madison were soon shocked to discover that people in the separate States were prepared to reject ratification of the Constitution if the document remained unamended.

Madison, the Master Politician

Anti-Federalists such as Patrick Henry forced Federalists, particularly James Madison, to concede that without the promise of amendments that would restrain the powers of the new national government, the Constitution would have failed to achieve ratification in the key states of Virginia and Massachusetts.

During the first Federal election campaign, the issue of amendments played a decisive role in some congressional races. For example, in the campaign for a Virginia House seat, James Madison won against Anti-Federalist James Monroe principally because he publicly pledged to work for the enactment of a bill of rights in the First Congress.

James Madison proved to be a masterful politician during his four-month ordeal to have Congress enact a Federal bill of rights. He successfully defeated efforts by allies of Patrick Henry to enact amendments that would have crippled the powers of the new government. Yet in order to have Congress accept amendments, he had to push and pull his Federalist allies, who either were apathetic, or opposed outright any amendments. He also had to defeat efforts to have debated some 200 amendments submitted by the States.

James Madison's political dexterity is illustrated by how he handled demands of Anti-Federalists for a total constitutional ban on a peacetime professional army. By offering the Second Amendment, giving citizens the right to keep and bear arms, and the Third Amendment, banning the quartering of troops in private homes in peacetime and requiring a law to do so in wartime, he provided practical and yet politically acceptable checks on the abuse and danger of a domestic professional military.

Creed of Compromise

Just as the Constitution was the product of compromise, the Bill of Rights that James Madison floor-managed through the House was also the product of the same process of compromise that has continued to determine our national political creed for two centuries.

When the Bill of Rights went to the Senate, Congressman Madison was bitterly disappointed that the upper house killed a provision that would have made the Bill of Rights applicable to the individual States by overriding the constitutions of the various States.

One can feel the weariness in Madison's words when writing of his ordeal of steering the Bill of Rights through Congress; he noted that "the difficulty of uniting the minds of men accustomed to think and act differently can only be conceived by those who witnessed it."

Patrick Henry, who with others had demanded a bill of rights as the price for ratification of the Constitution, was equally bitter over the Bill of Rights sent to the States. The former Virginia Governor thought it "would do more harm than benefit." What he wanted were amendments that drastically curbed the powers of the three branches of the new national government and left the separate States politically supreme and independent. Instead, the document focused almost exclusively on personal rights, most of which had already been established in the American and English experience, and left virtually untouched the power of the new national government.

Credit for the Bill of Rights

The Bill of Rights owes its existence as much to Patrick Henry as to James Madison. Without the pressure from former Governor Henry at the Virginia Ratifying Convention, and from his supporters later in Congress, it is doubtful that the United States would have had a Federal Bill of Rights in its present form.

Paradoxically, neither Patrick Henry nor Congressman Madison had a burning zeal to provide a bill of rights, whereas their fellow Virginian, Colonel George Mason, did. He was the first to propose such a bill at the Philadelphia Convention only to have it rejected — setting the stage for the fierce ratification debates in the States. Both Madison and Henry had their own political reasons for supporting amendments, which the reader will discover as the drama unfolds.

The purpose of a bill of rights in the late 1780s was to appease the critics of the Constitution, who opposed a central government, and to create a political consensus in the country. Yet it was the first step in defining the future American political division: Federal power versus State independence. It is a debate that continues to the present.

Untrodden Ground

The importance of the first Federal elections, the First Congress, and the first months of George Washington's administration was that altogether they defined the American Republic. What was done in the eighteen months that are covered in this volume would cast a long shadow over the future of the United States. President Washington was well aware of this when, after his swearing in, he wrote, "I walk on untrodden ground," and observed that his conduct as America's first elected executive would establish precedents for the future. As indeed it did.

It was similar for the First Congress. In fact, the multitude of issues the First Congress had to confront is reflected in the first decades of the American Union's experience. The possibility of secession of dissatisfied States, for example, confronted the First Congress; North Carolina and Rhode Island had not yet joined the Union; whereas Vermont and Kentucky, caught up in the cross currents of Indian and international conflicts, sought admission as new States.

Perhaps the most dangerous problem facing President Washington and the First Congress was the presence of Spain and Great Britain on America's southern and western frontiers. Spain had closed the Mississippi River to U.S. navigational trade and the British had shut the St. Lawrence River to American trade. Both European powers used native Indian tribes to attack American frontier settlers. These acts were viewed by the Federal government as perilous to its future, particularly since it still had a swollen domestic and foreign war debt and lacked the funds to maintain an army.

In 1789 the debt stood at the staggering sum of $79 million. The fate of the Constitution and the existence of the new national government depended on how these financial obligations would be met.

Future Beyond the Frontier

President Washington and members of the First Congress, with a few dissenting exceptions, were convinced that the future of the American Republic was to be found in the Indian-occupied forests and plains on either side of the Mississippi River. The sale of western public lands to American settlers, along with an increase of trade abroad, was viewed as a means to reduce, or pay off, the national debt. An American frontier inflamed by Indian wars, fueled by foreign powers, represented a clear and present peril to America's future.

For this fundamental reason, almost 80 percent of the initiatives President Washington submitted to the First Congress related to western issues, particularly those covering Indian and military affairs. Because he had been a land surveyor and a veteran of the French–Indian Wars, President Washington approached western issues with greater confidence than he demonstrated with other issues.

On the debt issues, for example, President Washington did not pretend an understanding but left them largely with Secretary of the Treasury Alexander Hamilton. The President was deeply distressed when his Treasury Secretary's proposals to fund the debt kindled a lengthy firestorm of congressional debate. Those proposals also proved to be the prelude to the historic political conflict between Alexander Hamilton and Thomas Jefferson. In the wake of that conflict were formed the first political parties: the Federalists (Hamilton) and the Republicans (Jefferson).

Defining the Political Future

A principal disagreement between Hamilton and Jefferson was over the French Revolution, which broke out in Paris in summer 1789 while the first U.S. Congress was laboring to lay the foundation for the new national American government. President Washington was among the first to grasp the destructive potential of the French Revolution, notwithstanding the fact that the American War owed much to France for its success and, in turn, had fueled the French cry for freedom from monarchical control.

We now know what George Washington only surmised in the fall of 1789: the French Revolution was to take a path radically different from, and far more destructive and bloody than, that of the American Revolution. We also know that the French Revolution would influence and define the politics of Europe and Latin America during much of the nineteenth century and the early decades of the twentieth. Lenin would emulate the French Revolution in his 1917 bloody seizure of power and with the establishment of the Soviet Union.

In a very real sense, the fears and warnings of the American founding generation of the consequences of unchecked and centralized political power became a nightmare reality with the establishments in Europe nearly two centuries later of Nazi, Fascist, and Communist totalitarian regimes.

It remains a moot question whether George Washington would have approved of America's involvement in four armed conflicts on foreign soil in this century alone. It is also a moot point whether he and other Founding Fathers would have approved of the creation of a vast American military establishment to contain Communism for over four decades.

Ironically, the collapse of the Soviet system in Russia and in Eastern Europe in the late 1980s occurred during the bicentennial of the creation, ratification, and implementation of the Constitution of the United States of America. This paradoxical development raises two important questions: Has the pernicious influence of the French Revolution finally come to an end? Is the beneficial influence of the American Revolution now spreading worldwide?

When George Washington enunciated his famous phrase to stay clear of "foreign entanglements," he did so as the President of an infant Republic that was weak politically, economically, and militarily, and when the French Revolution was proving disruptive in the 1790s to the politics of the country in much the same way that Communism proved disruptive to American politics in this century.

By remaining neutral during the Reign of Terror of the French Revolution and the Napoleonic dictatorships and wars for the first twenty years of the American Republic, the United States not only acquired from France the Louisiana Purchase at a bargain price but also was given the necessary time to allow the novel ship of state to have a successful trial run without crashing on the reefs of disaster, which President Washington clearly saw as a possibility.

"Sure I am," he wrote, "if this country is preserved in tranquility twenty years longer, it may bid defiance in a just cause to any power whatever; such in that time will be its population, wealth and resources."

This volume is not a definitive report of the first Federal elections and the establishment of the national government. Rather, it is a report on the political process that defined America's future and briefly covers the evolution — despite all of America's real and imagined shortcomings viewed from the perspective of the 1990s — of a nation in a way radically different from that of Europe and the rest of the world. Perhaps in understanding the founding process, the reader may come to understand how the United States of America evolved from an infant Republic on a wilderness continent to a world power in less than two centuries.

Occasionally the reader will notice an unusual spelling or contraction. The author has preserved the original text (appearing within quotes), even when misspellings may have occurred in the original.

Roanoke Station
Randolph, Virginia

ACKNOWLEDGMENTS

★

Although the research and writing of this work were a solitary effort, many minds and hands helped along the way.

The author wishes to express his most expansive appreciation to Warren E. Burger, retired Chief Justice of the United States Supreme Court. His support as chairman of the Commission on the Bicentennial of the United States Constitution and the Bill of Rights during the writing of this volume, and his support of the previous two books, as well as writing forewords to all three works, must stand as a record for steadfast support of a work of history by a public official.

Indebtedness is also due the Commission's staff director, Dr. Herbert H. Atherton, who not only provided constant encouragement, but as a former Yale scholar also offered germane and important criticisms of the initial draft and in the process provided greater depth and breadth for the third volume.

Equally helpful were the critiques and comments of four academics who were among those who served as members of the Commission on the Bicentennial: Harry M. Lightsey, Jr., President, College of Charleston; Thomas H. O'Connor, Professor of History, Boston College; Bernard H. Siegan, Professor of Law, University of San Diego Law School; and Charles Alan Wright, Professor of Law, University of Texas Law School.

As with the previous two volumes, Dr. Forrest McDonald, University of Alabama, reviewed this volume and his suggestions were as indispensable as they were invaluable. His ten published books on the American Founding period were for the author a primary education, particularly his seminal and perceptive *Novus Ordo Seclorum: The Intellectual Origins of the Constitution* (Lawrence:

xxix

University Press of Kansas, 1985). Dr. McDonald's blend of scholarship and realistic perception of the politics of the eighteenth century is what makes all his works unique.

Two newspaper editors deserve the author's appreciation for publishing excerpts of selected parts of this work: Roderick Nordell of the *Christian Science Monitor* and Rich Martin, deputy managing editor of the *Roanoke Times & World News*, Roanoke, Virginia.

Two college libraries, critical in my researching the first two volumes, were equally crucial in the research of this volume: one is the Joseph duPuy Eggleston Library, Hampden-Sydney College, Hampden-Sydney, Virginia. Hampden-Sydney College was founded in 1776 and two of its founders were James Madison and Patrick Henry. The other is the Dabney S. Lancaster Library, Longwood College, Farmville, Virginia.

My sole associate in this work, as well as the entire trilogy, was my wife, Kathryn Boggs St. John, who has added clarity and accuracy by her editing and her sharp eye in the manuscript preparation and the verification of all quotes and sources. I am deeply grateful and fortunate, for she has enjoyed as much as I becoming acquainted with our Founders — Federalists and Anti-Federalists alike — whom we now consider our friends.

CHAPTER 1

★

July 4, 1788

Pageant Marks Independence
Federalists Eye Elections

Sunrise cannon shot and the peeling of bells at Christ Church signaled the start of a lavish day-long procession through the narrow cobblestone streets of Philadelphia to celebrate a dozen years of American independence and last month's ratification of the new Constitution.[1]

The patriotic pageant also signaled the start of a Federalist campaign to sweep the first national elections mandated by the document. Federalist leaders concede that some of the same issues debated during the bitter ten-month ratification struggle are likely to resurface in the coming election campaign for control of the new government.

Sounds of the cannon salute from the sloop *Rising Sun*, moored in the Delaware River, had hardly faded away when ten nearby ships ran up on their masts white pennants with the names, in gold letters, of the States that had ratified the Constitution.[2]

Late last month, exhausted mounted express riders brought the news that New Hampshire, in the North, had become on June 21 the necessary ninth State to give the new Constitution legal life. From the South came the news that on June 25 powerful, populous, and all-important Virginia had by ten votes become the tenth State to approve the document.[3] (Without Virginia's approval, General George Washington, a resident of that State, could not be considered as a nominee for President.)

1

Bounty from Ballots

Philadelphia's Federalists decided that they would turn their planned Fourth of July celebration into the most elaborate and expensive public pageant ever — with one eye toward luring the seat of the new national government away from New York City, and the other eye on the first Federal elections for President, Vice President, and House and Senate seats.

James Wilson, Scots-born Pennsylvania Signer of the Declaration and the new Constitution, told a capacity crowd gathered on the city green, renamed "Union Green" for the occasion, that the benefits expected to flow from the Constitution would not become a reality unless each person regarded his vote as crucial in the forthcoming first Federal elections.

"Let no one say," Mr. Wilson, with a pronounced burr, told the sea of upturned faces, "that he is but a single citizen; and that his ticket will be but one in the box. That one ticket may turn the election. In battle, every soldier should consider the public safety as depending on his single arm. At an election, every citizen should consider the public happiness as depending on his single vote." [4]

The Federalist election themes appeared in today's procession of elaborate floats and 5,000 marching participants, extending for a mile and a half through the city and, according to organizers, taking over three hours to pass by viewers. An estimated 17,000 spectators, half the population of the port city of Philadelphia, lined the narrow city streets, stood at open windows or on rooftops to watch the horse-drawn floats that depicted the last dozen years of American history — from the Declaration to the new Constitution. [5]

The most spectacular float of the procession was the "Grand Fœderal Edifice" drawn by ten white horses. Standing some thirty-six feet high, it consisted of a domed building made of painted papier-mâché and was supported by thirteen Corinthian columns. Three columns remained incomplete to symbolize that New York, North Carolina, and Rhode Island have not yet ratified the Constitution. [6]

Republic's "New Roof "

Mounted militia and military units afoot stepped smartly to fife and drum playing a specially composed "Federal March." They were joined by parading merchants, tradesmen, mechanics, craftsmen, and representatives of over a dozen other manual trades to demonstrate their belief that "IN UNION THE FABRIC STANDS FIRM."[7]
The Constitution is a "New Roof" for the infant Republic that will shelter all, insist many parade officials, in safety, happiness, and prosperity. Especially if bricklayers and carpenters who marched in today's parade should participate in the physical construction of buildings for the new national government in Philadelphia, where the Declaration was signed and the new Constitution debated, drafted, and signed.

Francis Hopkinson, poet, Signer of the Declaration, and one of the main planners of today's procession, penned "The New Roof" as a metaphor for the Constitution. It would, he writes, replace the rotting and leaky shingles represented by the Articles of Confederation. In another piece, "The Raising: A New Song for Federal Mechanics," he placed emphasis on the democracy of the document:

> COME muster, my lads, your mechanical tools,
> Your saws and your axes, your hammers and rules;
> Bring your mallets and planes, your level and line,
> And plenty of pins of American pine:
> *For our roof we will raise, and our song still shall be,*
> *Our government firm, and our citizens free.*[8]

Pageant of Past, Present, and Future

Every business, trade, and occupation was represented in the seemingly endless stream of marchers and floats. The past was represented by horse-drawn floats depicting Independence, the French Alliance, the Constitutional Convention, and the Federal Roof.

The future was represented by the Manufacturing Society's float, the huge wagon covered with cotton cloth of its own make. Many spectators were puzzled by the new inventions on the wagon. This correspondent was told they are lace loom, a printing mill, and a carding machine and a spinning jenny of eighty spindles for the mass production of cotton cloth.[9]

The greatest cheers went up from the crowd when the "Federal Ship *Union*" came into view. On the foreheads of the ten horses drawing the float was painted the name of a ratifying State. The float was built in only four days, its wheels and machinery hidden under a sheet of canvas painted by the portrait artist Charles Willson Peale. The bottom of the "ship" was the barge taken from the *Serapis*, which had been captured by American naval hero John Paul Jones.[10]

Behind a troop of light dragoons and a colorful collection of emblematic flags came the "Constitution" float mounted on a light blue carriage. Twenty feet long with rear wheels eight feet in diameter, and decorated with Liberty Caps, the float displayed a framed copy of the Constitution mounted over a painted banner proclaiming "The People." In the center of the float stood a thirteen-foot-high eagle emblazoned with thirteen silver stars in a field of blue, the eagle's talons gripping an olive branch and thirteen arrows.[11]

Following the "Constitution" float was Grand Marshal Francis Hopkinson leading a long line of city and State politicians and members of diplomatic corps. A printer's float was producing fresh copies of the "Ode" the politician-poet had composed for the parade, printers flinging them to the crowds as they passed. Carrier pigeons were released with toasts of the day and the "Ode" for delivery to the ten ratifying States, which read:

> Hail to this festival!—all hail the day!
> Columbia's standard on her roof display!
> And let the people's motto ever be,
> "United thus, and thus united, free!"[12]

Sober Toasts — Sign from Heavens

When the last of the procession had reached Union Green, dinner was served to the 17,000 souls who were not too exhausted to eat and to join in the ten toasts to the new Union with American porter, beer, and cider. In the shade of the floats "Grand Fœderal Edifice" and "Federal Ship *Union*," thousands of cups filled with cider were raised as each toast was offered at a trumpet blast. Each was answered by ten artillery salutes and repeated by the sloop *Rising Sun* at her moorings in the Philadelphia harbor.

"To the people of the United States," went the first of the ten full-throated toasts; the concluding one: "To the whole family of mankind." [13]

Mr. Hopkinson said later that as the clock in the Philadelphia State House struck six, the 17,000 celebrants "*soberly* retired to their respective homes." [14]

As bonfires illuminated the streets, the sky shone bright and beautiful with the appearance of the aurora borealis. For many this is a sign that the heavens look with favor on what has gone on before and what is yet to come. [15]

One observer has told this correspondent that today's procession employed for the first time on a massive scale poets, painters, actors, and musicians in the services of a national political celebration and forthcoming election. Dr. Benjamin Rush, Signer of the Declaration and one of the key sponsors of the pageant, confirms that today's procession was deliberately staged to form a long historical link between liberty and the arts in the minds of those who watched and who are expected to vote in the first Federal elections this fall.

"The connection," the prominent and pioneering Philadelphia physician observes, "of the great event of independence, the French alliance, the Peace, and name of General Washington with the adoption of the Constitution was happily calculated to unite the most remarkable transports of the mind which were felt during the war with the great event of the day, and to produce such a tide of joy as has seldom been felt in any age or country. Political joy is one of the strongest emotions of the human mind." [16]

Politics of Protest

A decidedly different July 4 celebration was held in the central Pennsylvania town of Carlisle, stronghold of Anti-Federalist foes of the new Constitution. Militia units drawn up in the town square discharged a volley for each of thirteen toasts offered. One toast called for amendments to "be speedily framed, and unanimously adopted, as may render the proposed Constitution for the United States truly democratical." [17]

During the just-concluded ratification struggle in key States, the issue of amendments — demanded by critics of the Constitution in the form of a bill of rights — forced Federalists to promise consideration of amendments or face defeat in the ratification conventions.

Observers predicted to this correspondent that during the forthcoming first Federal elections, candidates for Congress will be supported or attacked solely on their stands on the issue of amendments. [18]

Celebrants at the Carlisle July 4 rally rejected the idea put forth by Dr. Benjamin Rush that the new Constitution represents a continuation of the American Revolution. Rather, as many of the thirteen toasts indicated, the document is viewed as a repudiation of the Revolution since it consolidates power in a centralized government with control over the separate States that had jointly waged the War of Independence for the preservation of local liberties. Only the adoption of a bill of rights, the Anti-Federalists argue, that curbs the power of the new national government can check this potential tyranny. [19]

"May America remain forever free from tyranny, anarchy, and consolidation," rang out the thirteenth and final toast in Carlisle, Pennsylvania, followed by the militia's firing three musket volleys. [20]

Later the *Pennsylvania Chronicle* mocked the Anti-Federalist celebrants by insisting the volleys would have "astonished" the generals of Prussia: "The great misfortune that attended them was, they could not muster *cash* for more than three rounds. Oh poverty! thou curse of curses." [21]

Power Will Be Election Issue

Behind that printed barb is the reality that during the last ten months of the ratification battle in State conventions, Anti-Federalists have had none of the resources that their Federalist opponents have had. The well-financed and elaborately staged Philadelphia pageant, compared with the austere Carlisle Anti-Federalist celebration, is only one illustration. The same handicap will be faced by the Anti-Federalists in the upcoming Federal elections.

One observer has noted that no other issue raised by the Anti-Federalists has struck a more responsive chord and proved more popular than that of demands for amendments in the form of a bill of rights. Although Federalists view the demands as efforts to emasculate the Constitution, during ratification conventions they agreed to consider amendments but no promises were made about concerns relating to the powers of the new national government.[22] The powers of the government will be an important issue in the upcoming first Federal elections.

A Rum Riot in Albany

North Carolina, which will hold a ratifying convention later this month, is expected to demand a bill of rights. The issue of amendments has also preoccupied New York's ratifying convention delegates, who are meeting in the capital, Poughkeepsie, but who are taking a one-day recess for a friendly July 4 celebration. According to one observer, Federalists and Anti-Federalists alike gave dinners and mingled with one another to toast the twelfth year of American independence.[23]

In sharp contrast, early reports from Albany, New York, tell of a July 4 celebration marked by violence and bloodshed. One observer states that Anti-Federalists paraded into the heart of the city and watched with approval as a copy of the Constitution was burned. Federalists retrieved the charred document and began parading up the streets only to encounter an angry Anti-Federalist crowd. The resulting riot left eighteen injured. An Anti-Federalist leader blamed both sides, charging each with having more rum than reason.[24]

Responsible leaders on both sides hope that the Albany riot is an isolated incident and not a forecast of future explosions of political passions over the new Constitution.

CHAPTER 2

★

July 5–31, 1788

Attack on Powers to Tax
Seen As Conspiracy to Destroy Constitution

Virginia Congressman James Madison has alleged that a "conspiracy" has been hatched by enemies of the newly ratified Constitution to "destroy and discredit" the document in a drive to preserve the powers of the individual States.

The 37-year-old Federalist leader from Virginia returned to New York and his seat in the Continental Congress this month to assume a leading role in the forthcoming Federal elections. Congress must first pass an ordinance setting a date for the election of President and Vice President. Following that, the individual State Legislatures will determine their own dates for congressional elections.

Federalists are hailing Mr. Madison for answering clearly and logically each disputed issue and thereby achieving the June 25 narrow victory over Patrick Henry at the Virginia Ratifying Convention held in Richmond.[1] However, he did not prevail two days later when the Virginia Assembly voted to retain a recommended amendment to the document that would limit the powers of the new Congress to lay direct taxes or excises. Mr. Madison considers this power the cardinal virtue of the new Constitution, that the new Federal government would be free to establish and collect taxes on its own authority. Foes of the Constitution fear this power is the document's most dangerous vice.[2]

"The conspiracy agst. direct taxes is more extensive & formidable than some gentlemen suspect," Congressman Madison wrote to a friend. "It is clearly seen by the enemies of the Constitution that an abolition of that power will re-establish the supremacy of the State Legislatures, the real object of all their zeal in opposing the system."[3]

Foes' Plans and Purpose

One proposed amendment attached to New York State's July 25 ratification also proposed to limit the power of Congress to levy direct taxes. In addition, the New York Ratifying Convention sent to the other States a Circular Letter calling for a second Federal convention to approve a long list of amendments. Mr. Madison is convinced that a second Federal convention would be a dangerous Anti-Federalist device to "mutilate" the new Constitution before it even has an opportunity to prove itself in actual operation.[4]

He is reported to have warned General George Washington that Patrick Henry and his allies will now seize the first opportunity "for shaking off the yoke in a *Constitutional way*" by seeking to convince two-thirds of the States to convene a second Federal convention to undo the work of the first. Or, he gloomily suggests, Anti-Federalists in the first elections under the new Constitution may elect a majority to the Congress who will then "commit suicide on their own Authority."[5]

Since New Hampshire and Virginia approved the Constitution last month, and New York this month became the eleventh State to ratify (by only three votes), Federalists North and South have congratulated themselves. Nevertheless, Mr. Madison is convinced that Anti-Federalist opposition to the document's powers and to its implementation is still strong.

"I am so uncharitable as to suspect that the ill will to the Constitution will produce every peaceable effort to disgrace and destroy it," he warned Colonel Alexander Hamilton. He added that Mr. Henry declared previous to the final question in the Virginia Ratifying Convention that although he would submit as a quiet citizen, he would wait with impatience for the favorable moment of regaining "in a *constitutional way* the lost liberties of his country...."[6]

Wrath of George Washington

Informed observers have told this correspondent that the issue of amendments in the form of a bill of rights will be a critical matter in the forthcoming Federal elections, as it was during the long and often bitter ratification battle. Both Mr. Madison and General Washington view a bill of rights issue as politically explosive, requiring skillful management by the Federalists.

An issue of immediate concern to General Washington, giving him alarm and causing anger, is the fear that Federalists may lack access to the press to make their case public during the coming elections. He told John Jay in a July 18 letter (a copy has been obtained by this correspondent) that the current Continental Post Master General, Ebenezer Hazard, should be sacked for stopping the free exchange of newspapers among printers throughout the States.

It was an economy measure to ease postal operating losses, but General Washington is angered because the move comes just as the campaign for the first Federal elections is about to begin and because a majority of the country's newspaper publishers are Federalists.

"The interruption in that mode of conveyance [of information]," the General angrily wrote to the Confederation government's Secretary of Foreign Affairs, "has not only given great concern to the friends of the Constitution . . . but it has afforded its enemies very plausible pretexts for dealing out their scandals, and exciting jealousies by inducing a belief that the suppression of intelligence, at that critical juncture, was a wicked trick of policy, contrived by an Aristocratic Junto."[7]

During the ratification campaign, Anti-Federalists alleged that Federalist "aristocrats" had bribed postal officials to delay or destroy their letters, pamphlets, and newspapers. Since the first of the year, poor mail service has been a source of bitter complaints by both the Federalists and the Anti-Federalists. One source concludes that having incurred the anger of General Washington, Post Master General Hazard's efforts to economize will cost him his job. If so, he will be the first political casualty of the new national government.[8]

Sectional political disputes in the Continental Congress during all of July stalled passage of an ordinance setting a date for holding elections for President and Vice President. On July 2 the Continental Congress declared that the necessary nine States had ratified the Constitution, and since then there has been an intense struggle over which city will become the temporary seat of the new Congress.

One source has told this correspondent that Continental Congressmen and their supporters are conducting active campaigns and offering political deals; there are even unconfirmed reports of bribe offers. Cities frequently mentioned are Wilmington, Delaware; Lancaster, Pennsylvania; and Baltimore and Annapolis, both in Maryland; but the most intense competition is between New York and Philadelphia.[9]

The financial impact of New York's losing the seat of the national government was, according to an informed source, one of several economic considerations that forced an Anti-Federalist majority to ratify the Constitution by a narrow margin. Delegate John Jay told the New York Ratifying Convention on July 12 that all of the hard money in the city of New York came "from the Sitting of Congress there."[10]

The Politics of Parades

Philadelphia on July 4 staged a lavish "Federal Procession" to celebrate ratification and to launch the Federalist election campaign. It was also staged partly to influence selection of the city as the seat of the new national government.

Not to be outdone, even though the State had not yet ratified, New York City on July 23 staged its own smaller procession to celebrate ratification by ten States. New York's spectacle was designed, in part, with an eye to influencing ratification convention delegates who were meeting up the Hudson River in Poughkeepsie, and as a competitive response to Philadelphia's campaign to capture the seat of the new national government from New York City, where the Continental Congress meets.[11]

In a drizzling rain that elated New York Anti-Federalists, 5,000 pro-Constitution marchers, representing all the professions and trades, along with horse-drawn floats, extended in a line estimated to be a mile and a half as they marched through New York City streets. The horse-drawn frigate *Hamilton*, with its thirty-two guns and a crew of thirty, was designated the masterpiece of the procession. Firing thirteen-gun salutes, the float symbolized the newly launched Ship of State, and honored Colonel Alexander Hamilton's signing of the Constitution as well as his active role in ratification.[12]

Privately, Congressman Madison is reported to be less than happy with the concessions Colonel Hamilton and other New York Federalists granted to gain their State's approval of the new Constitution. For instance, according to one source, Mr. Madison could see "no worthy motive" in their agreeing to a Circular Letter calling for a second convention, which would pose a direct danger to the powers of the newly ratified Constitution. He bitterly commented to General Washington that the expedient motive of the Federalists and of Colonel Hamilton was fear that if New York were not a ratifying State, it would lose its chance for the new Congress, thus incurring a financial loss.[13]

Colonel Hamilton and Congressman Madison worked closely during the long ratification struggle, jointly authoring, under the nom de plume "Publius," a series of "Federalist" newspaper essays defending and explaining the Constitution.* Now, the relationship is reported to be under strain because of their disagreement over the provisional location of the seat of the new national government. Colonel Hamilton favors New York, as does General Washington, who suspects that it would be temporary and that a permanent choice could be made later by the first elected national Congress. Mr. Madison is urging the General to support a more central location.[14]

Delay Endangers Federal Elections

Deadlock in the Continental Congress over what city to choose as the seat — temporary or not — for the first Federal Congress may delay start of the Federal elections and has pitted Congressman Madison and Colonel Hamilton against each other. Some

---

* John Jay also contributed to the series but was forced by illness to discontinue his association after five articles.

Federalists are expressing alarm that the delay is playing into the hands of Anti-Federalists who are urging a second convention and demanding amendments. A long delay would also allow Anti-Federalists an organizational advantage in their drive to elect a majority to the new Congress.[15]

Although the debates of the Continental Congress this month have been conducted in secret, the French envoy to the United States has provided this correspondent with a copy of his journal notes on the debates. According to Comte de Moustier's July 28 entry, southern Congressmen favor Philadelphia because the city is less a commercial rival than New York.

"Other delegates had less patriotic motives," he observes. "One voted for New York because his wife's family is settled there, another because he courts several young ladies, a third because the air agrees with his health, etc. It is believed that Mr. [James] Madison has been so strongly in favor of Philadelphia only because he is to marry a woman who holds an annuity there."[16]

The French envoy in a later entry also reveals that Virginia's congressional delegation is split, although each State has a single vote. Mr. Madison and Edward Carrington favor Philadelphia, and Colonel Richard Henry Lee is championing northern Virginia along the Potomac. Colonel Lee fears that the new government, if in Philadelphia, will fall victim to some of the same "financial operations" and "pernicious stockjobbing which had ruined the states" during the recent War of Independence.[17]

"Mr. [Alexander] Hamilton alleged," the French diplomat confides in his notes, "that the delegates from New York were going to lose their popularity if the new Congress did not remain in that State because they had solemnly promised it at the [New York] Convention if the new Constitution were ratified there.... It is astonishing that the personal interest of each delegate is so active in attracting Congress to his own state."[18]

French Envoy and Mr. Madison

Arriving earlier this year to take up his diplomatic duties, Minister de Moustier astonished New York society by bringing

along his mistress and making no effort to conceal the liaison. Mr.
Madison, who once contemplated becoming a minister, has written
to Thomas Jefferson, the U.S. Minister to France, asking for de
Moustier's recall.

"... He is *unsocial proud and niggardly,*" Mr. Madison wrote in
code to the American diplomat in Paris, "*and betrays a sort of fas-
tidiousness toward this country. He suffers also from his illicit connection with Madame de Brehan* which is *universally known* and
offensive to American manners—she is *perfectly soured toward this
country....* On *their journeys* it is *said they often neglect the* most
obvious *precautions for veiling their intimacy....*" [19]

While John Adams was in France serving with Thomas Jefferson
and Dr. Benjamin Franklin, he was highly vocal in his disapproval of
French morals. Last spring he returned to his native Massachusetts
after serving as U.S. Minister to Great Britain. Since his return, the
Signer of the Declaration of Independence has been widely mentioned as a Vice Presidential running mate for General George
Washington.

Despairingly, Mr. Adams believes that his absence for a decade
of diplomatic service in Europe has made his earlier service to the
American Revolution forgotten by his fellow countrymen. Writing
from his Braintree, Massachusetts, home to his 22-year-old mar-
ried daughter, he predicts that his prospects for future public
office are bleak.

"I will tell you my dear child, in strict confidence," he writes in a
July 16 letter, a copy having been obtained by this correspondent,
"it appears to me that your father does not stand very high in the
esteem, admiration or respect of his country, or any part of it. In the
course of a long absence his character has been lost, and he has got
quite out of circulation." [20]

Replying on July 27, Abigail Smith assures her 53-year-old father
that far from having been forgotten, he has a political rival in John
Hancock. She warns him to be on guard against the Massachusetts
Governor's recent displays of friendship.

"It is my opinion," Abigail adds, "that you will either be elected
to the second place upon the continent, or first in your own State.
The general voice has assigned the presidentship to General

Washington, and it has been the opinion of many persons whom I have heard mention the subject, that the vice-presidentship would be at your option. I confess I wish it, and that you may accept it. But of the propriety of this, you must judge best. . . . "[21]

CHAPTER 3

★

August 1788

Secret Spanish Designs on
Kentucky Frontier Disclosed

The deadlock of the old Confederation Congress over a new temporary capital and a date for the first Federal elections could aid
Spain's secret efforts to annex the Kentucky frontier territory.

Congressman James Madison has made that explosive charge in
coded correspondence, obtained by this correspondent.

Last October, Mr. Madison as a member of the Congressional
Committee on Indian Affairs, alleged that Spain had inspired and
even financed a series of savage settler-Indian clashes on Georgia's
southern borders. Spain had also been accused by others of encouraging Indian tribes to make war on settlers in the Carolinas and in
Virginia's western territory of Kentucky.[1]

Now a new and more explosive charge has been made by Mr.
Madison in an August 23 letter to the U.S. Minister to France,
Thomas Jefferson. In code, the Congressman alleges that Spain has
secretly made overtures to Kentucky to become a permanent part of
its territorial empire. This approach follows the failure of the
Continental Congress to act in July on Kentucky's application to
become the fourteenth State, leaving the issue for the new Federal
government next year.[2]

"... There is *even good ground to believe*," Congressman Madison
confides in code, "*that Spain is taking* advantage of *this disgust in
Kentucky* and is *actually endeavoring* to *seduce them from the*

17

union holding out a darling object which will never be obtained by them as part of the union." [3]

Kentucky's "darling object" is Spain's reopening the vital Mississippi River to American traffic and trade. One source reports that Spain's Minister to the United States has secretly offered to conclude a trade treaty with Kentucky if the frontier province of Virginia will declare itself an independent State. [4]

Explosive Political Constellation

The Madrid government's inciting the Indian tribes along the southern and western frontiers of the United States is one thing. But to strive secretly at the same time to annex U.S. territory when the Continental Congress is deadlocked over putting in place the machinery for the new national government confronts Federalist leaders with a constellation of problems.

Virginia's Patrick Henry argued during the Richmond Ratifying Convention that the Mississippi River would be lost to Spain through secret negotiations made under the new Constitution. Although this was adamantly denied by James Madison and others, a majority of the Kentucky delegates in Richmond believed former Governor Henry and voted to reject the Constitution.

One source has told this correspondent that hostility to the powers of the new national government by frontiersmen in the interior of Virginia, Kentucky, and now North Carolina could create a crisis of confidence in the new Union. Such a crisis, this same source believes, could worsen into threats to dismember the Union if, as now rumored, Spain by treaty were given absolute control of the Mississippi. [5]

In the summer of 1786, the Continental Congress first debated the issue of negotiating to have the Mississippi reopened to American trade after Spain had closed it the year before. When it was suggested the United States give up its claim to Spain for ten years to gain access to the waterway, sectional divisions grew so fierce that serious consideration was given to the creation of two or three separate confederacies. [6]

Now the same sectional divisions that have produced the current congressional deadlock over the location of the new capital have encouraged, according to one source, Spain to make overtures to Kentucky to break away after the delay in its application for statehood. Eastern States oppose Kentucky's admission, fearing it would affect the congressional balance of political power between North and South. Others oppose its admission from fear that Kentucky might reject the new Constitution. However, if Kentucky is not admitted, it might in frustration yield to the offers of the Spanish.[7]

West Crucial to America's Future

Mr. Madison makes it clear in his correspondence to Minister Jefferson and General Washington that the explosive problems in the West will be made worse if a central geographical location for the new government is not selected. The long journey to New York, which would have to be undertaken by the southern and western elected officials, might furnish fresh reasons for opposing the operation of the new government, he confides to General Washington, "especially as the legislative sessions will be held in the winter season." He believes also that a site in the eastern States would be for the Anti-Federalists decisive proof of eastern States' power.[8]

One of the principal reasons the Confederation Congress was regarded as weak and inefficient was the chronic absenteeism of its members. Many members sailed through rough seas during winter months, or traveled long distances over bad roads or were delayed by spring rains that turned most roads into rivers of mud. Travel is particularly difficult, and at times dangerous, to and from the distant southern States, whose current boundaries extend hundreds of miles inland and out of reach of Atlantic shipping ports. A trip by horseback from the interior to the seacoast can take weeks over old Indian trails, with homesteads too scattered to guarantee nightly warmth, food, and accommodations. Travel is hazardous to human life and a strain on horses.

General George Washington, for example, narrowly escaped death or serious injury when returning in late September 1787 from the Philadelphia Constitutional Convention to Mount Vernon, near Alexandria, Virginia. His journey required at least four full days through wilderness areas and on narrow rutted dirt roads that were badly maintained. His carriage was crossing a wooden bridge spanning the rain-swollen Elk River in northeast Maryland when it fell through the rotting planks. The terror-stricken horses were suspended midair until nearby residents came to the rescue.[9]

Mr. Madison, unlike some of his Federalist allies from the older Atlantic and New England States, is acutely aware of these problems. Nor does he harbor a fear or dislike of the frontier "wild men"; he always champions the West. He believes the political and financial future of the new government depends on the encouragement of the West's settlement and development, and realization of revenues from its resources.[10]

Last May, for example, he wrote a fellow Virginian proposing that the new national government should promote the sale of western public lands as one way of paying off the swollen public debt that the new national government is inheriting from the Confederation.[11]

Deadlock Aids Anti-Federalists

In the meantime, General Washington has issued a warning to his supporters in the current Congress that the continuing deadlock over which city should be chosen as the temporary seat of the new national government will give the Constitution's dedicated foes in the various States the opportunity to weaken, or even wreck, the document.

"... attempts will be made," warned General Washington in an August 28 letter from Mount Vernon, "to procure the election of a number of antifœderal characters to the first Congress, in order to embarrass the wheels of government and produce premature alterations in its Constitution. . . . it will be advisable, I should think, for the fœderalists to be on their guard so far as not to suffer any secret machinations to prevail, without taking measures to frustrate them."[12]

The source of General Washington's information is believed to be Congressman Madison. During the last six weeks, the 37-year-old lawmaker has been a major participant in the deadlocked debate over whether New York or Philadelphia should be the temporary seat of the new national government. The deadlock has delayed putting in motion the Constitution's provisions for holding the first national elections, with the anticipated unanimous choice of General Washington as President.

In writing to the General, Mr. Madison terms it "truly mortifying" that the "evil" of sectional prejudice "which has dishonored" the old (Confederated) government should already infect the new one and frustrate proceeding with the provisions of the Constitution.[13]

Ever since the Continental Congress certified on July 2 that the nine necessary States had ratified the new Constitution, a North-South deadlock has upset Federalist supporters. During the first week of August, for example, in order to keep New York or Philadelphia from being selected as the capital, a majority of seven States surprised everyone by approving Baltimore as the temporary seat of the new government.[14]

Then, on the very next day, Congress reversed itself and designated New York. This enraged Philadelphia and, of course, Baltimore. Also suffering from wounded pride, since each had been proposed as a site, were Wilmington, Delaware, and Lancaster, Pennsylvania. The French envoy to the Continental Congress, now sitting in New York, reports that South Carolina, for reasons of the heart and not the head, broke ranks with the southern States, which favor Philadelphia.

"The delegates from South Carolina," confides the Comte de Moustier in his private journal (and relayed to this correspondent by a confidential source), "incapable of making a firm decision and attached to some New York women, by means of being importuned by the New Yorkers, were not able to resist their entreaties and it was proposed to replace the word Baltimore with the word New York, which passed with a majority of seven States, 5 States being opposed to it and Georgia divided."[15]

Rhode Island, which earlier this year rejected the Constitution but still maintains its seat in the Confederation Congress, became an important pawn in the protracted sectional power struggle. Instrumental with its single vote that defeated Philadelphia in favor of New York, the tiny New England State lived up to its reputation for consistent opposition to the new Constitution when its delegates refused to join in a final vote approving an ordinance for holding the first Federal elections. The Rhode Islanders then enraged just about everyone by announcing they were heading for home, leaving Congress deadlocked for most of August.[16]

William Ellery, one of the few Rhode Island officials who favor the Constitution, summarized the frustrations and fears of the Federalists.

"The Feds here think it very strange," wrote the Rhode Island Signer of the Declaration of Independence to a friend in Newport, on August 31, "that after all the struggle there has been about the new Constitution, that now, when eleven states have agreed to it, Congress should not agree to do what is necessary on their part towards its operation. The Antifeds are pleased. . . ."[17]

Unnerving News from North Carolina

Foes of the Constitution were elated when the news reached other States that North Carolina, on August 2, had rejected ratification by the overwhelming vote of 183 to 84, but they left open the possibility of acceptance if amendments were added to the Constitution. The vote was reported to have been heavily influenced by the opposition Patrick Henry had mounted in neighboring Virginia during that State's Ratifying Convention. The surprising rejection by North Carolina officially brings to a close the eleven-month ratification campaign in the thirteen States.

General Washington and Congressman Madison had assumed that North Carolina would follow Virginia's example and approve the document with recommended amendments in a form of a bill of rights. As it now stands, North Carolina and Rhode Island are the only States not to have ratified the document.

According to one observer, North Carolina withheld its approval in the belief it would provide Anti-Federalists with political leverage for a second Federal convention in which to secure amendments, prior to the document's becoming effective. Mr. Madison, weary of the tiresome and often treacherous debates in the Continental Congress, greeted the news from North Carolina with grim alarm. In July the New York State Ratifying Convention had approved a Circular Letter calling for a second convention. Mr. Madison is convinced such a convention would aid the Anti-Federalists in their purpose to "mutilate the system." [18]

Fears over Foes and Friends

In an August 24 letter to General Washington, with whom he regularly corresponds, Mr. Madison reports that the Anti-Federalists have agreed to hold a meeting in Harrisburg, Pennsylvania, early next month to coordinate their plans for a second convention.

Privately, Mr. Madison blames fellow Federalists Colonel Alexander Hamilton and John Jay for making this dangerous development possible when they agreed to the New York Circular Letter, as demanded by the Anti-Federalist majority during last month's New York State Convention, to which both were delegates. He bitterly observed to General Washington that it would have been better if New York had rejected ratification, rather than "sacrifice every thing" in exchange for a chance at keeping that city as the seat of the new Congress. [19]

Congressman Madison's fears and frustrations with his Federalist friends appear to have been aggravated when he received a letter from Virginia Governor Edmund Randolph saying that he too supports a second convention. Apparently he is feeling the political heat generated by Patrick Henry and other Anti-Federalists in his State.

Mr. Madison replied with anger and sharpness. ". . . I cannot but think," he wrote on August 22, "that an *early* convention will be an unadvised measure. It will evidently be the offspring of party & passion, and will probably for that reason alone be the parent of error and public injury. . . . Should radical alterations take place therefore [in the Constitution] they will not result from the deliberate sense of the people, but will be obtained by management, or extorted by menaces. . . to the views of individuals & perhaps the ambition of the State legislatures." [20]

CHAPTER 4

★

September 1788

Old Congress Expires with
Passage of Election Ordinance

The old Confederation Congress ratified its own death warrant on September 13 when nine States approved a measure designating New York City as the temporary seat of the new national government and set specific dates for the first Federal elections of President and Vice President.

Passage of the historic Election Ordinance broke a bitter summer-long sectional deadlock. In bringing to legal existence the Federal government of the United States of America, the Confederation government in its last official act effectively brought about its own demise, with few mourners. The old Congress will act as caretaker until the new government officially begins to function.

The much-maligned single governing body for the thirteen States established under the Articles of Confederation, with its passage of the Election Ordinance, carried to its political grave a profound paradox. Chronic absenteeism of members contributed greatly to its ineffectiveness. Yet, the debate over the Election Ordinance commanded the greatest attendance of member States since the Declaration of Independence twelve years earlier.

"...this business being settled, Congress, I fear, like all other bodies about to expire, will scarcely have a Witness to its dissolution," lamented North Carolina Congressman John Swann before adjournment.[1]

In fact, city officials, eager to show their appreciation for being chosen as the temporary capital for the new Federal government, are already remodeling City Hall for the new Congress when it meets next March.

"... the workmen made such a continual noise that it was impossible to hear one another speek," complained Massachusetts Congressman George Thatcher of the hammers and saws already at work before the retiring members could take their leave.[2]

Avoiding a Stranglehold

The eleven States that ratified the new Constitution will set their own dates for elections of House and Senate members to the Federal Congress. But the September 13 Ordinance sets specific dates for the election of the President and the Vice President. States will choose Presidential Electors on the first Wednesday in January 1789; balloting will take place on the first Wednesday in February. The first Federal Congress is set to convene in New York City on the first Wednesday in March.[3]

Congressman James Madison, who fought unsuccessfully for Philadelphia as the new government's temporary seat, told General George Washington in a letter dated September 14 (a copy has been obtained by this correspondent) that had New York not been selected, a continued deadlock might have ended in "strangling the Government in its birth."[4]

As it now stands, he adds, the selection of New York City reinforces arguments by southern and western critics of the Constitution that northerners will dominate and control the national government.[5]

It appears that sectional strife will be as intense in the new government as it has been in the old Confederation.

Washington Works His Will

General Washington is expected to be elected unanimously as the first President under the new Constitution. The powers of the office were so shaped by the Philadelphia Convention because of this widely held assumption. His support of the Constitution and his prestige guaranteed its adoption and ratification in key States, including Virginia. It is widely agreed that his favoring New York as the temporary location for the new government broke the sectional deadlock in the Confederation Congress.

For example, he issued a warning in late August from Mount Vernon to his Federalist supporters that further delays in putting the new government into operation would allow enemies of the Constitution time to secure a majority in the first Congress "in order to embarrass the wheels of government and produce premature alterations in its Constitution."[6]

In a September 23 letter to Congressman Madison, the General focuses on the political threat from Anti-Federalist forces in the States, particularly in his native Virginia.

"To be shipwrecked in sight of the Port," General Washington stated, "would be the severest of all possible aggravations to our Misery; and I assure you I am under painful apprehensions from the single circumstance of Mr. H—'s* having the whole game to play in the Assembly of this State, and the effect it may have on others, it should be counteracted if possible.[7]

Senate Seats at Stake

Although Patrick Henry failed to defeat ratification of the new Constitution in Virginia, losing by a narrow margin, he still has enormous political power and influence in the Virginia Assembly. General Washington is known to have expressed the belief that if James Madison were in the Virginia Assembly at Richmond, rather than in the Continental Congress in New York, he might counter Mr. Henry's influence in "an irreproachably direct manner" — as he had during the State's ratification debate last June when they faced each other in Richmond.[8]

The General is also known to favor Mr. Madison's election by the Virginia Assembly as the first of two U.S. Senators from the State.

---

* Patrick Henry.

He would be a valuable ally for the first President for securing Senate approval of appointments and treaties. However, Patrick Henry is reportedly working to elect his own handpicked candidates for the two U.S. Senate seats from Virginia.[9]

In the meantime, the French Consul-General in New York has told his superiors in Paris that Federalists and Anti-Federalists each fear that the other will gain control of the new Congress and have too much influence over national affairs.

Antoine R. C. M. de la Forest contends, in a September 14 secret diplomatic dispatch, that it was this fear in the Federalists that led them to accept New York as the temporary seat of government. Further delay would have given Anti-Federalists an opportunity to organize their forces for the State legislative elections. Their candidates, if elected, might in turn have sufficient power to elect the first Senators to the new Congress.

"Pennsylvania in particular has just had a conference among the Antifederalists of all the counties of the state under specious pretexts," the French envoy writes, "and they have secretly agreed to the list of officers whom their party must appoint; the Ordinance of Congress appears to be in time to permit the legislature currently seated at least to assure itself of Federal Senators. It is because of this circumstance that the State had to vote in favor of the New York residence."[10]

Failure of Anti-Federalists

What precise influence the September 3-6 Anti-Federalist Convention, held in Harrisburg, Pennsylvania, had on breaking the deadlock in the Continental Congress in New York is not clear at this writing. Federalists have known for weeks of their opponents' conclave, fearing it was a crucial step toward calling a second constitutional convention to undo or water down the work of the Philadelphia Convention.

One observer reports that Congressman Madison and other Federalists were concerned that the Harrisburg Convention would ignite a nationwide firestorm for amending the new Constitution. It turned out to produce more smoke than fire. A handful of Anti-

Federalists organized the conclave to advance their own prospects for election to the new Congress.[11]

As delegate William Petrikin later insisted, "I am Clearly of opinion our Harrisburgh conference did more injury to our cause than all the strategems of our advarsaries. Our friends throughout the state expected something decisive from us and we spent our whole time Canvassing for places in Congress. . . ."[12]

In spite of the Anti-Federalists' poor attendance in Harrisburg and their failure to achieve the objective of calling for a second convention that would focus on a bill of rights, they did issue a public manifesto calling for "speedy revision" of the new Constitution by a second convention. But as one observer points out, the Harrisburg Convention's manifesto did not call for the one thing demanded by Anti-Federalists since the Constitution was first published — a bill of rights.[13]

"The Convention had not a Franklin, or a Washington at the head of it. . . ," angrily complained an Anti-Federalist in the September 20 issue of the *Pittsburgh Gazette*. "It may be observed, that in the amendments proposed we have said nothing about a *bill of rights, the liberty of the press, or the trial by jury.* It was found upon examination there was nothing in the Constitution which interfered with any of these."[14]

Nation Waits on Washington

News of the failed efforts of the Anti-Federalists in Harrisburg spread rapidly during the balance of September to gleeful Federalists in other States. Nevertheless, anxiety still prevails among many supporters of the new Constitution over a lack of news that General Washington will agree to his election as the first President.

Ever since the Constitution was published twelve months ago, and during the long and often stormy ratification debates in the separate States, the hero of the American War of Independence has received a steady steam of letters from friends and supporters urging him to declare his willingness to serve as the first elected President of the new national government. He sidesteps the issue by insisting that he would not have an answer until the Electoral

College meets next January in the separate States on the same date and makes its choice.[15] In taking this position, the General avoids the appearance of openly seeking the office and instead is fostering the appearance of genuine election by the Electors in spite of the opinion of many that his silence is consent. He does not need to declare, accept, or decline until his name is presented to the First Congress by the Electoral College.

Still the letters arrive at Mount Vernon.

Colonel Alexander Hamilton of New York, one of the Signers of the Constitution, is worried that the General's caution may mean a resolution to decline the position. He wrote the General this month arguing that by his agreeing to leave retirement and serve as President of the Constitutional Convention in Philadelphia, he is "by that act *pledged*" to take part in the new government.

"It cannot be considered as a compliment," Colonel Hamilton adds, "to say that on your acceptance of the office of President the success of the new government in its commencement may materially depend. Your agency and influence will be not less important in preserving it from the future attacks of its enemies than they have been in recommending it in the first instance to the adoption of the people." [16]

He made the observation, perhaps not lost on General Washington, that "the point of light in which you stand at home and abroad will make an infinite difference in the respectability with which the government will begin its operations in the alternative of your being or not being at the head of it." [17]

Fellow Virginian Henry Lee wrote the 56-year-old General with similar arguments. In reply on September 22, the master of Mount Vernon still refuses to state his decision, if indeed he has yet made one. He hedges by saying that he prizes "the good opinion of my fellow citizens," but that he "would not seek or retain popularity at the expense of one social duty or moral virtue." [18]

Finances Partly Behind Silence

The General explains himself to his long-time friend by adding, "While doing what my conscience informed me was right, as it respected my God, my Country and myself, I could despise all the party clamor and unjust censure, which must be expected from some, whose personal enmity might be occasioned by their hostility to the government.... certain I am, whensoever I shall be convinced the good of my country requires my reputation to be put in risque;* regard for my own fame will not come in competition with an object of so much magnitude. If I declined the task, it would lie upon quite another principle."[19]

Beyond General Washington's stated preference for retirement from public life, his reluctance to accept the Presidency may stem, in part, from the family financial woes he has reluctantly revealed in private correspondence.

"...I never felt the want of money," he confided last month to his family physician, Dr. James Craik, to whom he is indebted, "so sensibly since I was a boy of 15 years old as I have done for the last 12 months and probably shall do for 12 months more to come."[20]

One observer reports that while General Washington is land rich, he is cash poor and must scramble just to meet weekly expenses. As evidence of his financial woes, on three occasions the hero of the American Revolution has put off the local sheriff's demands for hard coin in payment of taxes due on Mount Vernon.[21]

Most southern plantation owners in America have almost all of their wealth in land, livestock, crops, and slaves, and General Washington is no exception. Cash receipts for crops or from land rental have been exceedingly difficult to obtain and are often painfully slow because of the chronic, often severe, shortage of gold and silver coin. The severe inflation of the past caused by printing paper money has ruled out a return to the practice to pay debts.

Thus, unsuspected by his friends and supporters is the nagging question whether General Washington's empty purse will allow him to become President. His problem is made worse by the fact that he has already pledged to serve in the new government without pay and is expected to do so if he accepts the Presidency.

---

* "Risk."

CHAPTER 5

★

October 1788

New England Vice President
Eyed As Running Mate for Washington

A New England Vice Presidential running mate for General George Washington is very likely, with the attention centering on two candidates: Massachusetts Governor John Hancock and former U.S. Minister to Great Britain John Adams.

Governor Hancock is being considered principally because of a secret political bargain with Federalists. According to reliable sources, he supported ratification of the new Constitution last January in return for support of his re-election as Governor and the pledge to support him for the Vice Presidency. It was even suggested at the time by the Federalists that should General Washington decline to run, Governor Hancock would be the "only fair candidate for President." [1]

However, the popular but vain Governor appears not to have deep political support beyond his native New England. Mr. Adams, on the other hand, is reported to have support for the second spot not only in the northern States but also in the mid-Atlantic and southern States.

In fact, the French Minister to the United States, Comte de Moustier, reported to Paris in a September 12 diplomatic dispatch (a copy has been obtained by this correspondent from Dr. Benjamin Franklin) that New England is solidly behind John Adams. In turn, the men of that region are pressing southerners to support Mr.

Adams for the Vice Presidency while they are pledging to vote for General Washington.

"Mr. Adams has said that it was arranged that the President would be from the South, the Vice President from the North, and the Chief Justice from the Center," according to the French diplomat, who is a very reliable source of inside information.[2]

Madison's Opposition to Both

James Madison, Virginia's representative to the Confederation Congress, intensely dislikes and distrusts both New Englanders. The young lawmaker and the confidant of General Washington made his views known to Thomas Jefferson, who is serving as U.S. Minister to France. In an October 17 letter, written in code, Mr. Madison describes Governor Hancock as "weak ambitious a courtier of popularity given to low intrigue." He also makes reference to Mr. Adams' "cabal" against General Washington during the War of Independence.[3]

"Knowing *his extravagant self importance*," Mr. Madison adds in code, "and... *considering his preference of an unprofitable dignity... and having an eye to the presidency conclude that he would not be a very cordial second to the General* and that *an impatient ambition* might *even intrigue for a premature advancement*."[4]

Mr. Madison is known to favor either John Jay, Secretary of Foreign Affairs, or Boston-born General Henry Knox.[5] Knox served as General Washington's Chief of Artillery during the War of Independence and currently is Secretary of War for the Confederation government.

Mr. Adams has expressed anger and hurt that General Knox has allegedly joined Governor Hancock and Colonel Alexander Hamilton in "secret Whispers Prejudices and Calumnies against me"[6] in an effort to deny him the Vice Presidency. Mr. Adams noted that he has known General Knox since he was a small boy and that he "had done at least as much as any man in the world and I believe much more towards bringing him forward in Life and in the Army...."[7]

Adams' New England Advocates

Apparently aware that John Adams has powerful political enemies, his friends in New England have launched a campaign to persuade General Washington that the political poison being spread about Mr. Adams is really an Anti-Federalist plot.

General Benjamin Lincoln, a Massachusetts military leader whom General Washington trained, has written to Mount Vernon and, according to one source, insists that the character assassination campaign against Mr. Adams is unfounded and is an effort by Anti-Federalists to secure the number two spot. He writes, according to this source, that during the War, John Adams acknowledged every "virtue in your character" which the most intimate of your friends have discovered." [8]

Circumspect as always, General Washington in his reply, dated October 26 (a copy having been obtained by this correspondent), did not mention Mr. Adams by name. However, he did indicate that because of "the extent and respectability of Massachusetts it might reasonably be expected, that he [the Vice President] would be chosen from that State." [9]

At this writing, it is difficult to determine whether General Lincoln and other Adams supporters will view this as an endorsement, particularly since General Washington added that he would be bound by the choice of the Electoral College.

As for the office of President, General Lincoln, Colonel Hamilton, and others are keeping up a steady stream of letters to Mount Vernon, urging General Washington to declare openly his willingness to accept unanimous election. He steadfastly refuses, even though an early declaration might help Federalist candidates for Senate and House seats. He recognizes the mounting Anti-Federalist opposition to the new government and may be inching toward a decision, but with great reluctance.

"... if I should receive the appointment," he writes to Mr. Hamilton, "and if I should be prevailed upon to accept it, the acceptance would be attended with more diffidence and reluctance than I ever experienced before in my life." [10]

Senate Seats at Stake

General Washington and his Federalist supporters have had an uphill struggle opposing Patrick Henry at the Virginia Assembly, which met this month to decide elections of the first two U.S. Senators to serve in the U.S. Congress under the newly ratified Constitution.

The Assembly convened in Richmond on October 20 to consider the Election Ordinance approved last month by the Continental Congress in New York. As part of the first Federal elections, each State chooses Electors who will vote for their choices for President and Vice President. The Legislature in each State — in Virginia it is the Assembly — will elect two U.S. Senators, while voters at large will elect House members.

General Washington's influence narrowly carried Virginia's Ratifying Convention last June, over the vigorous objections of five-time Governor Henry. Nevertheless, the prestige of the hero of the American Revolution may be inadequate to break the iron hand that Mr. Henry holds over the Virginia Assembly.

One source says, for example, that the power of the former Governor is so absolute that he is in a position to dictate the choice of the first two U.S. Senators from Virginia. He can also dictate, this source believes, the rules for electing the House members and the Presidential Electors to ensure Anti-Federalist victories in Virginia's first Federal elections.[11]

Support for Madison

General Washington is known to favor James Madison for one of Virginia's Senate seats. Colonel Edward Carrington conferred with the General at Mount Vernon before arriving in Richmond to take his seat in the Assembly. He reported to Mr. Madison that the General is "alarmed" at the prospect of Anti-Federalists taking control of the first U.S. Senate. It is the General's decided opinion, Colonel Carrington noted, to urge Mr. Madison to seek a Senate seat.[12]

"I am persuaded," the Colonel wrote on October 22 to Mr. Madison, who is attending the Confederation Congress in New

York, "that an attempt will seriously be made for getting two Antifederalists for Senators. . . .I am convinced that it will be in vain to try any Federalist but yourself, & am decidedly of opinion that you ought to be put in nomination." [13]

Governor Henry may have successfully sealed the defeat of Mr. Madison on October 31 when he engineered the re-election of his Federalist foe to the Continental Congress, which will sit until the Federal elections are completed. Mr. Madison is thus effectively barred from returning to Virginia to run for a Federal Senate seat. [14]

Patrick Henry's absolute power over the Assembly was demonstrated when he offered and had adopted, on October 30, a Resolution calling for a second Federal convention of the States to approve amendments to the new Constitution.

The Resolution says that without amendments, "all the great essential and unalienable rights" of Virginia are "rendered insecure" under the Constitution. A second convention for proposing amendments would quiet "the minds of good citizens," secure "their dearest rights and liberties," and prevent "those disorders which must arise under a government not founded on the confidence of the people." [15]

Federalists believe that a second convention will emasculate the powers of the new national government and make it subservient to the individual States. In the Virginia Assembly, Federalists sought to head off adoption of Mr. Henry's Resolution by a substitute that pledged enactment of a bill of rights in the First Congress. Displaying his considerable power, Mr. Henry ordered the measure defeated, and so it was, by an overwhelming 85 to 39 vote. [16]

Randolph: A Reed in the Wind

Patrick Henry's tireless efforts to amend the new Constitution were anticipated. What was not expected is Virginia Governor Edmund Randolph's open support for a second convention. One observer charges that the Governor is caught between his conscience and his vanity. [17]

"He will injure his political Reputation," Virginia Assemblyman Francis Corbin wrote to Mr. Madison of Governor Randolph, "by his doublings and turnings. He is *too Machiavellian* and not *Machiavellian Enough.*" [18]

Governor Randolph refused to sign the new Constitution in Philadelphia, and since then he has been regarded as a reed in the wind, bending first in the direction of the Henry Anti-Federalists and then toward the Madison Federalists. He supported ratification last June, but by siding with the Anti-Federalist proposal for a second convention he appears as the man in the middle, without firm convictions.

One observer reports that the Governor is deeply wounded that his independent course has cost him dearly in friends and has earned him many enemies for "marching to the beat of his own drum." [19]

Across the Potomac, Maryland's elections have taken a more violent turn, transcending verbal disagreements about a bill of rights. Word has reached Virginia that candidates' arguments resulted in "a few broken heads" and smashed windows, and that several ladies lost their dignity in a hair-pulling match.[20]

The Humor of Patrick Henry

Without a physical blow, a single attempt to challenge openly Patrick Henry in the Virginia Assembly ended shamefully for the Federalists.

Francis Corbin, young, wealthy, and English-educated, rose in the Assembly and attacked Mr. Henry for his assertion that he bows to the majesty of the people. It is "the people," Mr. Corbin sarcastically said, with an exaggerated bow, whom Mr. Henry has opposed during every stage in the evolution of the new Constitution.

"It was of little importance whether a country was ruled by a despot with a tiara on his head, or by a demagogue in a red cloak, and a caul-bare wig," Mr. Corbin said, in a pointed reference to Mr. Henry's wig and his red cloak on a nearby chair, "although he *should profess on all occasions to* bow to the *majesty of the people.*" [21] And with another exaggerated sweeping bow, similar to those in European courts, he sat down.

Former Governor Henry raised himself "heavily" from his chair to answer the youthful Corbin, who was satisfied that he had oratorically muted the "Trumpet of the Revolution."

Appearing older than his 52 years, Mr Henry responded that he had indeed lacked the advantage of a British education, of wealth, of the favor of an English King as had Corbin and his Tory father during the War of Independence.

"While that gentleman was availing himself of the opportunity, which a splendid fortune afforded him, of acquiring a foreign education, mixing among the great, attending levees and courts... I was engaged in the arduous toils of the revolution...," Mr. Henry said with a deliberately awkward clownish bow. "The gentleman, I hope, will commiserate the disadvantages of education under which I have labored, and will be pleased to remember that I have never been a favorite with that monarch, whose gracious smile he has had the happiness to enjoy." [22]

Waves of laughter broke over the Virginia Assembly as young Francis Corbin, according to one observer, "sank at least a foot in his seat." [23]

CHAPTER 6

★

November 1788

Washington and Madison Suffer
Defeat at Hands of Henry

General George Washington suffered a severe political defeat at the hands of Patrick Henry this month when Continental Congressman James Madison was, by a narrow vote, denied one of the two U.S. Senate seats from the Commonwealth of Virginia.

Instead, the Virginia Assembly on November 8 chose two hand-picked candidates of former Governor Henry: Congressman Richard Henry Lee and William Grayson. Both had voted against ratification of the new Constitution, and their election was seen by one observer as a demonstration of Patrick Henry's dominance of the Assembly and Virginia politics.[1]

Congressman Madison took his defeat much more philosophically than did the master of Mount Vernon.

"The whole proceedings of the Assembly," General Washington wrote on November 17 to Mr. Madison in New York, "*it is said* may be summed up in one word, to wit, that the Edicts of Mr. H——* are enregistered with less opposition by the majority of that body, than those of the Grand Monarch are in the Parliaments of France. He has only to say let this be Law, and it is Law."[2] Although a transcript of the Assembly debates has yet to be released, those who were present have told this correspondent that former Governor Henry savagely attacked Mr. Madison, warning that his election to

---

* Henry.

41

the U.S. Senate would elevate a Federalist who could not be counted on to keep his word.

Mr. Madison heard also from Henry Lee: "Mr. Henry on the floor exclaimed against your political character & pronounced you unworthy of the confidence of the people in the station of Senator. That your election would terminate in producing rivulets of blood throughout the land."[3]

Other supporters of Mr. Madison, outraged at such assertions, maintain that had he been in Richmond, he would have been elected. Edward Carrington wrote assuring him that despite the calumnies delivered against him by Mr. Henry and other Anti-Federalists, he received 77 votes, Congressman Lee 98, and Colonel Grayson 86, thus the majority vote was not dishonorable to him, but was the result of those Anti-Federalists "who mediate mischeif against the Govt."[4]

One intimate believes that Mr. Henry deliberately ensured Mr. Madison's re-election to the soon-to-be-dissolved Continental Congress in order to keep him in New York and out of Virginia as a way to block his election to the Federal Congress.[5]

House Race: Madison vs. Monroe

Colonel Edward Carrington has been pressing Mr. Madison to return to Virginia and stand for a seat in the U.S. House of Representatives from his home district of Orange County.

The member of the House of Delegates wrote from Richmond, on November 26, that Mr. Madison's opponent would be his long-time friend James Monroe. "I have already apprised you of the *political* Hostility of Monroe, and it will be well for you to pay some regard to it," Colonel Carrington warned.[6]

One observer has told this correspondent that former Continental Congressman Monroe was handpicked by Patrick Henry. The Virginia Assembly agreed to redraw Mr. Madison's home district of Orange County to include Mr. Monroe's county, Anti-Federalist Spotsylvania. It also voted to require candidates for the House of Representatives to be residents of the district they are to represent, thus effectively excluding Mr. Madison from running in the Virginia Tidewater coastal counties that might favor him.[7]

Henry's Power Limited to State Level?

Patrick Henry's behind-the-scenes efforts in Virginia are bids to influence the new Congress and political events at the national level. He is reported to be backing for Vice President the Governor of New York, George Clinton, who is the prime promoter of calling a second convention to approve amendments to the Constitution. This move has only confirmed for Federalists that Patrick Henry is determined to render the new government impotent, having failed to defeat its ratification by his own State.[8]

Nevertheless, Senate elections in other States favoring Federalists and political realities indicate that Patrick Henry's power to influence events outside the Commonwealth may be limited.

For instance, Colonel Alexander Hamilton of New York points out in a November 23 letter to Congressman Madison that he doubts that the effort to elect Governor Clinton as Vice President is likely to succeed, principally because the Anti-Federalist Governor would not want to risk his current secure position and popularity.

Colonel Hamilton reports in the same letter that support from New England to the South is growing for John Adams as Vice President, now that General Washington let it be known last month he would have no objection to the former U.S. Minister to Great Britain. As a New Englander, he would provide geographical balance.

"On the whole I have concluded to support Adams; although I am not without apprehensions on the score," Colonel Hamilton added. "Either he must be nominated to some important post for which he is less proper, or will become a malcontent and possibly espouse and give additional weight to the opposition to the Government."[9]

Mr. Madison had made it clear that he opposes John Adams for the Vice Presidency. But that was before General Washington made it known he would not object to Mr. Adams' selection by the Electoral College because of the geographical balance.

In a letter to General Washington this month, a copy having been obtained by this correspondent, Mr. Madison voiced none of his bitter criticism of John Adams, former U.S. envoy, or of Massachusetts Governor John Hancock.

In the same letter, he observed that despite Patrick Henry's dictating in Virginia the selection of two Anti-Federalist candidates for the Senate, Federalist candidates for the U.S. Senate have been swept to victory in other States.

"A decided and malignant majority," Mr. Madison cautions, "may do many things of a disagreeable nature; but I trust the Constitution is too firmly established to be now materially vulnerable....Indeed Virginia is the only instance among the ratifying States in which the Politics of the Legislature are at variance with the sense of the people expressed by their representatives in [the Constitutional] Convention." [10]

Slavery Issue in South Carolina

Anti-Federalists in South Carolina did manage to sidestep Federalist control of the State Legislature and capture three out of five House seats.[11]

The most bitter House contest fought out in the South Carolina newspapers was a clash of personalities between two candidates, each of whom had supported ratification of the Constitution. William Smith, a 30-year-old son of a wealthy Charleston merchant, alleged that his opponent, Dr. David Ramsay, a 39-year-old physician, not only favored abolishing slavery, but also was, because he was born in Pennsylvania, a "foreigner" and not a native South Carolinian.[12]

"It is very well known that *he is principled against slavery*," Mr. Smith wrote in a published November 22 statement to Charleston voters, and "...his handing about *pamphlets* imported from the northward *against slavery is strong proof of his inclination to abolish it*." [13]

Dr. Ramsay denied the charge and countered that because Mr. Smith had been in Europe as a British subject all during the War of Independence, he had not been a citizen for seven years as required by Article I, Section 2 of the new Constitution.

"I declare," Dr. Ramsay replied in print on November 24, "that I never approved of the emancipation of the Negroes of this country, and I hold, that the adoption of such a measure would be ruinous both to masters and slaves. Experience proves, that those who have grown up in the habits of slavery are incapable of enjoying the blessings of freedom." [14]

Mr. Smith won the election, which Dr. Ramsay says he will challenge when the First Congress meets next year. The challenge is likely to be the first contested election to be considered by the House and, therefore, may set important precedents. [15]

Fear over Foreign Developments

Despite Mr. Madison's optimistic outlook that Federalists will command a solid majority when the First Congress meets next March, the young lawmaker has expressed concern over what effect a second convention, as demanded by Patrick Henry and others, might have on foreign opinion and future finances of the new national government.

In a November 2 letter to a friend, Mr. Madison observes that beyond weakening the powers of the new national government domestically, a second convention might endanger future loans from European countries. A second convention, he warns, "would be viewed by all Europe as a dark and threatening Cloud hanging over the Constitution just established, and perhaps over the Union itself," postponing or canceling any economic and political benefits realized by the reforms.

"It is a well known fact," he continues, "that this event has filled that quarter of the Globe with equal wonder and veneration, that its influence is already secretly but powerfully working in favor of liberty in France. . . . We are not sufficiently sensible of the importance of the example which this Country may give to the world; nor sufficiently attentive to the advantages we may reap. . . . " [16]

Equally worrisome to the Federalists is the presence of Spain to the South and West of their small nation and of Great Britain to its North and West. Spain has been accused of inciting Indian massacres against settlers in Georgia.

In a November 5 letter to James Monroe, Mr. Madison reveals that Spain is willing to offer emigrants money and land to settle on the western, Spanish-controlled side of the Mississippi River. In return, he reveals, they would be required to become "Spanish

Subjects; to be under Spanish laws, and be the instruments of Spanish Policy.... A watchful eye ought to [be] kept on the machinations of Spain."[17]

Spain has closed the Mississippi River to American transshipment of its commodities and the issue has produced a political firestorm, particularly in Virginia. Patrick Henry, during the recent ratification debate in the State, accused supporters of the new Constitution of wanting to give up U.S. rights to the river.

In fact, during the debate this month over election of the first U.S. Senators from Virginia, former Governor Henry accused Congressman Madison of secretly favoring giving up the Mississippi and of opposing a bill of rights. He predicted that Mr. Madison would not obey instructions to vote against direct taxation if he were elected to a Senate or a House seat.

"Thus gentlemen," Patrick Henry told the Virginia Assembly, "the secret is out, it is doubted whether Mr. Madison will obey his instructions."[18]

Foreign Influence in Pennsylvania

Although there is no evidence that either Spain or Great Britain has sought to influence the first Federal election campaign, a foreign influence has nevertheless shaped the political outcome in the parts of Pennsylvania that have a sizable German population.

Currently, one-third of the population in Pennsylvania is composed of German immigrants. Printers in Philadelphia took note of this in September 1787 when they published the text of the newly signed Constitution in both English and German.

During the campaign in that State for Senate and House seats, Federalists and Anti-Federalists sought to capture the loyalty of the German vote. This led to a spirited public debate in Pennsylvania newspapers after a demand was made that candidates for office be placed on ballots exclusively because they were German.

On November 13, for example, newspapers published a statement from an unnamed writer addressed "To the German Inhabitants of the State of Pennsylvania" asserting that the elections favored Englishmen for Congress and as Presidential Electors.

"This shows how little intention," the writer argued, "there is to pay to the industrious and useful Germans their due regard. Is this not degrading the character of the Germans to the lowest degree?... If this is the proceeding at the first election, what will be the consequence in the new government, when the English believe they can gain their point without the Germans, then they will be totally excluded, and the German nation in Pennsylvania, will be, and remain the hewers of wood and carriers of water."[19] In reply, the *Pennsylvania Packet* published on November 25 an article signed "A German" denouncing both Federalists and Anti-Federalists for courting the German vote. In matters of government, national distinction should be set aside, he asserted.

"If any national distinctions can possibly be made in the future laws of the empire," the writer argues, "why are not these anxious writers equally concerned for the Scotch and for the Irish? Why are they not desirous that they also should have their due proportion of federal representation? Nay, distinctions of this kind may be carried to any extent; and there seems to me just as much reason that the *tall* citizens should be jealous of the *short*, and that there should be a *fat* ticket in opposition to a *lean* one; or that each should insist upon their proportional share of representation in the great federal assembly."[20]

Wartime Corruption Issue

Unofficial returns from eight House races in Pennsylvania show that the Federalists won six and that the German vote proved decisive. The bitter two-month campaign was in part a continuation of the ratification debate over the Constitution. The Anti-Federalists demanded amendments or a bill of rights. The Federalists either denied that amendments were necessary or urged waiting until the new national government was in operation and experience reveals their need.[21]

However, the major issue mounted by the Anti-Federalists centered on Robert Morris, one of the two Federalists who won election to the U.S. Senate from Pennsylvania. Anti-Federalists alleged that as the former Superintendent of Finances during the War of

Independence, Mr. Morris converted millions in public money to his private use.

"Eleven years have now elapsed," wrote "Centinel" in the November 20 issue of the *Independent Gazetteer*, "since Mr. Morris was entrusted with the disposition of near two millions of specie dollars, and no account of this immense sum has yet been rendered by him. What conclusion must every dispassionate person make of this delinquency? Is it not more than probable that he has converted the public money to his own property, and that, fearful of detection and reluctant to refund, he has, and will as long as he is able, avoid an investigation and settlement of these long standing accounts?" [22]

Senator-elect Morris responded that the "repeated slanders of my enemies" have been mounted in an attempt to "wound the Federal cause" by attacks on his reputation. Maintaining that he has been in New York attempting to settle his accounts with the impoverished Confederation government, Mr. Morris pledged, "I shall do everything in my power to obtain a final settlement of them before the meeting of Congress under the new Constitution." [23]

Decline of Constitution Critics

In the five months since ratification of the new Constitution, Anti-Federalist critics of the document have demonstrated increasing confusion and political weakness in other States as well as in Virginia.

In New York, for example, reliable sources have told this correspondent that, unlike Patrick Henry in Virginia, Governor George Clinton does not have the solid support needed to exert Anti-Federalist control over the State Legislature when it meets next month. Moreover, the *Pennsylvania Gazette* reported on November 5 that Connecticut, Delaware, and Pennsylvania have already elected six Federalists to Senate seats. [24]

Political allies of Governor Clinton have demonstrated what may be an act of desperation to offset a possible Federalist sweep of the new Congress. On November 13 a group of New York Anti-Federalists met at Fraunces's Tavern. Using the name "Federal Republican Society," the group drafted a circular letter to other

States calling for the election of Governor Clinton as Vice President as a means to secure a bill of rights.

"It is highly probable," the committee observes, "if your State would unite with Virginia and ours, that Governor Clinton will be elected—We need not make any observations to shew, the influence that the Vice President will have in the administration of the new government—"[25]

One observer of New York politics predicts the embryonic effort will be stillborn, principally because the Anti-Federalist committee numbers only ten members, who have almost no political influence or power. This same observer points out, moreover, that since ratification of the Constitution five months ago, Anti-Federalist criticism of the document in the printed press has virtually vanished now that the Federalists have pledged themselves to take up amendments when the newly elected Congress meets next year.[26]

Colonel Alexander Hamilton, a bitter foe of Governor Clinton's, would use all of his influence with General Washington if there were the remote possibility that he would consider an Anti-Federalist as a Vice President. According to one source, Colonel Hamilton has reluctantly decided to support John Adams for Vice President since he is a reliable opponent of a second constitutional convention. The New York lawyer has warned Federalists to keep a watchful eye on Governor Clinton, conceding that he might garner votes in New York, Virginia, and South Carolina among the Anti-Federalists.[27]

Colonel Hamilton's support of John Adams for Vice President, according to one well-placed source, virtually ensures the election of the former envoy to Great Britain to the second spot on the Federalist ticket. Apparently he has calculated that despite his dislike of Mr. Adams, it is better to support him than to risk alienating the majority of New England Federalists.[28]

At the same time, Colonel Hamilton has raised with Mr. Madison the possibility that George Washington and John Adams might split the votes evenly, which would cause a deadlock in the Electoral College. The Constitution does not mandate voting separately for President and Vice President. The one with the majority of votes is named President. The Vice Presidency falls to the one who receives the second highest number of votes. By supporting

John Adams, as opposed to less favorable candidates, Federalists might inadvertently cast for him a number of votes equal to that cast for General Washington.

"If it should be thought expedient," Colonel Hamilton wrote to Mr. Madison on November 23, "to endeavour to unite in a particular character, there is a danger of a different kind to which we must not be inattentive—the possibility of rendering it doubtful who is appointed President. You know the constitution has not provided the means of distinguishing in certain cases & it would be disagreeable even to have a man treading close upon the heels we wish as President." [29]

CHAPTER 7

★

December 1788

Second Convention Idea Sinks
Beneath Wave of Federalist Wins

Anti-Federalist hopes for a second constitutional convention to secure amendments in the form of a bill of rights may prove to be "a hopeless pursuit" in the wake of widespread Federalist congressional election victories this month.[1]

In an apparent effort to capitalize on their sweep of Senate seats in the new Congress, Federalists have for the first time openly attacked former Virginia Governor Patrick Henry, who is leading the campaign for a second convention. The most widely revered figure of the American Revolution, next to General George Washington, has been Mr. Henry until he opposed the new Constitution.

In the December 20 edition of the *Federal Gazette*, printed in Philadelphia, the publishers call for support of a Federalist slate of Electors, who are to cast their ballots for President and Vice President. The *Gazette* asserts that the choice is between General Washington and former five-term Virginia Governor Henry. Without equivocation, the newspaper states:

"The contest will be between the FIRST BENEFACTOR of the United States, and an ambitious demagogue in Virginia [Patrick Henry], who has placed himself at the head of the debtors and speculators of that state, and who sees that the establishment of the federal government must forever make him a contemptible state bawler; for he well knows he has not talents to influence a federal assembly of the pitched characters of the United States."[2]

51

Although Mr. Henry was instrumental last month in securing the appointment of Anti-Federalists to Virginia's two Senate seats, in seven other States the Federalists handily won seats in the upper house. Senators are chosen by the State Legislatures; House members are chosen by the people in general elections. Federalists are confident that when the races for the House are completed, they will hold a majority of seats in both legislative branches of the new Congress.

In the wake of such overwhelming defeats, Anti-Federalists in New York, Pennsylvania, and elsewhere are reported to be secretly combining their forces to persuade Patrick Henry to oppose openly General Washington for President.[3]

Other reports indicate that he will not sanction such a challenge. Instead, according to one observer, Mr. Henry is supporting New York Governor George Clinton for Vice President in a bid to be represented and to secure a bill of rights once the Federal government is formed. During a meeting in New York last month, Anti-Federalists sent letters to allies in other States urging them to support Governor Clinton for Vice President, saying that the move had the approval of Patrick Henry.[4]

Colonel Alexander Hamilton, a bitter political foe of Governor Clinton, is mounting a campaign to block these efforts by supporting John Adams, former U.S. Minister to Great Britain. Colonel Hamilton is saying that Mr. Adams will prove to be "a trustworthy opponent of a second convention."[5]

Second Convention Stillborn

Governor Clinton convened a special session of the New York legislators this month for the purpose of electing Presidential Electors and U.S. Senators. New York is the only State that has not yet elected Senators and Presidential Electors for the Federal government. The session erupted into a bitter quarrel between Federalists and Anti-Federalists, with one observer reporting that the session was a resumption of the bitter battle New York had during its ratification sessions last summer.[6]

Governor Clinton may have helped to fuel the factional fighting with his formal address to the Legislature, when he called on the lawmakers to support a Circular Letter "to our Sister States" for a second convention and for suspension of the powers of the new Constitution "until it should undergo a revision by a General Convention of the States."[7]

The Anti-Federalist ally of Patrick Henry's is reported to be angered that he has not received Virginia's formal message calling for a second convention. One observer says that the New Yorker believes Federalists in control of the mail service have taken steps "to retard delivery of it so as to defeat its utility."[8]

Melancton Smith, a moderate Anti-Federalist and an ally of Governor Clinton's, wrote in the December 11 issue of the *New York Journal* that a second convention is imperative before a revolution against the original American Revolution becomes a reality.

"... An entire revolution," he wrote of the new Constitution, "is about taking place without war or bloodshed.... It has been urged by those who are opposed to it that the great principles of the revolution has been too little attended to in its formation—that it embraces objects not necessary to be committed to the care of the general government—that sufficient checks are not placed in it to restrain the rulers from an abuse of power—that it will annihilate the state governments on whom we must depend for the preservation of our liberties; and, that it will operate to deprive the people of those rights...."[9]

James Madison has expressed the belief that the Patrick Henry–George Clinton Anti-Federalist push for a second convention is for the express purpose of destroying the new Constitution and thus preserving the powers and influence that the individual States held under the Articles of Confederation, which did not constitute a central government.

He expressed confidence lately — in a December 8 letter to Thomas Jefferson in Paris — that the Federalists' sweep of Senate seats and the anticipated wins in the House will give Federalists a majority in the new Congress when it meets for its first session in March 1789. This political fact, Mr. Madison believes, has doomed the Henry-Clinton drive for a second convention.

In the eight States that have elected or appointed U.S. Senators as 1788 comes to a close, the Federalists have won in seven States: South Carolina, Maryland, Delaware, Pennsylvania, New Jersey, Connecticut, and Massachusetts. Only in Virginia have two Anti-Federalists been elected to the Senate to oppose fourteen Federalists. And only in New York do the Anti-Federalists have any prospect of electing two of their own to Senate seats. North Carolina and Rhode Island yet remain out of the Union for they have not ratified the Constitution.

"Notwithstanding the formidable opposition made to the New federal Government, first in order to prevent its adoption, and since in order to place its administration in the hands of disaffected men," Mr. Madison relates to Mr. Jefferson, U.S. Minister to France, "there is now both a certainty of its peaceable commencement in March next, and a flattering prospect that it will be administered by men who will give it a fair trial." [10]

Mr. Madison is well aware that one of the main goals of the Anti-Federalists in convening a second convention is to draft amendments to the Constitution in the form of a bill of rights. A Federalist-controlled Congress next spring will be forced to deal with that divisive issue since many Federalists were elected on the promise that once Congress convened it would consider amendments as had been demanded during ratification debates.

Madison to Run for House Seat

Although Mr. Madison was narrowly defeated last month for a U.S. Senate seat, through Patrick Henry's efforts, he has made it known that he will seek a seat in the House of Representatives. Mr. Henry tried to head off Mr. Madison by pushing through the Assembly a law requiring that candidates for the House must reside in the district they represent. Mr. Henry also had the Virginia Assembly expand the Orange district's boundaries to include Amherst, an Anti-Federalist stronghold. Originally, Mr. Madison had hoped to stand for election in the safe Tidewater counties, although his home is in Orange County, a considerable distance inland. [11]

Mr. Madison traveled as far as Philadelphia in early November with the intent of continuing on to New York for the winter, where the Continental Congress is sitting until the Federal government is formed. But a steady stream of letters from Virginia urging him to return to Virginia and run for a House seat proved to be a powerful inducement.

His close working relationship with the hero of the American War of Independence may offset Patrick Henry's support of James Monroe, another Anti-Federalist, who is running as an opponent to Mr. Madison.

An observer says that Mr. Henry and his supporters are putting forth the argument that a vote for Mr. Madison is a vote against a second convention, particularly against amendments to the Constitution. As part of his own strategy to head off a second convention, Mr. Madison has repeatedly pledged that he would work for passage of a bill of rights in the new Congress.[12] His pledges have not persuaded Mr. Henry, however.

An Ill and Reluctant Candidate

Mr. Madison's decision to return to Virginia and run for the House may have been influenced by General Washington's support of his original candidacy for the Senate. Moreover, his friend Richard Bland Lee had written from Richmond that his election prospects "seem to be gaining ground," despite efforts of his political enemies, and that if he campaigned in the district it would do much to "dissipate the plots" being formed to secure his defeat.

"If you were to visit the Counties previous to the election and attend the Culpepper election yourself—I think there would be little doubt of your success," the 27-year-old member of the Virginia House of Delegates added.[13]

Mr. Madison confided his concerns about campaigning in a letter to General Washington, written while he was still in Philadelphia: "I have an extreme distaste to steps having an electioneering appearance." Additionally, he revealed that he was still "much indisposed with the piles" (hemorrhoids), made even more painful by the carriage trip over the rough roads to Philadelphia.[14]

Mr. Madison had fallen seriously ill several times during the ordeal of the Constitutional Convention and of ratification. The first time was toward the end of the exhausting Philadelphia Convention in the summer of 1787, after he had been taking detailed daily notes while actively taking part in the extensive debates. His second illness forced him to a sickbed during the Virginia ratification debates in Richmond last June when he had to face Patrick Henry.

George Washington's Gloom

Heeding his friends' advice, Mr. Madison returned to Virginia, with an eight-day stopover at Mount Vernon before resuming the painful journey by stage and then by a two-wheeled chair to his home in Orange County. It is assumed that the hero of the War of Independence and the principal advocate of the Constitution discussed in some detail a wide-ranging strategy for the Federalists.

In a December 2 letter to a friend, the General made it clear that the Virginia Assembly's rejection of Mr. Madison as a Senator and its opposition to the Constitution were "most malignant" in motives.

"Sorry indeed should I be, if Mr. Madison meets the same fate in the district of which Orange composes a part, as he has done in the Assembly; and to me it seems not at all improbable," the General added.[15]

As winter snow and ice closed over Mount Vernon, the weather may have matched the General's mood. Despite the optimistic news that Mr. Madison brought with him during his visit, the General is troubled by past loyalties and current conflicts, while having to consider possible leadership responsibilities, which he is reluctant to assume.

For example, the Anti-Federalists' promotion of New York Governor Clinton for Vice President has revived memories for the General of the crucial role the New York political leader played during the War.

As wartime Governor of New York, George Clinton endeared himself to General Washington when he rushed foodstuffs to the starving troops at Valley Forge. The aid enabled the Continental Army to survive the bitter winter of 1777–78, when 2,500 of a total

10,000 troops perished from cold, hunger, and disease.[16] But Governor Clinton's alliance now with Patrick Henry for a second convention has forced General Washington to support John Adams as a safe running mate and "the only certain way to prevent the election of an Anti-Federalist."[17]

General Washington knows by now that his letters to friends are read by officials of the Postal Service or are circulated by recipients to strengthen the case for election of a Federalist majority in the new Congress. In a December 4 letter, for instance, the General expressed happiness at the election of Federalist candidates for the Senate in several States, with the exception of his native Virginia.

"... Much will depend upon having disinterested and respectable characters in both Houses," the General said. "... And then, if the government can be carried on without touching the purses of the people too deeply, I think it will not be in the power of its Adversaries to throw every thing into confusion by effecting premature amendments."[18]

Whether by coincidence or by design, the *Maryland Journal* (Baltimore) on December 30 echoed the General's call for election of a Federalist Congress. It published a statement signed by a group of Baltimore merchants who argued that only a Federalist Congress could induce the owner of Mount Vernon to accept unanimous election as President.

"... there ought to be a certain prospect," the merchants stated, "of his meeting men in both Houses of Congress, in whom he can place confidence, from their well known character and attachment to the New Constitution. It would indeed be imposing upon that GREAT MAN a most irksome and painful task to associate him, in the evening of his days, with men whose opinions and measures will be at perpetual variance with his."[19]

The Logic of Washington's Election

The General having been pressed for months by his friends and supporters to declare his willingness to be elected, his open support for election of a Federalist Congress has forced him to consider some kind of compromise. According to one observer, he has nearly concluded that perhaps he could accept election, set the wheels of the new national government spinning, and then resign and return to his retirement at Mount Vernon.[20]

"The future is all a scene of darkness and uncertainty to me, on many accounts," General Washington confided to a friend on December 23. "It is known, that when I left the army, it was with a fixed determination, never to be engaged again in any public affairs. Events, which were not then foreseen, have since turned up.... It is my most earnest wish that none but the most disinterested, able and virtuous men may be appointed to either house of Congress; because, I think, the tranquility and happiness of this Country will depend essentially upon that circumstance."[21]

The logic of the General's election, despite his ardent desire to remain in retirement, can be summarized as follows:

• Having led the new nation to independence militarily, he cannot now be expected to become a detached spectator at the political birth of a new national government formed to safeguard that independence.

• His acceptance of the presidency of the Philadelphia Convention, which drafted the Constitution, and his behind-the-scenes efforts to secure its ratification make him the most logical choice to lead the new government. Further, this is particularly true because the powers of the office of President were framed with him in mind.

• He has expressed strong support of a Federalist majority in the new Congress to frustrate Anti-Federalist efforts to dominate it; and he has urged others to serve. If he remains in retirement and rejects all entreaties to accept the office of President, it will appear as an act of renunciation of his own duty and of his sincerely expressed beliefs in the new government.

"... I certainly will decline it," he wrote on December 23, "if the refusal can be made consistently with what I conceive to be the dictates of propriety and duty. For the great Searcher of human hearts knows there is no wish in mine, beyond that of living and dying an honest man, on my own farm."[22]

CHAPTER 8

★

January 1789

Washington Will Accept Presidency
Electors Chosen in Ten States

General George Washington has made a series of private decisions that clearly signal he is reluctantly prepared to leave retirement at Mount Vernon and accept election as America's first President.

A reliable source reveals that on New Year's Day the General drew up detailed and "elaborate instructions for the management of his farms" during his anticipated absence in New York City as chief executive officer of the new Federal government.[1]

The hero of the American War of Independence made his decision before ten of the eleven State Legislatures had appointed or elected Electors for President and Vice President. Despite a severe winter freeze along the East Coast, the process on January 7 of choosing Electors from New England to the South went off as planned, giving the first phase of the Electoral College system its trial test.

The second phase of the proposed system, mandated in the new Constitution, will come on February 4 when Electors in the ten States will simultaneously cast two ballots each, choosing the President and Vice President. The third phase, on March 4, will be the counting of Electoral ballots when both houses of the new Congress meet in New York City to certify winners, or to break a tie if there should be one in the vote.

Rhode Island and North Carolina will be left out of the Presidential election because they failed to ratify the Constitution. New

York ratified the document, but its Legislature has been deadlocked since mid-December over the selection of Electors. According to one source, neither the New York Federalist Senate nor the Anti-Federalist Assembly has been able to agree on the method of selecting candidates for New York's two U.S. Senate seats.[2]

Ploy to Prevent Anti-Federalist President

Colonel Alexander Hamilton, 34, a New York lawyer and former military aide to General Washington, maintains the deadlock is a last-ditch effort of the Anti-Federalists, motivated by "the vanity and the malignity of some men" to embarrass the national government at its onset.[3]

Colonel Hamilton is more concerned, according to one source, that the Electoral balloting may produce a victory for someone other than General Washington. The Constitution does not require Electors to use their two ballots to vote separately for President and Vice President. Instead, they can cast two ballots without specifying the office, and the individual with the majority automatically becomes President and the runner-up is Vice President.

Federalists have agreed to support General Washington and John Adams, but Colonel Hamilton believes that the Federalists' zeal for Adams could jeopardize their choice of President. If the Anti-Federalists withhold a few votes from Washington, the Presidency could go to Adams.[4]

"Men are fond of going with the stream," he warned in a January 25 letter to James Wilson of Pennsylvania. "Suppose personal caprice or hostility to the new system should occasion half a dozen votes only to be withheld from Washington—what may not happen? Grant there is little danger. If any, ought it to be run?"[5]

In this letter, a copy having been obtained by this correspondent, Colonel Hamilton proposes that "it will be prudent to throw away a few votes say 7 or 8; giving these to persons not otherwise thought of" to ensure that John Adams will have enough votes to become Vice President but not President, and at the same time to ensure that George Clinton, New York's Anti-Federalist Governor, is checkmated in his effort to gain either office.[6]

Colonel Hamilton admits that he has already gained the concurrence of Electors in Connecticut and New Jersey to follow this formula. He asked Mr. Wilson to use his influence to do the same in Pennsylvania.[7]

Washington — A Potential Caesar?

The *Pennsylvania Packet* (Philadelphia) reported in its January 7 edition that a plot has been hatched by the Anti-Federalists to run Patrick Henry of Virginia for President and Governor Clinton of New York for Vice President. The newspaper urged Pennsylvania Electors to cast their ballots for the Washington-Adams Federalist ticket so they "may have another glorious opportunity of saving their country from ruin."[8]

While General Washington is still considered by most to be the unanimous choice for President, a lone, dissenting voice calling himself "Cato" enraged readers of the January 10 edition of the *Delaware Gazette* by daring to urge that the hero of the recent war not be elected. The essay, addressed to the Electors of Delaware, draws parallels between the extraordinary popularity of the General as President and Commander-in-Chief and the Caesars of the ancient past.

"Let me intreat you therefore," the unknown dissenter stated, "to shew more regard for the liberty of your country, than Rome did, in giving Caesar repeatedly the command of armies!... think that the excess of popularity, is a rapid advance towards the slavery of your dear fellow citizens, and that man who has gained the affections and esteem of your country, and has endeared himself to your countrymen, is utterly unworthy to be elected to a dangerous and important office, and should by no means be intrusted with the command of an army."[9]

Cato sparked a firestorm of criticism, as indicated by an angry reply printed in the January 31 *Delaware Gazette*. "Delawarensis" maintains that Cato's arguments could be compared to a "madman, who attempts to batter down stone walls with bullets of snow" while entrenching himself behind "an immense rampart of fustian, ignorance and self-conceit;...

"In what part of the United States, gentlemen," the essayist addresses the Presidential Electors, "can you find a man so fit to rule as our late general? If you wish to investigate his character—consult ten thousand vouchers and documents, that are now on record—ask the majority of the citizens of these states—consult the opinion of our allies—and even interrogate the late hostile nation of Britain. They are all warm in his commendations. Even envy herself groans with anguish at the contemplation of those virtues which she is obliged to acknowledge." [10]

Symbolic Suit for Swearing In

Besides having drawn up written instructions for the management of Mount Vernon, the General is reliably reported to have written to General Henry Knox, a close friend in New York, asking that he purchase "superfine American Broad Cloth" for a new suit of clothes.

"Mrs. Washington would be equally thankfull to you," he added in his January 29 letter, "for purchasing for her use as much as of what is called (in the Advertisement) London Smoke as will make her a riding habit." [11]

It is assumed that the cash-poor General would not have placed the order for any other purpose than for a new suit of clothes to wear when he is sworn in after the Congress certifies his election. Yet, publicly he continues to maintain a silence on whether he will serve, insisting to all except very close friends that he will not make known his decision until the Electors' votes are counted in March.

General Knox, former artillery chief and close personal friend, has already informed General Washington that the majority of Presidential Electors selected on January 7 is expected to give him, on the eve of his 57th birthday next month, a unanimous mandate to serve. [12]

The symbolic importance the General attaches to wearing a suit made of American cloth for his swearing in, rather than one of imported English fabric, was clearly stated in a letter to the Marquis de Lafayette in Paris written the same day he asked General Knox to order the material.

"I hope it will not be a great while," he wrote to his former military aide, "before it will be unfashionable for a gentleman to appear in any other dress. Indeed we have been too long subject to British prejudices. I use no porter or cheese in my family, but such as is made in America...."[13]

One source reports that with the appearance of the New Year, the General's worry over the outcome of the first congressional elections under the new Constitution has largely vanished. In his January 29 letter to General Lafayette, he noted with satisfaction that the elections of Senators, Representatives, and Electors were "vastly more favorable than we could have expected" and that this was due in some measure to "the good sense of the Americans....

"I think I see a *path*," he added about his hopes for achieving the permanent economic well-being for the nation, "as clear and as direct as a ray of light, which leads to the attainment of that object. Nothing but harmony, honesty, industry and frugality are necessary to make us a great and happy people."[14]

Since January 7, when the Presidential Electors were chosen, General Knox and many other supporters have provided General Washington with, in addition to published reports, a steady stream of political intelligence. General Benjamin Lincoln of Massachusetts, for example, reported in a letter to the General that the chosen Electors in New England are solid for his election and that supporters of the new Constitution have secured a majority of congressional seats.

In reply, General Washington revealed that Electors in Maryland and Virginia have already "been advised" that he looks with favor on their casting votes for John Adams as Vice President as "the only certain way to prevent the election of an Anti-Federalist."[15]

Federalists Sweep House Races

Unofficial returns from ten States that have held elections for seats in the House of Representatives reveal that at least forty Federalists have won seats, while only nine seats were captured by the Anti-Federalists. The nine seats were won in South Carolina, Virginia, Pennsylvania, and Massachusetts, the four States in which the Constitution was bitterly contested. Federalists swept House races in Maryland, Delaware, New Jersey, Connecticut, and New Hampshire. This means that when the First Congress convenes, it will be overwhelmingly Federalist.

Anti-Federalists in Massachusetts were stunned and angry when one of the early leaders of the American Revolution, 66-year-old Samuel Adams, was defeated in his race for a House seat by Fisher Ames, a 30-year-old lawyer. Mr. Adams' supporters stressed his service to the American Revolution, although his defeat may have been principally due to the fact that the voters wanted someone in Congress who would champion their commercial interests. Mr. Adams is widely known to have been a repeated failure at business even though a success at revolutionary political agitation.[16]

Nevertheless, Massachusetts Anti-Federalists had reason to be consoled by winning at least two House seats, one of them captured by a successful Boston merchant and an ally of Mr. Adams, Elbridge Gerry. The 44-year-old outspoken critic of the new Constitution has made it clear that he will not be intimidated by the Federalist majority in the new Congress and that he plans to pursue amendments in the form of a bill of rights.

Mr. Gerry was a Massachusetts delegate to the Philadelphia Convention and he refused to sign the Constitution. He vigorously opposed his State's ratification of the document without a bill of rights. In seeking a congressional seat in the new Congress on this single issue, he has been attacked by Federalists in a bitter, nasty campaign. His foes even spread the false rumor that he had withdrawn from the congressional race.

"Amendments, every citizen has still a right to urge, without exciting a spirit of persecution," Mr. Gerry complained in a published statement on January 22. "Every friend to a vigorous government must, as I conceive, be desirous of such amendments, as will remove the just apprehensions of the people, and secure their confidence in, and affection for, the new government."[17]

Embracing Anti-Federalists' Bill of Rights

The most conclusive evidence that General Washington has made up his mind to serve as President is the disclosure by a reliable source that he has already drafted a sixty-five-page speech he proposes to deliver to the new Congress. This source believes that both James Madison and Colonel Hamilton have been secretly asked to review the draft.[18]

A partial copy of the draft, obtained by this correspondent, reveals a concern for placing the economy on a sound footing and, at the same time, offers an olive branch to the Anti-Federalists by supporting amendments to the Constitution, or a bill of rights.

By taking this stand, General Washington hopes to win Anti-Federalist support for the new government and to head off amendments he believes various States will offer that would forbid direct taxation, denying the government necessary revenue for its operation.[19]

In the draft, the General discloses a firm opinion he did not publicly display during or after the Philadelphia Convention. He notes, for example, that if a "promised good" of the new Constitution were to terminate in an unexpected evil, it would not be the first instance of folly in "short sighted mortals."

"Should, hereafter, those who are intrusted with the management of this government," he observes in his speech draft, "incited by the lust of power and prompted by the Supineness or venality of their Constituents, overleap the known barriers of this Constitution and violate the unalienable rights of humanity: it will only serve to shew... that no Wall of words, that no mound of parchmt. can be so formed as to stand against the sweeping torrent of boundless ambition on the one side, aided by the sapping current of corrupted morals on the other."[20]

Madison Outflanks Henry

Ironically, James Madison in his race against James Monroe for a Virginia congressional seat has been subjected to rough campaign attacks similar to those against Mr. Gerry in Massachusetts.

Patrick Henry has been accused of spreading rumors among minority groups such as the Virginia Baptists that Mr. Madison opposes amendments, particularly safeguards for religious minorities, and thus has "ceased to be a friend to the rights of conscience."

Baptist Minister George Eve demanded that Mr. Madison provide a statement refuting the charge.[21]

Bending to pressures in his State, Mr. Madison, on January 2, wrote the minister: "It is my sincere opinion that the Constitution ought to be revised, and that the First Congress meeting under it ought to prepare and recommend to the states for ratification the most satisfactory provisions for all essential rights, particularly the rights of conscience in the fullest latitude, the freedom of the press, trials by jury, security against general warrants etc."[22]

By firmly pledging to work for a bill of rights if elected to the First Congress, Mr. Madison may have effectively stolen the Anti-Federalists' remaining issue, ensured his own election over James Monroe, and denied the Anti-Federalists justification for convening a second convention, which he believes would seek to undo the work of the Philadelphia Convention.

His personal relationship with opponent James Monroe, nevertheless, has been cordial. They have even traveled together the last two weeks, presenting opposing views to groups congregated in churches throughout the Virginia counties each hopes to represent.

"Service was performed and then they had music with two fiddles," Mr. Madison related of observers at one stop. "They are remarkably fond of music. When it was all over we addressed the people and kept them standing in the snow listening to the discussion of constitutional subjects. They stood it out very patiently— seemed to consider it a sort of fight of which they were required to be spectators. I then had to ride in the night twelve miles to quarters; and got my nose frostbitten, of which I bear the mark now."[23]

CHAPTER 9

★

February 1789

Washington and Adams Elected
Madison Wins House Seat

Secret ballots were simultaneously cast by 138 Presidential Electors from New Hampshire to Georgia on February 4 resulting in the election of Virginia's George Washington, 56, as President and John Adams, 53, of Massachusetts as Vice President.

Heavy snow covered most roads and ice-bound rivers made water transport impossible during the last month. Dispatch riders have struggled over near-impassable roads to deliver Electoral ballots to officials in New York City for certification by the new Congress as called for in the Federal Constitution.

One observer later stated that never was an election so much a foregone conclusion yet so tortuous in its official consummation.[1]

The First Congress is to meet in New York on March 4 to count the Electoral College ballots from the ten States. However, official congressional certification may be delayed if the severe winter weather continues, preventing the required quorum from traveling long distances.[2] According to one source, the votes unofficially at this writing are:

George Washington	69
John Adams	34
John Jay	9
John Hancock	4

George Clinton 3
All Others............................. 19
TOTAL................................. 138 [3]

The number of Electors per State was based on the combined
number of Senators and Representatives:

Massachusetts......................... 10
Pennsylvania.......................... 10
Virginia............................... 10
Connecticut 7
South Carolina......................... 7
Maryland.............................. 6
New Jersey 6
Georgia............................... 5
New Hampshire 5
Delaware.............................. 3
TOTAL................................. 69 [4]

Adams Tie with Washington Averted

In the participating States there is little information to explain
why Electors cast their secret ballots as they did. A 69 to 69 tie
between General Washington and John Adams was feared, had all of
the second votes been cast in favor of Mr. Adams. Each Elector had
two votes. The unofficial February 4 results indicate that all Electors
cast their first ballot for George Washington, with their second vote
scattered among John Adams and sectional or political choices.

New York, North Carolina, and Rhode Island did not participate
in the Presidential balloting. If they had, their sizable Anti-
Federalist factions might have thrown the majority to someone
other than General Washington. This could have clouded the outcome, forcing the new Congress to break a tie, if one had occurred,
in the newly elected House of Representatives as required by the
Constitution.

Rhode Island and North Carolina refused to ratify the
Constitution, leaving them outside the Union and preventing their
participation in the first Presidential election to be held in any

nation in the world. New York, the eleventh ratifying State, has been deadlocked over choosing Electors as well as electing Senators to the first Federal Congress.

Campaign to Cut Adams Vote

A preliminary analysis of the returns from the ten states reveals that John Adams failed to receive any votes in Delaware, Maryland, South Carolina, and Georgia.[5] Dr. Benjamin Rush of Philadelphia assured Mr. Adams in a February 21 letter, a copy having been obtained by this correspondent, that the results in the four States were in part the product of "jealousy of the New England States" and because those States voted for retaining New York City as the temporary capital instead of choosing Philadelphia.[6]

There may have been other behind-the-scenes maneuvering, however. Just before the February 4 balloting, New York's Colonel Alexander Hamilton secretly circulated a proposal among key Federalists in Connecticut to have their Electors cast votes for someone other than John Adams in order to minimize the risk of a tie; or, worse yet, to avoid a total upset with Mr. Adams possibly securing more votes than General Washington should the Anti-Federalists have prevailed in some States.[7]

At this writing, because of delayed communications, it is not known whether the four States that abstained from voting for Mr. Adams did so because of Colonel Hamilton's intervention.[8] Dr. Rush was not totally forthright when he wrote to Mr. Adams, for he confirmed to others that when Pennsylvania's Electors met in Reading, several votes were "thrown away from Mr. [John] Adams, to prevent his being equal in votes to General Washington."[9]

Vice President-elect Adams' personal and political pride has been deeply wounded by the pre-election intriguing and plotting. He has told friends that it is astonishing to him that anyone would have doubted that General Washington would secure every Electoral vote for President.

"For myself I only regret," he states, "that the first great Election should be tarnished in the Eyes of the World and of Posterity with the appearance of suspicion and of an Intrigue. Who were the

Knaves and who the Fools I neither know nor care; but there is a strong appearance that a proportion of each Species must have been concerned." [10]

Deep Distrust of Adams

At least one Elector, David Stuart of Virginia and a close friend of General Washington through marriage connections, privately concedes that he regrets voting for Mr. Adams. He maintains that the Vice President-elect has made himself unpopular.

"As I consider it very unfortunate for the Government," he wrote to General Washington, "that a person in the second office should be so unpopular. I have been much concerned at the clamor and abuse against him—" [11]

It has also been asserted that the thirty-four Electoral votes he secured were principally to prevent selection of an Anti-Federalist Vice President and were not based on his own merits. One observer says that a genuine lack of personal or political support for Mr. Adams is also due in some measure to his contemptuous attitude toward those who lack his keen mind.[12] Thomas Jefferson and James Madison believe that he harbors monarchist leanings after serving so long as a diplomat in Europe, first in France, later in Holland and in Great Britain. Congressman Madison wrote Minister Jefferson last fall, insisting that Mr. Adams' "impatient ambition" to be President would not make him "a very cordial second to the general." Mr. Madison also alleges that during the War of Independence, the Signer of the Declaration of Independence conspired against General Washington while he was a member of the Continental Congress.[13]

Fair-minded opponents can charge only against his character and a "foolish jealousy towards Washington," one observer believes. He also argues that at no time was there ever a danger that Mr. Adams would equal General Washington in the Electoral College.[14]

If this is the case, and the preliminary counts indicate as much, it raises the question why Colonel Hamilton sought to make the issue central to the voting. One suggestion is that the anti-Adams campaign was mounted to diminish the Vice President-elect's prestige, to curtail his influence in the new administration, and to diminish his demonstrated capacity to pursue an independent course rather than the Federalist party line.[15]

It is expected that Colonel Hamilton will become an important member of General Washington's administration, and his relationship with Mr. Adams is likely to ripen into a fierce personal feud, predicts an observer.[16]

Federalists Target Foes

Paradoxically, while Colonel Hamilton was working to deny John Adams Electoral votes, the most outspoken and most powerful Anti-Federalist, Patrick Henry, was desirous of ensuring General Washington as many votes as possible. Virginia Federalist Elector James Wood, Jr., reported on February 17 that when the State's Electors met in Richmond, Patrick Henry as one of them "attended in perfect good humour and was extremely anxious that Genl. Washington shou'd not lose a single vote in this or any other State."[17] This correspondent has learned that despite Mr. Henry's strong opposition to the Constitution, he placed General Washington's name first on his ballot. His second vote went to Anti-Federalist George Clinton of New York.[18]

Before the Virginia Electors met on February 4, the popular five-term Governor had been widely mentioned as a Vice Presidential candidate, as well as a Presidential candidate. But he had not permitted his name to be advanced as urged by Anti-Federalist supporters and he did not receive a single vote in the balloting.

Despite the apparent Federalist election sweep, supporters are still targeting Anti-Federalist leaders in bitter published attacks. For instance, Patrick Henry for the past two months has been the target of "Decius" in the *Virginia Independent Chronicle*, published in Richmond.

No stranger to personal attacks, he is now accused of opposing the Constitution because of "AMBITION, AVARICE, ENVY, HATRED AND REVENGE." Mr. Henry assumes these attacks are inspired by Federalists who wish to dilute his political influence.[19]

He was instrumental in securing three Electoral votes for New York Governor George Clinton, who also has become the target of slashing attacks in the press this month. A series of articles in New York newspapers, signed by "H.G.," calls into question Governor Clinton's wartime service against the British.

"No man can tell when or where he gave proof of his generalship, either in council or in the field," the writer charges.[20] Governor Clinton is standing for re-election this year and the attacks are believed to be part of an effort to defeat him and thus prevent his appointment of two Anti-Federalists to the U.S. Senate.[21]

General Washington and Governor Clinton continue to have a close, cordial friendship, forged during the War of Independence, despite their current disagreements over the powers of the new national government. President-elect Washington has maintained a discreet silence about his own election, but expressed delight over the Federalist sweep of House and Senate seats.

"All the Political Manœvers which were calculated to prevent or to impede the execution of the new Government," the General wrote on February 5, "are now brought to a close until the meeting of the new Congress; and although the issue of *all* the Elections are not yet known, they are sufficiently *Displayed* to authorize a belief that the opposers of the government have been defeated in almost every instance."[22]

Indian Wars and Balloting

General Washington may have a sense of deep disappointment that one of his most daring military commanders in the War of Independence, Major General Anthony Wayne, failed in Georgia to secure a Senate seat. Despite the fact that Georgia gave General Wayne an 800-acre rice plantation in recognition of his role in liberating Georgia from British military rule, the State Legislature did not elect him to the Senate principally because it insisted that he was a citizen of Pennsylvania and not of Georgia. General Wayne affirms he has lived in the State for three years.[23]

The most southern and least populous State did elect Federalists to the two Senate seats and the three House seats in the middle of an on-again off-again savage Creek Indian war that has been raging on the Spanish-Florida frontier since September 1787. Georgia is strongly Federalist in the belief the new national government will aid it in settling the conflict. The strife may have been the reason for a small voter turnout in contests for the three House races; only 4,000 ballots were cast in seven election districts for a slate of twenty-eight candidates.[24]

Georgia's two Federalists who take their Senate seats next month will be joined by Federalist Senators from other States, and that will bring the Federalist total in the upper house to eighteen. The sole State to send two Anti-Federalists to the Senate is the State with the most-admired citizen: General Washington, from Virginia. However, the largest and most populous of all the States elected a majority of Federalist Congressmen; only two Anti-Federalists were elected.[25]

Madison Secures House Seat

General Washington is particularly pleased that James Madison won a U.S. House seat handily on February 2, defeating James Monroe. One observer credits his victory to last-minute personal campaign appearances and a published pledge in the Orange district's newspapers promising to support amendments to the Constitution after the First Congress formally convenes in New York City.[26]

Anti-Federalists are privately convinced that Mr. Madison's public pledge was an election ploy and are skeptical that he will carry it out. They have reasons to be concerned, since the Congressman-elect had opposed amendments during the ratification struggle in the States. He and other Federalists agreed to consider amendments in the form of a bill of rights only when they faced certain defeat in the key ratifying states of Massachusetts and Virginia.

Deep snows, frozen rivers and streams, along with bad roads, have persuaded Mr. Madison that the March 4 convening of the First Congress is likely to be delayed. He arrived at Mount Vernon on February 23 to wait for a thaw and break in the weather. The delay is giving him time to confer privately with President-elect Washington, who may be seeking Mr. Madison's advice on what course of action to pursue as President.[27]

General Washington has drafted a sixty-five-page speech for delivery to the new Congress but Mr. Madison has counseled the President-elect not to deliver the address, arguing that it reveals too much of his personal feelings and is too specific in its legislative proposals.[28] He predicts that the forthcoming Congress will be beset by "contentions" between Federalists and Anti-Federalists and between "Northern & Southern parties, which give additional disagreeableness to the prospect."[29]

Even though the General may take Mr. Madison's advice, he indicates in the draft his sincere belief in his countrymen and in the new Congress's ability to rise above its partisan and sectional differences and to adopt measures promoting the general welfare.

"It belongs to you to make men honest in their dealings with each other, . . ." he exhorts them. "I trust you will not fail to use your best endeavors to improve the education and manners of the people; to accelerate the progress of arts and Sciences; to patronize works of genius; to confer rewards for inventions of utility; and to cherish institutions favorable to humanity."[30]

Maryland House Races Rigged

The President-elect was not only pleased with the Federalist win of eight House seats in Virginia, but with the win of all six congressional seats in Maryland. The General on February 2 expressed to Maryland Governor John E. Howard his belief that "the large majority by which they were chosen" will silence any future charges that the sentiment of the people was not in unison with the Maryland State Convention which ratified the Constitution.[31] Anti-Federalists in Maryland have repeatedly charged that the State Ratifying Convention approved the new Constitution without offering the critics of the document an opportunity to propose amendments.

What Governor Howard did not reveal to the President-elect is that the Maryland Legislature allowed for only seventeen days between passage of its election law and the opening of the polls. The law provided for a State-wide at-large election with six districts. Each voter was entitled to vote for six candidates, one in each district rather than from the voter's district; thus the Federalists effectively neutralized Anti-Federalist voting strength in at least three counties and virtually ensured the sweeping victory that so gratified General Washington.[32]

"This shameful daring violation of the constitution was made by *the federals* in our Assembly," angrily stated an Anti-Federalist in the February 13 edition of the *Maryland Journal* of Baltimore, "and not from ignorance or inattention, but *design* to prevent the election of *particular characters*. This conduct of the federals in the House of Delegates was dishonourable, and in the Senate disgraceful."[33]

Bad Weather and Ballots

Severe snow and plunging temperatures made voting from Virginia to Massachusetts in December, January, and February difficult and in some cases impossible. One Maryland Presidential Elector, for example, was unable to reach Annapolis from his home on the Eastern Shore because of heavy ice in the Chesapeake Bay.[34]

General Washington reported that when he left Mount Vernon on February 2 to vote in nearby Fairfax County for congressional candidate Richard Bland Lee, the temperature ranged from twenty degrees the previous night to twenty-six degrees at high noon.[35]

Elsewhere in Virginia, voters who cast their ballots for either James Madison or James Monroe in the tricounty congressional race had to do so in temperatures that had fallen to ten degrees below zero.[36]

The *Pennsylvania Mercury* (Philadelphia) lamented on January 8 that many freemen in that State apparently assigned the severe snow and ice as reasons for not attending town meetings to make known their choice of Federal Representatives and Presidential Electors. "The chilling frosts of winter, are but trifling compared to the consequences which will result from choosing men to govern us, who are unworthy of our trust and confidence...."[37]

In Massachusetts eight inches of snow fell throughout most of the State the day before elections. The snow and resulting impassable roads hindered the voter turnout as well as the collection of the vote totals.[38]

CHAPTER 10

★

March 1789

New Congress Convenes
Snow and Ice Delay Start

Severe snow and ice storms roared down from Canada in the last month, delaying the official convening of the First Congress, scheduled for March 4. A majority of absent members struggled over snow-covered roads or waited for rivers and harbors to thaw. Congressman James Madison of Virginia, after his arrival in New York City on March 14, reported that "the badness of the Roads & the weather" required him and some fellow lawmakers to spend twelve days on the road, traveling the 225 miles from Alexandria, Virginia, with stops in Baltimore and Philadelphia.[1]

Anxiety over the absence of a quorum moved eight Senators and eighteen House members to address two separate letters on March 11 to missing members, saying that "no arguments are necessary to evince to you the indispensable necessity of putting the Government into immediate operation; and therefore earnestly request, that you will be so obliging as to attend as soon as possible."[2]

The First Congress will have a total of eighty-one House and Senate members, representing eleven States. Rhode Island and North Carolina failed to ratify the Constitution and remain out of the new Union. Of the eighty-one men sitting in the new Congress, fifty-four had been active in earlier delegations regarding the new government. They either had been delegates to the Philadelphia Convention, which drafted the Constitution, or had participated in their State Ratifying Convention; some had been active in both. Only seven of the eighty-one members of the First Congress had opposed ratification.[3]

New York City celebrated the unofficial convening of Congress on March 4 by a day-long ringing of church bells and firing of guns.[4] According to New Hampshire Senator Paine Wingate, the city spent $50,000 on refurbishing Federal Hall to accommodate the First Congress in the hope the city will be chosen as the permanent seat of the new national government over its rival, Philadelphia. General Wingate noted further that the "expence of living" was considerable, said to be "one third dearer than at Philadelphia."[5]

"It is *solely* to the public spiritedness of our Citizens," noted the *New York Morning Post* of the former City Hall in its March 14 edition, "that we may attribute the erection of such a superb Edifice—an Edifice that would grace any Metropolis of Europe.... by far the most extensive and elegant of any in America...."[6]

In fact, the City Council of New York retained the French architect Pierre L'Enfant to supervise the Federalist-style refurbishing of the building that had previously housed the Confederation Congress from 1785 to its official expiration this year.[7] One source reports that the cost to the city was really $65,000, financed by lotteries and a special local tax.[8]

Ghosts of Confederation Congress

When the First Congress finally achieves a quorum, its first order of business will be to verify the ballot count of the first Electoral College and put into motion procedures for inaugurating General George Washington as the first President and John Adams as the first Vice President. The new Congress also faces the task of drawing up legislation creating various departments of the executive, establishing a system of Federal courts, and creating a Supreme Court as called for in the Constitution.[9]

Many members of the new Congress fear the body may repeat the principal failure that did much to destroy the effectiveness of its predecessor. As one observer points out, one of the persistent problems that crippled the Confederation Congress was chronic absenteeism, caused by bad weather, family matters, or private business. The lack of a quorum meant a delay of legislative decisions and gave the appearance of ineptitude and inefficiency.[10]

Throughout most of this winter the old Congress failed to achieve a quorum. As a result, the single-branch Confederation government could not function as a bridge to the new, three-branch Federal government. As one member points out: "... the Appearance in Europe, and perhaps even here, of the old Congress being in full operation and tranquilly yielding the seats to the new would have a good effect." [11]

As it now stands, the old Congress is expiring without making "a last will and testament," and members of the new Congress, some of whom were members of the Confederation Congress, have while waiting during much of March wondered whether the ghost of old failures and unresolved problems will haunt them.

As a member of both the old and the new, Congressman Madison is concerned that the delays will damage the credibility of the new national government, particularly as it relates to the swollen foreign and domestic debt and the government's empty purse.

"A considerable delay will be unavoidable," he forecast on March 29, "after the ballots are counted, before the President can be on the spot, and, consequently, before any Legislative act can take place. Such a protraction of the inactivity of the Government is to be regretted on many accounts, but most on account of the loss of revenue." [12]

New York Federalist Surprise Win

While members of the new Congress waited impatiently throughout most of March, the New York Legislature managed a partial break in its political deadlock when it set March 3–6 for election to its six House seats. Unofficial returns over the last few weeks indicate a surprise upset: the Federalists captured four seats to the Anti-Federalists' two.[13]

One observer has told this correspondent that the Anti-Federalists, expecting to do well in the balloting, were as severely disappointed at their defeat as the Federalists were pleased "at their surprising strength." Federalists now maintain that the capture of the four House seats signals "growing public acceptance of the Constitution."[14]

However, the Legislature in Albany adjourned on March 3 without appointing two U.S. Senators. It has been deadlocked since last December over the appointment of Presidential Electors and Senators. Speculation is widespread that New York City might not remain the temporary capital if it fails to elect Senators. Colonel Alexander Hamilton suggested to allies on January 29 that it was possible to force the selection of Federalist Senators by using the threat of the loss of the temporary capital to Philadelphia.[15]

To force Anti-Federalists to vote for ratification of the Constitution last July, Federalists pointed up the dire economic consequences of losing the seat of government. The threat may have also played a part in the surprise Federalist victory in the House races this month and could eventually prove crucial in the selection of the two Senators from New York.

Fraud Alleged in New Jersey

In New Jersey's election for House seats, Governor William Livingston declared on March 19 the election won by four Federalist candidates. Supporters of defeated Anti-Federalist candidates Abraham Clark and Jonathan Dayton alleged fraud and manipulation by allowing the polls to remain open until Federalist candidates were assured of victory. One observer has said that the Legislature set no closing hour for the polls, allowing local officials to leave the polls open until the at-large elections produced the desired majority.[16]

Mr. Clark and Mr. Dayton, both Signers of the Declaration of Independence and the new Constitution, ran in northern New Jersey counties close to New York, while their opponents ran in southern counties nearer to Philadelphia. In the wake of the long Confederation congressional debate last year over the temporary capital, the New Jersey elections have proved to be a continuation of this debate, with Governor Livingston certifying southern candidates who favor Philadelphia.[17]

Supporters of Mr. Clark and Mr. Dayton say they will ask the new Congress to overturn the Governor's decision. (Congress is already faced with having to decide a disputed House race in South Carolina.) Mr. Clark sought the help of New York lawyer Colonel Alexander Hamilton, one of the principal advocates of the Constitution, but, according to Mr. Clark, Colonel Hamilton advised him not to mount an appeal, saying it would be disruptive to the start of the new Congress which is faced with more pressing problems.

"I feel myself out of all patience with Col. Hamilton," Mr. Clark bitterly wrote to a friend. "He really appears to be, what I have some times thought him, a shim sham politician.... His politics are such as will not stand the test. He will soon refine them to nothing...." [18]

Problems Facing First Congress

During much of March the restive and anxious members of Congress have had many discussions even though they could not take any formal action without a quorum. According to a reliable source, one topic of conversation is the eventual location of the permanent seat of the government. Other subjects they have discussed among themselves are the problems of forming the new government, organization of a judiciary, and establishing a system for raising revenues. [19]

Pressure for a Bill of Rights

Besides concerns about swollen debts and an empty purse, there is the political pressure for amendments to the new Constitution. Mr. Madison of Virginia was elected to a House seat on a campaign pledge to work for amendments in the First Congress. By making this pledge last month, he hoped to nullify the need for a second convention, which he fears would destroy or mutilate the work of the Philadelphia Convention.

One observer has pointed out that while some Anti-Federalists consider "the first Congress as a second Convention," [20] Federalist domination of the House (49 to 10) and the Senate (18 to 2)* will

---

* New York's Senators have not yet been appointed by the Legislature.

make it difficult for Mr. Madison to move his Federalist colleagues to act on amendments.

Thomas Jefferson wrote Mr. Madison a long letter from Paris, a copy of which has been obtained by this correspondent, that may serve as support for amendments in the form of a declaration or a bill of rights. Minister Jefferson views a bill of rights as a way to restrain the power of the new Federal government; such restraints have also been demanded by more moderate critics of the Constitution.

"The executive in our governments," the U.S. Minister to France wrote on March 15, "is not the sole, it is scarcely the principal object of my jealousy. The tyranny of the legislatures is the most formidable dread at present, and will be for long years. That of the executive will come in its turn, but it will be at a remote period.... I am much pleased with the prospect that a declaration of rights will be added; and hope it will be done in that way which will not endanger the whole frame of the government, or any essential part of it." [21]

Pressure from the States on Madison to deliver a bill of rights is already enormous. One observer points out, for example, that at least five of the eleven States that ratified the Constitution have demanded a bill of rights and that eight States have proposed a total of 210 amendments. When the duplications are omitted, the number stands at about 100. [22]

Mr. Madison faces a balancing act in the First Congress. He will have the task of selecting a dozen or so amendments to frame a basic bill of rights, guarding essential personal liberties. At the same time he must defeat those designed by foes of the Constitution, amendments that would, for example, curb the new government's power to tax and to regulate commerce. He must also overcome the apathy or the opposition of many Senate and House members who are Federalist colleagues.

Mr. Madison may find opposition to amendments from one of his principal allies at the Philadelphia Convention, Roger Sherman of Connecticut. Elected to a House seat in a Federalist sweep of the State, the widely respected 67-year-old Signer of the Declaration of Independence, the Articles of Confederation, and the new Constitution has gone on record as opposing amendments.

"On the whole," he wrote in the *New Haven Gazette* last December 18, "it is hoped that all states will consent to make a fair trial of the constitution before they attempt to alter it, experience will best shew whether it is deficient or not, on trial it may appear that the alterations that have been proposed are not necessary, or that others not yet thought of may be necessary, every thing that tends to disunion ought to be avoided. Instability in government and laws, tends to weaken a state and render the rights of the people precarious." [23]

Plums of Power

Aggravating the problems of the close political adviser to General Washington is the steady stream of requests for appointments in the national government. In March alone, even before his election was verified, Mr. Madison received correspondence filled with pleas for appointments, ranging from clerks to both Houses, to customs collectors and naval commissions.

He has even received a request that Congress consider funding a discovery that would allow mariners to determine longitude when navigating on the high seas. Another plea was from the inventor John Fitch, asking Mr. Madison to present to Congress his petition for respecting his claims of exclusive right to his "Invention of Steam-boats." [24]

In the late summer of 1787, a number of delegates to the Constitutional Convention in Philadelphia viewed Mr. Fitch's demonstration of his steam-powered boat on the Delaware River. Dr. Benjamin Franklin, America's most famous inventor, concluded that he did not see much of a future for the invention. [25]

In the meantime, at Mount Vernon (awaiting certification by Congress that he has been elected the first President) General Washington, too, has been overwhelmed with letters from friends and admirers seeking appointive posts in the new government.

"Scarcely a day passes in which applications of one kind or another do not arrive," the General wrote in a letter on March 21. "... I would not be in the remotest degree influenced, in making nominations, by motives arising from the ties of amity or blood. ..." [26]

The General made it clear that while he wants appointees of character, he astutely wants the appointive plums of power distributed evenly in the different States to minimize jealousies. Otherwise, "fatal consequences" might arise and compromise all that had been hard-won and set into motion, by raising "a flame of opposition that could not easily, if ever, be extinguished.

". . . I can with truth declare," the General added with great compassion, "that several of the candidates, who have already come forward. . . are men of unquestionable talents, who have wasted the flower of their lives, in the civil or military service of their Country; men who have materially injured their properties, and excluded themselves from obtaining a subsistence for their families by the professions they were accustomed to pursue. There are some, I might add, who have shed their blood and deserved all that a grateful Country has to bestow."[27]

Washington's Own Woes

Although it has been a tightly held secret, a source has revealed that as General Washington prepares to assume the office as first President of the American Republic, he has been forced to borrow 600 pounds sterling at 6 percent interest to pay his most pressing debts and to meet anticipated travel expenses to New York City for himself and his wife, Martha. Mrs. Washington has made no secret of her great bitterness at the pending destruction of her domestic life — blaming fate, not the General — as her husband reluctantly prepares for what he considers is his duty.[28]

Compounding his personal money woes is the illness of his mother. The General left Mount Vernon for a two-day trip south to Fredericksburg to visit his 80-year-old mother, who is reliably reported to be slowing dying of breast cancer. Anticipating a long absence from Virginia, he apparently viewed the visit as a final one, the "last act of personal duty I may ever have it in my power to pay [her]."[29]

On his return to Mount Vernon, the General reviewed plans with his nephew for the management of his farms while he is away. He is also reported to have made it clear to Congressman Madison in a

March 30 letter why he declined New York Governor George Clinton's offer to use his private home until an official residence is provided.

The General, conscious that his every action will be watched, wants "to be placed in an independent situation" and therefore believes that rooms in "the most decent tavern" are preferable to a private home.

". . . I mean to avoid private families on the one hand," he explained to Mr. Madison, "so on the other, I am not desirous of being placed *early* in a situation for entertaining. Therefore, hired (private) lodgings would not only be more agreeable to my own wishes, but, possibly, more consistent with the dictates of sound policy. For, as it is my wish & intention to conform to the public desire and expectation, with respect to the style proper for the Chief Magistrate to live, it might be well to know. . . what these are before entering upon it." [30]

Madison: "Prime Minister"

Although General Washington expressed to Congressman Madison his sympathy that delay in getting the new government into gear "must be very irksome to the attending members," [31] he did not admit that he was grateful for the delay.

". . . For myself," he confided to his closest personal friend, General Henry Knox, "the delay may be compared to a reprieve; for in confidence I assure *you*, with the *world* it would obtain *little credit*, that my movements to the chair of Government will be accompanied by feelings not unlike those of a culprit who is going to the place of his execution: so unwilling am I, in the evening of a life nearly consumed in public cares, to quit a peaceful abode for an Ocean of difficulties, without that competency of political skill, abilities and inclination which is necessary to manage the helm." [32]

The General is almost certain to rely on Mr. Madison for political advice and assistance. In fact, one source has told this correspondent that the Virginia lawmaker is likely to function as President-elect Washington's "prime minister," acting as a bridge between the legislative and executive branches during the critical months ahead as the new Federal government takes concrete form.[33]

The principal intellectual advocate of the new Constitution took his seat in the new Congress two days before turning 38. Almost twenty years the junior of General Washington, Mr. Madison occupies a position of influence and power second only to that of the President-elect. Having spent years perfecting new and novel theories of republican government, he is now on the eve of having those theories undergo the acid test of actual experience under the document he so vigorously supported.

CHAPTER 11

★

April 1–20, 1789

Congress Begins Business
Adams Sworn in As Vice President

Members of the first Federal Congress of the United States, with pent-up impatience in many after four weeks of delay, turned to the task this month of organizing itself and certifying the election of George Washington as President and John Adams as Vice President of the United States.

The House of Representatives began its first formal business on April 1 with a bare majority of thirty-five members, although some were ill at ease with the fact that the convening date was All Fools' Day. After agreeing to the establishment of rules of procedure for the House, the appointment of a staff of seven — including a Clerk and Door Keeper — the House elected its Speaker, Frederick Augustus Muhlenberg. The German-educated minister and Pennsylvanian Federalist politician, who speaks better German than English, was chosen, according to one source, because he provides geographical balance between a Virginia President and a Massachusetts Vice President.[1]

Maryland Congressman William Smith has revealed to this correspondent that the Pennsylvania congressional delegation is threatening to make a motion to move the temporary capital from New York to Philadelphia after the House and Senate count the Electoral ballots and certify the election of George Washington and John Adams.

"... Indeed the members of both houses," Congressman Smith said, "seem much dissatisfied with this place—Boarding is very high & by no means so good, as at Phila. or Baltimore, nor do I think this the proper place for the permanent residence of Congress on many accounts."[2]

Electoral Ballots Counted

The threatened motion had not materialized by April 6 when the Senate convened with the arrival of Virginia Senator Richard Henry Lee — the necessary twelfth member for a majority.[3] The Senate and House met in a joint session in the Senate Chamber of the newly renovated Federal Hall and watched as the Electoral ballots from ten states were counted.[4] A Senate and a House member each sat at the Clerk's desk and jointly tabulated the predictable results for President: 69 for George Washington; and the other votes totaled 34 for John Adams and 35 for ten other candidates. The Speaker and the House members then withdrew.[5]

"I AM directed by the House of Representatives," Congressman James Madison later reported to the Senate, "to inform the Senate, that the House have agreed, that the notification of the election of the President and of the Vice President of the United States, should be made by such persons, and in such a manner, as the Senate shall be pleased to direct."[6]

Historic Messengers

Immediately, the Senate dispatched two special messengers — Charles Thomson rode South to General Washington at Mount Vernon, and Sylvanus Bourne sailed north to Braintree, Massachusetts, to the home of John Adams. Mr. Bourne, a 33-year-old Boston merchant, first met the Vice President-elect when he was engaged in Netherlands trade and Mr. Adams a diplomat in Holland. He left New York by Rhode Island packet boat and, with a fine wind, made the trip in fifty hours.[7]

Mr. Thomson required seven days to reach Mount Vernon, explaining that he was "much impeded by tempestuous weather, bad roads and the many large rivers I had to cross. . . . "⁸ At the Hackensack, New Jersey, ferry, on his first day, for example, the wind was so strong and water so rough that he had to wait until midmorning the next day before crossing. "Such is one of the blessed effects of Congress being cooped up in the midst of so many rivers," he observed.⁹

An Irish-born former schoolmaster, Mr. Thomson, now 60, served as Secretary of the Continental Congress from 1774 to its demise, where he had the duties of one of the "principal civil departments of government." One observer told this correspondent that Mr. Thomson was chosen to inform General Washington of his election since he was the perfect symbol of the old Congress passing the torch to the elected executive head of the new national government.¹⁰

During Mr. Thomson's long service without interruption he made many friends, and many enemies. It was his political enemies in New England and the South, this correspondent has learned, who successfully blocked his appointment as Secretary of the Senate. While Mr. Thomson was on his way to Mount Vernon, the Senate voted Samuel A. Otis into the post after many ballots. Mr. Otis is the former Speaker of the Massachusetts House of Representatives and brother of the early Revolutionary hero James Otis, Jr.¹¹

Danger of Congressional Delay

Before the departures of the two messengers, John Langdon, Senate President pro tempore, authorized Mr. Thomson to apply to the Board of Treasury "for such sums as you may judge necessary for the expenses of the journey." Mr. Bourne was authorized "one hundred dollars towards defraying the expenses" of his journey.¹² Their expenses were undoubtedly kept to a minimum, for as just about everyone knows, the Congress of the Confederation expired a pauper. The financial health, if not the very life of the new government, depends on revenues raised from import duties. Most importation is done in the spring, with part of the duties paid customs agents upon docking and the balance due approximately six months later.

If Congress delays approving a list of tariffs, the new government cannot count on revenue for twelve to eighteen months more.

The political consequences of this could mean, at worst, that the Federal government might not survive past its birth.[13]

On April 8, Congressman James Madison of Virginia introduced a plan in the House, not unlike the one first adopted by the Confederation in 1783, consisting of specific duties on imported spirits, wines, teas, pepper, sugars, cocoa, and coffee. Hopes for a smooth sailing hit a sandbar when other lawmakers sought to add to the list, raising greater debate and with it more delay.[14] Mr. Madison proposed, for example, an 8 cent per gallon tax on molasses, which is imported from the Caribbean and used by New England distillers to manufacture rum. The proposal was vigorously objected to by Massachusetts Representative Fisher Ames. Rum making, the 30-year-old* Congressman pointed out, is a direct source of wealth for New England. It would shipwreck the region's distilleries, he asserted, since the imports of molasses helped pay for the production of rum which was then exported. Not only that, such a tax was a tax on the poor who used molasses rather than sugar.

"I conceive, sir," he added, with pointed references to Mr. Madison, "that the present Constitution was dictated by commercial necessity more than any cause.... We are not to consider ourselves, while here, as at church or school, to listen to the harangues of speculative piety; we are here to talk of the political interests committed to our charge."[15]

Adams Tastes "Wine of Popularity"

Rum toasts were offered throughout Boston after Sylvanus Bourne arrived at Mr. Adams' Braintree farm on April 9 to inform him officially of what he has unofficially known since March. Already prepared for his journey, the Vice President-elect left the next day for Boston, escorted by 150 mounted militiamen and 40 carriages of local and state officials, and along the way greeted by 13-gun artillery salutes.[16]

---

* Fisher Ames celebrated his 31st birthday on April 9.

Boston church bells announced the entourage's arrival as cheering, hat-waving crowds shouted John Adams' name. One observer noted that he has become more popular in the last few weeks than his famous cousin, Samuel Adams, who lost a House seat to Fisher Ames. John Adams is tasting "the strong wine of popularity" and drinking deeply of its intoxicating effect after being so long overseas and out of sight, suffering slights and wounds.[17]

The short, rotund, and intense Vice President was met by the handsome, trim, and vain, yet popular, Governor John Hancock at his official residence. The Governor, who ordered all of the public honors for Mr. Adams, gave no outward indication of his deep disappointment that he had not received the post promised by Federalists in exchange for supporting ratification of the Constitution.[18]

Positioning for Presidential Succession

During his six-day journey from Boston to New York, traveling by land rather than by ship, the Vice President-elect was met at major cities and small towns alike by cheering crowds, effusive officials, mounted military escorts, and cannon salutes.[19]

Upon his arrival in the temporary capital on April 20, he was escorted into the city by officers and mounted troops, who were joined by citizens on horseback and in carriages, as a Senate and House committee welcomed Mr. Adams.[20] The following day, after he took the oath of office as Vice President, he gave a speech to the new Senate, over which he will preside as its president. Mr. Adams said: "A trust of the greatest magnitude is committed to this Legislature—and the eyes of the world are upon you."[21]

But according to one observer, the Vice President has his eyes on members of the Senate who, he believes, are rivals harboring an ambition to succeed General Washington. Some Senate members are already accusing Mr. Adams of promoting the idea that the President-elect, reluctant to serve in the first place, might resign in Mr. Adams' favor once the wheels of the new government are set in motion.

"I am Vice President. In this I am nothing, but I may be everything," Mr. Adams is reported to have said in private.[22]

Some comments about Mr. Adams are not flattering. Senator William Maclay of Pennsylvania is one of those who supported Mr. Adams for the Vice Presidency, with his own purposes in mind. He was anticipating that New England would vote to move the new capital to Philadelphia.

"But his Pride Obstinacy And Folly Are equal to his Vanity," Senator Maclay privately observed of the Vice President. "... Yet John Adams has served to illustrate Two points at least to me, viz That a fool is the most Unmanageable of all Brutes— and That Flattery is the Most Irksome of All Service." [23]

Philadelphia physician Dr. Benjamin Rush, a political ally of Senator Maclay's, has sought to flatter the Vice President by insisting that his role as presiding officer over the Senate will give him "great weight" in making appointments to the first offices in the new government. Dr. Rush urged that he support James Wilson for Chief Justice of the Supreme Court. The Pennsylvanian was a Signer of the Declaration of Independence, one of several delegates at the Philadelphia Convention who helped to frame the Constitution, and a Signer of that document.

Dr. Rush wrote to Mr. Adams: "... His Abilities & knowledge in framing the constitution, & his zeal in promoting its establishment, have exposed him to a most virulent persecution from the antifederalists in this state.... Should Mr. Wilson be left to sink under this opposition, I shall for ever deplore the ingratitude of republics." [24]

Mr. Wilson, a 47-year-old lawyer who as a Pennsylvania Elector voted for President Washington, has already written Mount Vernon offering to serve as Chief Justice. [25]

Hero's Welcome

Most members of the House and Senate realize that no substantive business of Congress can be concluded until General Washington arrives in New York and is formally sworn in as the first elected President under the new Constitution.

The President-elect is expected to arrive in New York on April 23 and a joint congressional committee composed of three Congressmen and two Senators will meet the General in New Jersey and escort him by barge to the lower tip of New York City. The city of 23,000 is expected to swell by twice that number as, in the words of Congressman Smith of Maryland, "a great deal of parade & ceremony will take place" to welcome the military hero of the American Revolution.[26]

"All the world here and elsewhere," noted Pennsylvania Federalist John Armstrong, Jr., "are busy in collecting flowrs & sweets of every kind to amuse and delight him in his approach and at his arrival.... Yet in the midst of this admiration there are Sceptics who doubt its propriety and wits who amuse themselves wt. its extravagance. The first will grumble, and the last will laugh and the Presidt. should be prepard to meet the attacks of both with firmness and good nature."[27]

Satirical Drawing of Washington

Mr. Armstrong was undoubtedly referring to a printed drawing that has been circulating in the last two weeks on the streets of New York City. Entitled "The Entry," it satirizes the spirit of the day by depicting General Washington riding a jackass led by his aide David Humphreys. Beneath the drawing is printed:

> The glorious time has come to pass
> When David shall conduct an Ass ...[28]

The flyer illustrates that not everyone in New York City views General Washington with blind hero worship. Nonetheless, the regard with which he is held by most Americans nearly reaches a religious fervor. This magnitude of feeling is shared by most members of the new national Congress. New Jersey Federalist Congressman Elias Boudinot, former President of the Confederation Congress, for example, wrote to General Washington on the day the House and Senate jointly counted the Electoral ballots.

"The importance of this transaction," Mr. Boudinot wrote on April 6, "is so great in my estimation that I consider it, under Providence, as the key-Stone to our political Fabrick. It is from this Consideration alone, that I can rejoyce with you Sir, as a private

Friend, on your elevation to this dignified but difficult Office; by which you must again leave, all the sweets of domestic Felicity, which to yourself individually considered, cannot be repaid by all the honors of the world—I feel your delicate Situation—You have no choice in this great Business—Providence & your Country call, and there is no place for a refusal—The Sacrifice is required & the Offering must be made...." [29]

Outpouring in Newspapers

As the news slowly made its way north and south that the Congress in New York had certified the Presidential election, editorials, songs, and odes began appearing in newspapers from Boston to Baltimore. For example, the *Federal Gazette* published the following poem titled "TO THE FATHER OF HIS COUNTRY."

>   While *greater bards* invoke a muse of fire,
>   And, borne on Fancy's wing, to Heaven aspire;
>   In strains majestic sing thy well-earn'd fame,
>   And to a wondring world thy worth proclaim;
>   Shall thy untutor'd muse, with feeble lays,
>   Attempt a subject which transcends *their* praise?
>   Yes, gen'rous chief, the grateful talk be mine,
>   While simple truth shall dictate ev'ry line,
>   To give a plain, a just, but concise view
>   Of Freedom's darling Son, great Sir—of you.—
>   In Fancy's fields let tyrant's flatt'rers stray:
>   Wretches who make the human race their prey
>   Might shock mankind, if seen without disguise,
>   And bid their gen'rous indignation rise—
>   To sanction guild and varnish flagrant crimes,
>   Ignoble task! the fawning flatt'rer rhymes;
>   But rhymes in vain—Beneath the mask are seen,
>   Lurking, with haggard looks, and frightful mien,
>   Rapine and murder, avarice and pride,
>   With ev'ry vice the poet strives to hide.

Thus too th' abandon'd prostitute* presumes
With patches, paints; with washes, and perfumes,
To hide her loss of honor and of fame,
And strive, at least, *to form* a virtuous dame—
Unhappy female! all *her* wiles are vain;
The virtuous fair one, modest, neat, and plain,
(True tests of virtue!) needs no foreign art,
To warm, inspire, and captivate the heart:
For the chaste nymph, with secret pride, can boast
That she's, "when unadorn'd—adorn'd the most."—
Let then the muse all arts of flatt'ry shun,
Nor once offend the ear of Washington
With durgid bombast or high sounding praise—
Come, Candor, come and pen these honest lays.
First see the hero at his country's call
Leaving his peaceful home, his friends, his all,
Rushing impetuous to the hostile field
And forcing Britain's chosen troops to yield.
What toils what hardships did he undergo!
What variegated scenes of human woe,
Thro' eight successive years, did he withstand,
To purchase freedom for his native land!
With him the naked soldier could sustain
The winter's piercing frost, the snow and rain:
The gallant chief inspir'd each gen'rous soul
With freedom's sacred flame, and to the goal
Of glory led them on, 'till, peace procured,
Freedom obtained, and happiness restor'd,
The gallant hero sheath'd the deathful sword—
That sword which ne'er was drawn but to oppose
Fair virtue's, freedom's, and his country's foes—
Then crown'd with laurels to his sabine farm
Return'd with joy. No more the dire alarm
Of dreadful war invites him to the field,

---

* Great Britain.

Columbia's rights from foreign force to shield.
But other foes too soon their place supply'd—
Licentiousness with faction at her side,
Detested fiends! had almost overthrown
That glorious Freedom by his prowess won.
'Tis thus while mariners Charybdis shun,
That they oft' times by Scylla are undone:
Short-sighted mortals, ever prone to stray.
Seldom or never steer the middle way.
Lo now again th' illustrious Chief appears,
Relieves our sufferings, and dispels our fears,
Saves by his councils, what his arms have won,
And shows himself bright Freedom's fav'rite Son.
    Immortal worthy! long may'st thou preside
With honor o'er thy Country's peace, and guide
A grateful People to true happiness,
Oh may propitious Heaven thy measures bless!
May faction's cursed voice no more be heard;
May modest merit find its due reward;
May Science, parent of each useful art,
Her chearing influence to our land impart—
Long may'st thou live, and when to Heaven remov'd,
Oh may thy worth, thy virtue be approv'd!-—
May future ages still applaud thy fame,
And tyrants only shudder at thy name.[30]

CHAPTER 12

★

April 14–29, 1789

Wild New York Crowds Hail Washington at End of Seven-Day Triumphal Tour North

With a strong wind at their backs, thirteen experienced harbor pilots acting as oarsmen, wearing white smocks and black-fringed caps, rowed President-elect George Washington across Newark Bay to Staten Island where a collection of small craft joined the barge as it turned into the Upper Bay and headed for the tip of New York's Manhattan Island.[1]

A joint committee of the new Congress and civil representatives of New York City had made the two-hour boat trip to Elizabethtown, New Jersey, from Wall Street on the afternoon of April 23 to meet General Washington. The President-elect later described the display of decorated boats in the harbor, some with musicians aboard, the roar of ships' cannons, the decorations, and the wildly cheering crowds, as creating in him "sensations as painful. . . as they were pleasing."[2]

The General, dressed in a black cocked hat and a suit of blue and buff made from American woven fabric, stepped from the red moreen-curtained barge and mounted the carpeted steps to a platform where he was greeted by his old friend, Governor George Clinton. The New York Governor's formal words of greeting were lost in the ear-shattering roar of the crowd, the ringing of church bells, and the discharge of ship and shore cannon.[3]

One eyewitness reported that the thousands on shore waving their hats resembled "the rolling motion of the sea, or a field of grain waving with the wind. . . . The General was obliged to wipe his eyes" as he wended his way slowly and solemnly through the sea of wildly cheering humanity.[4]

"He frequently bowed to the multitude," another eyewitness told this correspondent, "and took off his hat to the ladies at the windows, who waved their handkerchiefs, threw flowers before him and shed tears of joy and congratulation. The whole city was one scene of triumphal rejoicing."[5]

Historic Moment at Mount Vernon

The President-elect's thunderous New York City reception climaxed a seven-day triumphal tour northward — an emotional tidal wave of a journey that one observer said took on in every town and city all of the trappings of a coronation.[6]

On April 14, as the clock in the hall at tranquil Mount Vernon struck the hour of noon, the clatter of coach and horse hooves announced the arrival of the General's old colleague from Continental Congress days, Charles Thomson. They exchanged greetings and compliments, the General aware from a letter he had received earlier from his former artillery chief Henry Knox that the old patriot was on his way to confirm officially what the entire country has anticipated for months.[7]

Standing in the brightly painted large, formal banquet room of Mount Vernon, the two faced each other. The General listened solemnly as Mr. Thomson made a short speech and then read from a letter signed by the President pro tem of the new Senate. The key sentence read: "I have now Sir to inform you that the proofs you have given of your patriotism and of your readiness to sacrifice domestic ease and private enjoyments to preserve the liberty & promote the happiness of your Country, did not permit the two houses to harbour a doubt of your undertaking this great this important Office to which you are called not only by the unanimous votes of the Electors but by the voice of America."[8]

Fumbling with his spectacles during an awkward silence, the General read from a prepared reply, conceding that the "unanimous suffrage in my favor" left him no choice but to accept the call to duty and explaining that his silence should evince his gratitude.

"While I realize," he quickly added in a voice whose emotion was well controlled, "the arduous nature of the Task which is imposed on me, and feel my own inability to perform it, I wish however that there may not be reason for regretting the Choice, for indeed all I can promise is only to accomplish that which can be done by an honest zeal." [9]

Two days later, at ten o'clock in the morning of April 16, the President-elect's carriage set out for nearby Alexandria, with General Washington accompanied by Mr. Thomson and Colonel David Humphreys. The General's secretary, Tobias Lear, left the previous day to prepare for the General's arrival in New York. [10] Colonel Humphreys is reported to have drafted some of the General's public speeches during his seven-day triumphal trip north. Copies of those speeches obtained by this correspondent contain none of the reluctance and self-doubt that the General has confessed privately to close friends or committed to his diary, a copy having been obtained by this correspondent:

"About ten o'clock I bade adieu to Mount Vernon, to private life, and to domestic felicity," he wrote with a melancholy resignation, "and with a mind oppressed with more anxious and painful sensations than I have words to express, set out for New York...with the best disposition to render service to my country in obedience to its calls, but with less hope of answering its expectations." [11]

Disruption of Domestic Felicity

Mrs. Martha Washington, after bidding farewell to her General, was reported to have said that "God only knows" when he might come home to stay and enjoy Mount Vernon in the graying twilight of their lives. "I think it was much too late for him to go into publick life again,—but it was not to be avoided," she added without any effort to disguise her unhappiness at the disruption of their family life. [12]

Mrs. Washington, age 58, is expected to join the President-elect in a month. Although she "cannot blame him for having acted according to his ideas of duty," her heart will remain at Mount Vernon and with her two growing grandchildren.

"... I know too much of the vanity of human affairs," she confided to a female friend, "to expect felicity from the splendid scenes of public life. I am still determined to be cheerful and to be happy, in whatever situation I may be; for I have also learned from experience that the greater part of our happiness or misery depends upon our dispositions, and not upon our circumstances. We carry the seeds of the one or the other about with us, in our minds, wherever we go."

With the utmost honesty, she did admit that her "new and unwish'd for situation" may not be a burden because of the kindness of friends and that if she were younger, she might indeed enjoy "the innocent gaities of life" in New York.[13]

During the General's first stop in nearby Alexandria, friends and neighbors drank thirteen toasts at a dinner, less a tribute to his uncertain future than a farewell to his pastoral past that had been filled with work on the Mount Vernon lands, shared with friends and neighbors only a short horseback ride away.

"All that now remains for me," he said with quiet anxiousness, "is to commit myself and you to the protection of that beneficent Being who, on a former occasion has happly brought us together, after a long and distressing separation. Perhaps the same gracious Providence will again indulge us with the same heartfelt felicity. But words, my fellow-citizens, fail me; *Unutterable sensations must then be left to more expressive silence: while, from an aching heart, I bid you all, my affectionate friends and kind neighbors, farewell!*"[14]

During the seven-day, 225-mile journey, the President-elect was seldom without a military escort and a delegation of local civil dignitaries and only then when out in the open countryside and away from a town or a city. These continual relays of mounted guards of honor at times threw up clouds of dust to the point that the General could barely see the countryside, and the settled dust was often so thick it was impossible to know the true color of his coat or trousers.[15]

Shining Eyes and Tight-Throated Cheers

In Baltimore on April 17 he was greeted by local artillery and feted at a dinner at the Fountain Inn[16] where an endless succession of toasts and speeches kept him up late. Determined to cover as much distance each day as official greetings and the outbursts of enthusiastic strangers would permit, he departed Baltimore before 5:30 A.M. to the roar of cannon. Prominent citizens on horseback escorted him seven miles until he stopped his carriage and persuaded them to return home.[17]

In the sparsely settled countryside of Maryland on April 18 and in southern Delaware on the 19th, farmers from their fields and workmen from shops turned out to greet him. Some were veterans who with shining eyes and tightness in their throats cheered their former military chief. Local church bells hailed his coming and his going and local militia cannon saluted him as well.[18]

He reached Wilmington on April 19, the fourteenth anniversary of American and British musket fire exploding at Lexington and Concord. Before his departure the following day, the city's elected officials expressed the by now familiar greetings, and their gratitude for his giving up his cherished retirement to answer the call of his country. The President-elect read a suitable reply drafted by his aide, David Humphreys. With this, his carriage set off for Philadelphia with an eager and ever-present mounted escort, described by one observer as "honorable but hampering."[19]

A Laurel Crown

With reluctant envy, a troop of horse from Delaware watched at the Pennsylvania State line as another troop stood at stiff and adoring attention, ready to conduct the "President-General" to Philadelphia. One troop had been waiting all night and after the proper military honors "due his rank and exalted character," the procession moved out to Chester, a hamlet fifteen miles from the city, to take breakfast and rest a few hours.[20]

The President-elect left Chester on a white stallion, while Colonel Humphreys and Mr. Thomson followed in his carriage. The nearer the procession got to Philadelphia, the longer it grew. At every crossroads a new detachment appeared. The entire formation would pause so that the General could accept the welcoming speeches of the riders, who would then fall in at the end of the steadily lengthening line.[21]

The *Pennsylvania Packet* reported that as the long column approached Philadelphia "every fence, field, and avenue" was lined with cheering faces. Cannon boomed, church bells rang, and ships on the Delaware River broke out their pennants in welcoming salutes. One observer estimated that at least 20,000 people waited hours in the city to glimpse the hero of the American Revolution who had led his ragged men through that same city twelve years before, wearing a sprig of green as an emblem of hope.[22]

When General Washington reached Mr. Grey's bridge on the Schuylkill River leading into the city, one eyewitness reported that at each end of the bridge "magnificent arches, composed of laurel emblematical of the ancient triumphal arches, used by the Romans...," were erected, having been designed by Charles Willson Peale. As he started across the bridge, there was dropped with precise accuracy "above the Hero's head, unperceived by him, a civic crown of laurel." [23]

Heading a long column of troops, which were joined by the cheering crowd as he passed, the General acknowledged with a dignified nod of his head the thousands who lined Philadelphia's Market and Second Streets. At City Tavern, a dinner for 250 was served as the General sat patiently through the endless effusive toasts and tributes. A fireworks display over the city ended the General's day. He retired, exhausted, at City Tavern rather than lodge at the lavish home of U.S. Senator Robert Morris, which would have left him open to the charge of partiality.[24]

A Hero's Welcome with Song and Flowers

When April 21 dawned with rain, the General deftly dissuaded a city troop of horsemen from escorting him to the Delaware River ferry landing for Trenton. He would not "think of traveling under cover, while they were exposed to the rain on horseback."[25] Upon arriving at the bridge south of Trenton, where thirteen years before he grieved as his troops bled and died, he saw a great arch, supported by thirteen pillars, each decorated in evergreens. The arch bore an inscription wreathed in flowers:

THE DEFENDER OF THE MOTHERS,
WILL BE THE PROTECTOR OF THE
DAUGHTERS[26]

As General Washington passed under the arch, "a number of young Misses, dressed in white and crowned with wreaths and chaplets of flowers," holding baskets of blossoms sang:

Virgins fair, and Matrons grave,
Those thy conquering arms did save,
Build for thee triumphal bowers,
Strew, ye fair, his way with flowers—
Strew your Hero's way with flowers.[27]

One eyewitness reported that each of the singers scattered at the feet of the General's horse blossoms from her basket. For a brief few moments all at the crowded bridge barely took a breath at the scene that "bathed many cheeks with tears." General Washington expressed later in a handwritten card addressed to the Ladies of Trenton that the scene and song "have made such an impression on his remembrance, as... will never be effaced."[28]

Tidal Wave of Tribute

After the obligatory dinner and speeches in Trenton, he was off at dawn the next day, April 22, to Princeton where he received a formal address from the college and made a brief reply. Then his carriage continued on the familiar road to New Brunswick. Another military escort and a band playing martial airs added to the enthusiasm of the townsfolk, nearly all of whom lined the streets.

At Woodbridge he passed the night as the New Brunswick escort stood watch. Away at the first light of dawn, he arrived by early afternoon at Elizabethtown, which was overflowing with officials from the town and delegations from New Jersey and New York State and City. From here the final fifteen miles were to be by barge. It seemed as if the entire population followed him to the dockside where he boarded a lavishly and expensively decorated barge built for the occasion and at the expense of leading citizens. Before embarking, he had refreshments and punctiliously acknowledged the three U.S. Senators and five House members who had come as the official delegation of the new Congress. His old friend Secretary at War Knox was on an accompanying boat.[29]

The barge passed by Staten Island, swung out into the Upper Bay, and then entered the inner harbor. As it approached the tip of Manhattan Island, porpoises offered playful greetings, flanked and followed by a flotilla of small ships flying pennants and flags. A Spanish packet broke out on its riggings twenty-eight foreign flags as the barge passed its anchorage; its thirteen-gun salute received a return salvo from a battery of eighteen pounders on shore.[30] Once he was ashore, official greetings were drowned out by the noise of crowds, cannons, and church bells, the scene obscured by the thick smoke of artillery salutes. The President-elect became for a time a prisoner of the crushing crowds in the human tidal wave of tribute. One eyewitness reported that the people were so close "you might have walked on people's heads for a great distance."[31]

The crush grew so great that the procession from the dock to the President-elect's official residence on Cherry Street was delayed and could only move at the command of officials and by their pushing and shouting and using staves. Later, after a review of yet another military honor guard, receiving officers who had served under him, and listening to welcoming speeches, barely heard above the church bells and beating of drums, the General and honored guests attended a dinner hosted by Governor Clinton. Afterward, the greatly fatigued hero retired amid the evening noise to rest, and to prepare for his swearing in as the new nation's first President. The heavy rain that evening did not dampen the joy that will live forever in the hearts of "every lover of the Saviour of our Land."[32]

"'This great occasion,'" stated the *Gazette of the United States*, "'arrested the publick attention beyond all powers of description—the hand of industry was suspended—and the various pleasures of the capital were concentered to a single enjoyment' — All ranks and professions expressed their feelings, in loud acclamations, and with rapture hailed the arrival of the FATHER OF HIS COUNTRY." [33]

CHAPTER 13

★

April 30, 1789

Washington Takes Oath
Urges Reliance on Providence and People

George Washington took the oath of office today, April 30, as the United States' first President under the new Constitution. It was immediately ratified by the largest and wildest crowd in New York City's history. The spectators packed the narrow cobblestone streets and cheered themselves hoarse while city bells and artillery offered ear-splitting salutes.[1] Dressed in a dark brown suit, made from cloth woven in Hartford, Connecticut, white silk stockings, and black shoes with silver buckles, his handsome head framed by finely powdered white hair pulled to the back, the 57-year-old hero of the American War of Independence stood at the portico of the Senate Chamber at Federal Hall and repeatedly bowed and nodded.

With one hand tightly grasping his steel-hilted sword and with his other on his heart, the General was clearly overcome by the waves of wild approval cascading upward from Broad and Wall Streets in the lower part of the island port city on the Hudson River.[2]

A hush fell over the throng when a little before one o'clock today, a day that began gray but gave way to golden sunshine, the solemn six-foot one-inch Virginian turned and took a few graceful steps inside the Senate Chamber toward a dais raised a yard above the floor.

Members of the newly elected Congress, State and city officials, and foreign diplomatic ministers rose from a semicircle of chairs. The General bowed to both sides and was escorted to the center of three chairs under the dais canopy by Vice President John Adams. They exchanged bows; Mr. Adams took a chair on the General's right and Speaker Frederick Muhlenberg on his left.[3]

Adams Momentarily Speechless

According to one observer, there was a moment of absolute silence, Vice President Adams then rose and for the first time in his political career, for the longest moment of his life, was struck speechless.[4]

"Sir, the Senate and House of Representatives of the United States," the Vice President finally said in a rush of words wrapped in his nasal New England accent, "are ready to attend you to take the oath required by the Constitution. It will be administered by the Chancellor of the State of New York."[5]

"I am ready to proceed," General Washington replied simply in a soft Virginian accent. Both then walked to the half-enclosed portico overlooking the street, where there was a small table draped in red cloth. On this had been placed a crimson cushion which held a large leather-covered Bible. The Bible was almost forgotten until, at the last moment, someone suggested its use and another fetched it from the nearby Masonic Lodge. Since those standing at the portico could be seen from the street, and from rooftops and windows across the street, Washington's reappearance turned the silent sea of expectant faces into renewed waves of wild cheering, which he returned with a bow, again and again, with his hand over his heart.[6]

A sudden silence fell as Chancellor Robert R. Livingston faced George Washington — two tall men separated by small, short Samuel Otis, Secretary of the Senate, holding the Bible on its crimson cushion. The General put his right hand on the book and repeated after Livingston the thirty-four-word oath of office in reverential tones, as if he were repeating a prayer. After adding the words "So help me God" to the oath, the President then bent down to kiss the Bible, relieving the short Mr. Otis of the embarrassing struggle to hold the book as high as his height would allow.[7]

Chancellor Livingston, a member of the Continental Congress when George Washington became military Commander-in-Chief fourteen years before, said quietly, "It is done."

He then turned to the crowd and in a voice of joyful triumph shouted: "Long live George Washington, President of the United States!" The cry was taken up by the crowd and with it came the clear benediction, "God bless our President."[8]

The American national standard with its thirteen stars and stripes was raised atop Federal Hall: a signal for a nearby artillery battery to fire a throaty thirteen-gun salute. The Spanish sloop *Galveston* shuddered at its anchor in response, the guns of war drowning out the church bells of peace.[9]

Like rolling thunder, thousands of human voices hailed President Washington with an explosion of emotion. At first responding with bows, he soon sensed the incoherent roar was not likely to subside quickly. He turned and went inside the Senate Chamber, pulling from his pocket his prepared speech that had been drafted with the help of Congressman James Madison of Virginia.

Religious Nature of Inaugural

One observer later reported that the President delivered his twenty-minute address in so low a voice that his audience had to lean forward to hear.

"This great man," one eyewitness related for this correspondent, "was agitated and embarrassed more than ever he was by the leveled cannon or pointed musket. He trembled, and several times could scarce make out to read."[10]

A third of the speech was given over to religious references, such as his "supplications to that Almighty being who rules over the universe," and he noted that every step of the Revolution "seems to have been distinguished by some token of providential agency...."[11]

He expressed his ardent love for his country, and linking the power of Providence from Heaven with the power of the people on earth, he told his awestruck audience: "...we ought to be no less persuaded that the propitious smiles of Heaven, can never be expected on a nation that disregards the rules of order and right...since the preservation of the sacred fire of liberty, and the destiny of the republican model of government, are justly considered as DEEPLY, perhaps as FINALLY staked, on the experiment entrusted to the hands of the American people."[12]

President Washington made only an indirect recommendation to the new Congress: consideration of amendments to the new Constitution. However, he cautioned that it should "carefully avoid every alteration which might endanger the benefits of an united and effective government...."[13]

Amendments, or a bill of rights, are potentially the most explosive political issue that is expected to come before the new Congress. In endorsing what he had earlier opposed, the President is apparently attempting to diffuse the issue that might disrupt his design for a harmoniously working relationship between the executive and the legislative branches of the new national government.

He concluded his unevenly articulated address by asking for a "divine blessing" and for "temperate consultations—and the wise measures on which the success of this government must depend."[14]

A Testament of Tears

President Washington's softly spoken final words died away in the large Senate Chamber. He folded his speech, as a long, awed silence prevailed. He bowed and sat down, his face etched in exhaustion, making him appear old.

After much handshaking, the President walked between lines of saluting militiamen to nearby St. Paul's Chapel "to hear divine service, performed by the Chaplain of Congress." Prayers were from a "Proposed" Book of Common Prayer, for the American Protestant Episcopal Church was younger even than the government. The Te Deum was sung with an overpowering effect.[15]

"Every one without exception," confided the Comte de Moustier, the French Minister, familiar with aristocratic pretensions and appearances, "appeared penetrated with veneration for the illustrious chief of the republic. The humblest was proud of the virtues of the man who was to govern them. Tears of joy were seen to flow in the hall of the senate, at church, and even in the streets, and no sovereign ever reigned more completely in the hearts of his subjects than Washington in the hearts of his fellow citizens. Nature, which had given him the talent to govern, distinguished him from all others by his appearance. He had at once the soul, the look, and the figure of a hero. He never appeared embarrassed at homage rendered him, and in his manners he had the advantage of joining dignity to great simplicity." [16]

A Squabbling Senate

President Washington was left to dine privately and to reflect on the problems he will confront in the next four years. Members of the Senate returned from St. Paul's Chapel to Federal Hall with the purpose of preparing a formal reply to the inaugural address.

An angry debate erupted, according to one observer, over whether the reply should include the words, "most gracious speech," used by the British Parliament in replying to the King of England. So many objections were raised that the wording of the response was postponed. But the Senate did decide today to strike out that phrase lest the people consider the words "the first step of the ladder in the ascent to royalty." [17]

With only the experience of monarchy for guidance, the dispute over possible contamination of the new American government had erupted earlier when Vice President John Adams, presiding over the Senate, suggested that the President be addressed as "His Most Benign Highness." A Senate committee voted for "His Highness the President of the United States of America and Protector of the Rights of the Same."

According to a reliable source, when General Washington was told this by Congressman Madison before the inaugural, he was greatly annoyed. Fearful that such "foolishness" might endanger unity between the executive and the legislative, he urged Mr. Madison to block the measure when Congress meets after today's inaugural. Nevertheless, a spirited congressional debate is expected over the issue.[18]

Standing on "Untrodden Ground"

When President George Washington officially begins his duties tomorrow, he heads a national government in name and form only, but not in structure or with financial substance.

There is nothing to the new United States government but a President and a Congress. He has only the precedent of the "imperfect" and "feeble" Confederated government to guide him. There are no departments, no official advisers, and no arrangements for the collection of revenue or for the management of the postal system.

The national army consists of a few scattered soldiers who face Spain to the South and to the West; Great Britain is to the North with her powerful fleets. The newly formed American government has no navy, no funds to build one, no ready cash reserves.[19]

President Washington faces much the same grim constellation of circumstances as he had in June 1775. Interestingly, it was Adams of Massachusetts, now Vice President, who offered the original resolution for Washington's appointment as Commander-in-Chief of the Continental Army. It was a political move to draw Virginia into the War of Independence against Great Britain.[20]

The President is also aware that unlike his role as a leader in military affairs, which were abundant with historical and recent precedent and guidelines, this novel government has no precedent to direct him as political leader. The task is made more difficult since the drafters of the Constitution said little about the role or style of the chief executive because it was assumed that George Washington would serve as the first President and that he could be trusted to define its role.

"All see, and most admire, the glare which hovers round the external trappings of elevated office," the newly sworn-in President observed to a friend. "To me there is nothing in it. . . . In our progress towards political happiness my station is new; and, if I may use the expression, I walk on untrodden ground. There is scarcely any part of my conduct wch. may not hereafter be drawn into precedent. Under such a view of the duties inherent to my arduous office,

I could not but feel a diffidence in myself on the one hand; and an anxiety for the Community that every new arrangement should be made in the best possible manner on the other." [21]

When darkness descended over this temporary capital of the new national government, illuminations and fireworks lighted the sky. Between the old fort and the Bowling Green a large illuminated transparent portrait of the President was displayed for the crowd. The illumination featured an emblem of "Fortitude" above his head, on his right hand was "Justice," symbolizing the new Senate, and on his left was "Wisdom," representing the House of Representatives.

After the evening festivities had faded, the press of people was so great that President Washington and his aides could not use their carriage. They had to walk, part of the way in darkness, to their lodgings. [22]

Such an end to this extraordinary day underscores the uncertainty that President Washington faces as he feels his way into the future. The President fears that the outpouring of public adulation signifies that the American people expect much more than his administration and the new Congress can possibly deliver. According to one source, some members of Congress fear that the adulation will convert the new President into an elected monarch. [23]

Today's edition of the *New York Journal* published a poem illustrating the intensity of feeling toward the President.

ODE
Sung on the arrival of the
PRESIDENT of the UNITED STATES
(Tune "*God save Etc.*")

HAIL, thou auspicious day!
Far let America
    Thy praise resound;
Joy to our native land!
Let ev'ry heart expand,
For WASHINGTON's at hand.
    With glory crown'd!

Thrice blest Columbians hail!
Behold, before the gate,
   Your CHIEF advance;
The matchless HERO's nigh!
Applaud HIM to the sky,
Who gave you liberty,
   With Gen'rous France.

Illustrious Warrior hail!
Oft' did thy sword prevail
   O'er hosts of foes,
Come and fresh laurels claim,
Still dearer make thy name,
Long as immortal Fame
   Her trumpet blows!

Thrice welcome to this shore,
Our leader now no more,
   But ruler thou;
Oh truly good and great!
Long live to glad our state,
Where countless honors wait
   To deck thy brow.

Far be the din of arms,
Henceforth the olive's charms
   Shall war preclude;
These shores a HEAD shall own,
Unsully'd by a throne,
Our much lov'd WASHINGTON,
   The great, the good.[24]

CHAPTER 14

★

May 1789

Foreign Plots Worry Washington
Bill of Rights Burning Issue

Agents of Spain and Great Britain are plotting in secret against frontier territories of the United States, which fact poses a potential external crisis for the newly formed Washington government.

A reliable source has told this correspondent that before leaving Mount Vernon in mid-April, President Washington received intelligence "too authentic to be disregarded, of private machinations by real or pretended agents both of Spain and Great Britain." [1]

According to this same source, Spain has decided that the vital Mississippi River will remain closed to the trade of American western frontier settlers as long as they remain politically affiliated with the new national government. Spain is holding out the prospect that should frontier settlers choose to "form an independent empire," the vital waterway would be reopened to their trade. The river is the primary source of transportation for these far-inland settlers.

Perhaps even more ominous is a report reaching New York that the British Governor of Canada, Lord Dorchester, has sanctioned a secret plan for the military seizure of New Orleans from Spain and for fortifying the mouth of the Mississippi. [2] Lord Dorchester is the former Sir Guy Carleton and he is regarded as one of the ablest British generals who fought during the recent War.

Kentucky Settlers Spanish Target

President Washington is well aware that a war between Spain and Great Britain would inflame America's frontiers and bring into use Indian tribes as surrogates of opposing sides. Tribes have already renewed savage hostilities against American settlers in the Kentucky territory and the Ohio Valley.

The President wrote the Governor of Virginia on May 16 expressing "great concern" over fresh "murders committed by the Indians" last month. He pointed out that recent treaties have been concluded with several tribes and that more accurate information needs to be supplied frontier military commanders to make certain the right tribes are held responsible for the alleged murder of white settlers.[3]

Representative James Madison received a warning from a close friend in the western territory that the national government must provide protection for western settlers from Indian attacks or Spain would profit from them.

"... I know fifty families of Dutch," relates George Nicholas in a May 8 letter, "who have been repeatedly driven by the Indians from their settlements, and are now living on rented land who are determined unless they can return with safety to their own land to go to the spanish Country where they are offered land and protection without paying for either."[4]

For the last two years, Spain has been accused of inciting and arming Indian tribes against American frontier settlers. President Washington has rejected suggestions that military force be used to put an end to Spanish efforts to inflame the American frontier. He fully realizes that the new national government has neither the men nor the money to mount a military effort.

Rather, he advocates perseverance of temperate policies and good dispositions that will produce "such a system of national policy, as shall be mutually advantageous to all parts of the American Republic."[5]

Bill of Rights: A Burning Public Issue

The President has made it clear in private conversations with Congressman Madison that he wants and needs a period of domestic political tranquility and unity in both foreign and domestic affairs if the government is to have any hope of success.

The single issue that could disturb domestic peace would be the failure of Congress to enact a series of amendments to the Constitution. A delay with amendments would almost certainly kindle a domestic firestorm and make it difficult for the Washington administration to deal with either domestic or foreign problems. Critics of the Constitution could immediately argue that the document was narrowly approved by key States principally because the Federalists pledged to support amendments after ratification.

To avoid being faced with such a threat, Congressman Madison, on May 4, gave notice to the House of Representatives that he had planned to bring up for debate on May 25 the issue of amendments. However, the debate about raising revenue has delayed his proposal until next month.

Outflanking Political Foes

One observer credits the soft-spoken Virginian with shrewdly preparing the groundwork for a congressional debate on amendments by maneuvering both the legislative and the executive to go publicly on record as favoring congressional debates on amendments. The President mentioned in his inaugural remarks that he approved amendments, and the House's reply also referred to amendments. Mr. Madison is believed to have briefed President Washington on what he plans to present on June 14.[6]

His announcement on the House floor May 4 was an effort to spike the guns of Anti-Federalist Patrick Henry and his congressional surrogate, James Bland of Virginia. For on the following day, Congressman Bland presented to the lower house a petition from the Virginia Legislature for a general and second convention to consider amendments.[7]

Virginia's document states that congressional discussion is likely to delay debate on amendments, but that the Constitution has provided an alternative "by admitting the submission to a convention of the states...."[8]

Mr. Madison is convinced that any convention of the States would be dominated by foes of the Constitution who would seek to curb severely the powers of the new national government. Adding to his concerns, if amendments are not presented soon in the Congress, are the arguments of House members who say they are satisfied with the document and favor a few years' trial before considering amendments. And there are those in the House who favor amendments but believe that Congress cannot afford to take time away from the immediate task of organizing the new government.[9]

New York State has deepened Mr. Madison's worries by following Virginia's lead and submitting to the new Congress on May 6 a petition from its Legislature calling for a convention of the States. The wording in one section of the petition is particularly worrisome since it proposes that "certain powers in and by the said Constitution granted, would not be exercised until a convention should have been called and convened for proposing amendments."[10]

A Powerful Politician

The amendment issue is also a matter of personal and political honor for Mr. Madison. He was elected to his House seat because he pledged to work in the First Congress for amendments to the Constitution. The public campaign pledge proved decisive in his victory over James Monroe, who opposed the Constitution and has fought hard for a bill of rights.

In just two years, the still youthful 38-year-old has emerged as the second most influential person in the new national government. President Washington's power comes from a public adoration and admiration of his wartime leadership. Patrick Henry's power extends from public admiration of his forceful personality and oratorical powers in support of freedom during the pre-Revolutionary days and afterward. Mr. Madison, by intellectual argumentation, quiet persuasion, and astute maneuvering, has become a key figure in the new government. He drafted President Washington's inaugural address, he wrote the May 5 reply of the House, and, in turn, the President's May 8 response to the lower house and his reply to the Senate of May 18. Hence, in the opening series of formal messages between the first President and the First Congress, Mr. Madison "was in dialogue with himself." [11]

Before entering politics, Mr. Madison studied theology with the idea of entering the ministry. It was not surprising that the first series of purely cordial exchanges between the President and the Congress made repeated religious references to ". . . the invisible hand which has led the American people through so many difficulties. . . ." [12]

Adams-Washington Exchanges

In Great Britain, it has been a long-standing tradition for the House of Commons and the House of Lords to reply to addresses from the King of England. The American Colonial Legislatures and later State Legislatures responded to a formal address of the respective executive by delivering the reply in person. [13]

On May 18 Vice President John Adams, as presiding officer of the Senate, followed this tradition by delivering the upper house's response at the President's temporary residence on Cherry Street as the President stood by and listened.

According to one eyewitness among the eighteen Senators who accompanied him, the Vice President's hands trembled as he read from a prepared text placed in his hat, which he held with both hands. This made it difficult for the short Vice President smoothly to turn the pages of the text while attempting to face the tall President. [14] Nevertheless, Mr. Adams struggled on with trembling voice:

> We feel, Sir, the force, and acknowledge the justness of the observation, that the foundation of our national policy should be laid in private morality; if individuals be not influenced by moral principles, it is in vain to look for public virtue. . . . [15]

In his brief reply, President Washington had as much difficulty as Mr. Adams. Pulling from his vest pocket the text of his prepared response with his right hand, while his left hand held his hat, the President had to balance his hat on his forearm to reach in his pocket for his spectacles. Finding too many objects in his hands and clearly embarrassed, the President finally set the glass case on the chimney mantel. He then awkwardly adjusted his spectacles while shifting his hat under his left arm and held his speech in his right hand.[16] He began with a stiff and halting manner:

> ... I now feel myself inexpressibly happy in a belief, that Heaven which has done so much for our infant nation will not withdraw its providential influence before our political felicity shall have been completed; and in a conviction, that the Senate will at all times co-operate in every measure, which may tend to promote the welfare of this confederated republic—[17]

The ordeal over, the President politely invited everyone to sit, only to have the Vice President and the Senators decline and abruptly end the occasion by bowing and filing out of the house.[18]

Presidential and Senate Power Struggle

The hasty exit may have been because the Vice President and the Senate had suffered what may have been to them an embarrassing defeat at the hands of the House. Earlier, the Senate had approved addressing the President as "His Highness the President of the United States and Protector of the Rights of the Same."

Vice President Adams had argued that the President and the Senate possess the shared power to make titles, and that without such a title for the President the common people, at home and abroad, "will despise him." [19]

One observer credits Congressman Madison with engineering the defeat of that proposal. On May 5 the House approved a joint committee report rejecting any titles beyond those contained in the Constitution.[20]

Privately, Mr. Madison has suggested that the proposed title for the President smacked of monarchy or of aristocracy and that had "the *project succeeded it would have* subjected *the president to a severe dilemma* and given *a deep wound to our infant government.*" [21]

Although on the surface the issue may appear comic, or of little importance, it manifests a deadly serious struggle for power by the collective Senate and by its individual members. Already a move is reported to be gaining ground in the Senate to require the President to obtain the approval of the upper house for the appointment and removal of all executive officers. Had the Senate succeeded in this first skirmish over titles, its whip hand over the President might have been strengthened considerably.[22]

A reliable source has told this correspondent that some New England and southern Senators went along with Vice President Adams' trivial title proposals to create a sectional political alliance in the mistaken belief that Mr. Adams has influence with President Washington.[23]

The Independent Vice President

John Adams is proving to be as independent in both branches of the new national government as he is unpredictable. Pennsylvania backed him for the office of Vice President in the expectation that he and New England, in turn, would support Philadelphia's bid as the permanent capital. He has also been pressured to support James Wilson of Pennsylvania for the post of Chief Justice. This position, called for in the Constitution, is still to be officially created.

Nevertheless, the Vice President has made it clear that he will remain neutral in regard to the selection of a permanent capital. On the issue of a candidate for Chief Justice, he wrote to Dr. Benjamin Rush of Philadelphia that he favors John Jay of New York. He may be angry at the supposition that Mr. Wilson as a Presidential Elector voted for him in exchange for a favor, but he reveals more of his personal ambitions than mere anger.

"I am not obliged to vote for a man," he wrote to Dr. Rush on May 17, "because he voted for me—had my office been ever so lucrative or ever so important. But ask your own heart, is not my Election to this office in the scurvy manner it was done, a Curse rather than a Blessing?... Is it not an indelible stain on our Country, Countrymen & Constitution?"[24]

The Vice President has apparently become aware that some Presidential Electors withheld their votes from him to make certain that his total would not tie or exceed General Washington's. Colonel

Alexander Hamilton of New York initiated this suggestion and involved Dr. Rush in the ploy. At this writing it is not clear whether Mr. Adams knows the principals, but he has made clear his anger and outrage, and personal humiliation, to those who have innocently written him and sincerely expressed congratulations on his election.

"As far as I am personally concerned in this Event," Mr. Adams wrote in a May 21 letter, "it was not a Subject of much congratulations; it was rather a mortification to me to see that in our first great Election, so great a portion of our Fellow Citizens have been artful and that so many more had been Dupes. It is only on the supposition that such Knavery and such Folly may be guarded against in future that I can congratulate you on the prospect of happiness under the new Government." [25]

CHAPTER 15

★

June 1789

Surgery Saves Life of President
Senate Challenges Appointment Power

The new national government has passed through a major crisis less than two months after its official beginning. President George Washington, on June 20, underwent emergency surgery for the removal of a life-threatening infected tumor deep in his left thigh.[1]

Diagnosed by attending physician Dr. Samuel Bard as caused by anthrax, almost always fatal in animals, the condition was reported to have started with a fever, followed by rapid inflammation and swelling of the upper thigh region. The illness appeared so swiftly that the President could not sit without acute pain.[2]

"I am not afraid to die, and therefore can bear the worst," the President told his aides and attending physicians when informed that he must submit immediately to surgery. "Whether to-night or twenty years hence, makes no difference. I know I am in the hands of a good providence."[3]

Tobias Lear, personal secretary to the President, reported that when the inflamed area was laid open by the surgeon's knife, it was discovered the infection and inflammation had spread under the skin and tissues and the tumor was "very large and the incision on opening it deep."[4]

Five days after surgery, the President's fever had faded, to the immense relief of everyone — especially Congressman James Madison. The latter told a friend, "... the alarm is now over. His

123

death at the present moment would have brought on another crisis in our affairs."[5]

One source close to the President has told this correspondent that his recovery is likely to be slow, very slow. This source speculates that the President's sword scabbard may have irritated his left thigh which subsequently became infected because of the constant rubbing. He has worn his sword frequently since coming to New York, whereas at Mount Vernon he had not carried it for many months.[6]

Appointment Powers Challenged

The life-threatening illness and slow recovery did not prevent the Congress from launching a challenge to the President's powers of appointment. His illness may have made some Congressmen feel it was imperative that such powers required discussion, that the hero of all America was human and subject to man's frailties. But Congressman Madison unwittingly set the stage for the power struggle when he offered a motion to establish the departments of treasury, war, and foreign affairs. The draft legislation included a clause declaring the secretaries of these three executive departments to be removable by the President alone, without the advice and consent of the Senate.[7]

Congressman William Smith of South Carolina on June 16 told the House that he and other members wished to have deleted the clause regarding sole responsibility for removing secretaries; the only way to remove a man, he believed, was by impeachment. Congressman Roger Sherman of Connecticut, who had been a delegate to the Philadelphia Convention, argued that if the Senate were empowered by the Constitution to provide advice and consent in Presidential appointments, the House should have a share of power in such removal.[8]

Mr. Smith cited a "Federalist" essay published during the Constitution ratification debates last year, that "the consent of that body [the Senate] would be necessary to displace as well as to appoint."[9] The "Federalist" papers were authored by Mr. Madison and Colonel Alexander Hamilton.

Separation of Powers Sacred

Not revealing whether he or Colonel Hamilton wrote that particular essay, the unruffled Mr. Madison insisted that the power to impeach the President and the prospect of re-election would be sufficient to make him responsible for the conduct of his appointees.

The power of the President to remove his appointments is "absolutely necessary," Mr. Madison warned, otherwise the balance of powers created in the constitutional system will be destroyed. It is not, Mr. Madison added, a question of taking power from one branch of government and giving it to another, but to which branch the Constitution has given such power.

"...I therefore shall only say," Mr. Madison concluded on June 22 after days of animated House debate, "if there is a principle in our constitution, indeed in any free constitution, more sacred than another, it is that which separates the legislative, executive and judicial powers; if there is any point in which the separation of legislative and executive powers ought to be maintained with greater caution, it is that which relates to officers and offices.... The legislature creates the office, defines the powers, limits its duration, and annexes a compensation. This done, the legislative power ceases. They ought to have nothing to do with designating the man to fill the office." [10]

Although Mr. Madison and his House allies prevailed on June 24 in preserving the power of the President to remove appointees, their colleagues in the Senate are expected to encounter spirited debate when the subject is taken up in the upper house. Members of the Senate who favor power sharing on appointments — and removing them — have an ingrained distrust of a powerful single executive, what with their experience rooted in British colonialism.

An observer has noted that the outcome of this debate is likely to define the office of the President in the future. [11] The subject of removing appointees was one great question left unanswered by the delegates at the Philadelphia Convention during the summer of 1787.

This correspondent has learned that a majority of the delegates to the conclave in Philadelphia, whose minutes have not yet been made public, agreed to the great powers conferred on the office primarily because they expected George Washington would be elected President. Apparently, they were aware that he would set the precedent for the future. One observer has pointed out that if any other person were occupying the office it is almost certain the House would have voted this month to subject the executive to the will of the Legislature. If that had occurred, the executive might be a powerless figurehead only two months after the office was first filled.[12]

Bill of Rights Resisted

The one issue that could politically impede the capacity of both the executive and the Congress to govern is the issue of amendments or a bill of rights. As promised, Congressman Madison on June 8 proposed nineteen amendments to the Constitution, out of the eighty, eliminating duplicates, submitted or suggested by seven States.[13]

Congressman James Jackson of Georgia led the opposition, suggesting a twelve-month postponement. The new Constitution, he argued, should be allowed a fair trial without amendments while the Congress attends to more urgent matters. "Our Constitution, sir," he said, as a clearly anxious Mr. Madison sat nearby, "is like a vessel just launched, and lying at the wharf; she is untried. . . . Let us gentlemen, fit out our vessel, set up the masts and expand her sails and be guided by the experiment in our alternations."[14]

Mr. Madison has been insistent during the debate, a departure from his usual softly laconic manner and speaking style that is never above a whisper. This may be due to the renewed agitation of Virginia and New York for convening a second constitutional convention if Congress delays consideration of a bill of rights.[15]

If Congress delays consideration of amendments, Mr. Madison warned his colleagues in the House, "it may occasion suspicions" and "may tend to inflame or prejudice the public mind" against the decisions of the new Congress. "They may think," he quietly argued, "we are not sincere in our desire to incorporate such amendments in the constitution as will secure those rights, which they consider as not sufficiently guarded. The applications for amendments come from a very respectable number of our constituents, and it is certainly proper for Congress to consider the subject, in order to quiet that anxiety which prevails in the public mind." [16]

Opposing Forces Join Against Madison

What clearly concerns Mr. Madison is the fact that both his Federalist allies and his Anti-Federalist foes in the House have united to oppose the consideration of amendments. At least four Anti-Federalist House members, among them Elbridge Gerry of Massachusetts, favor delay, although less than a year ago they had sought to block adoption of the Constitution altogether, complaining that it contained no bill of rights. [17] A major reason they now favor delay is the prospect of convening a second convention controlled by the Anti-Federalists.

Ironically, at the Philadelphia Convention, we have been told, Mr. Madison opposed a bill of rights when it had been proposed by fellow Virginian Colonel George Mason. Mr. Madison and his fellow Federalists continued to oppose a bill of rights during the ratification debates in key States. But being a realist, he relented and agreed to recommend amendments when the Constitution was in danger of not being ratified, and the continuously looming cloud of a second convention requires him to stay with that promise.

Mr. Madison's about-face was not lost on one partisan of Patrick Henry's. Colonel William Grayson, a Virginia Senator, maintains that Mr. Madison's June 8 speech in the House was the direct result of the influence of the former Virginia Governor.

Another observer notes, "In advocating his bill, Mr. Madison on the floor of Congress, presented a striking contrast to Mr. Madison on the floor of the Virginia Convention. He now urged some of the same arguments which Mr. Henry had presented and he had combated in the last named body...." [18]

Outflanking Friends and Foes

The Virginia convention had narrowly approved ratification after the Federalists, led by Mr. Madison, promised to consider amendments in the First Congress. After the conclave concluded a year ago this June, Mr. Henry drew up forty separate amendments. Half of these were concerned with civil liberties covering religion, press, speech, jury trial, petition, and assembly. Others dealt with limiting taxing power.

Two specific amendments proposed by Mr. Henry — preserving the rights of the people, and preserving the powers of the States not specified in the Constitution — were included by Mr. Madison in his nineteen amendment proposals presented to the Congress this month. This was to blunt the charge of Governor Henry and other Anti-Federalists that the Federalists intend to destroy the liberties of the people and the power of the States with the powerful, consolidated national government.[19]

Mr. Madison has admitted privately that amending the new Constitution will be a delicate operation, requiring a high degree of political skill. He has apparently chosen those amendments protecting individual civil liberties while disregarding those he believes would cut dangerously and deeply into the anatomy of the Federal government and perhaps cause a fatal hemorrhage of its power.[20]

"It will be a desirable thing," he told the House on June 8, "to extinguish from the bosom of every member of the community, any apprehensions that there are those among his countrymen who wish to deprive them of the liberty for which they valiantly fought and honorably bled."[21]

Failing to gain immediate consideration with an appeal to patriotism, and with the amendments still not brought before the House, Mr. Madison shifted tactics and proposed the appointment of a select committee. During his argument for adoption of this proposal, he took the opportunity to incorporate his nineteen proposals within his argument, thus submitting them to the House.[22]

Henry's Plans Go Up in Puff of Smoke

When the news of what Mr. Madison has done in New York this month reaches the ears and eyes of Patrick Henry in Virginia, he may conclude that his proposal for a second convention and for amendments limiting the powers of the new national government, particularly the power of taxation, have gone up in a puff of smoke.

Mr. Henry has written Senator Richard Henry Lee that amendments that do not go beyond just civil liberties "will injure rather than serve the cause of liberty" since they will "lull suspicion" that he deems it less important to limit the powers of the new government.[23]

He has predicted that it is only a matter of time before the States are swallowed up by the Federal government and that the agent will be the Federal judiciary. On the other hand, Federalists such as Congressman Madison view the State Legislatures and the State courts as the most dangerous enemies of the new union.[24]

Senator Lee has already indicated that he holds out little hope that amendments to limit the new national government's powers of taxation and to limit the powers of the judiciary have much chance of passage.

"I hope that if we cannot gain the whole loaf, we shall at least have some bread...," Senator Lee said of the anticipated amendments debate.[25]

First Act of Congress Signed

Three weeks before he fell ill, President Washington signed on June 1 the first law passed by Congress: "An act to regulate the time and manner of administering certain oaths." On June 2 House Speaker Frederick Muhlenberg administered the oath to defend the Constitution to eighteen Congressmen who had arrived after April 8, when the oath was first administered by the Chief Justice of New York.[26]

Since it began its formal sessions, the House has been open to the public while the Senate has met in secret, behind closed doors. Much of the time in each house has been in assembling a staff and working out questions of protocol between the two. In addition to setting down their own rules, members of each branch have sought to agree on how they will exchange messages, how messages should be sent to and received from the executive, and procedures for settling legislative disagreements.[27]

"The federal business has proceeded with a mortifying tardiness," complained Congressman Madison on June 30, "... principally resulting from the novelty and complexity of the subjects of Legislation. We are in a wilderness without a single footstep to guide us. Our successors will have an easier task." [28]

Congressman Fisher Ames of Massachusetts has a different view. He contends that the cause for the slow progress is the House's adoption of the parliamentary device known as the Committee of the Whole. Mr. Ames termed it "a great, clumsy machine" made up of many House members all wanting to speak and refine subjects — "correct spelling or erase *may* and insert *shall*" — that could better be handled by fewer members in special or select committees.

In fairness, he adds that House members have demonstrated "less party spirit, less of the acrimony of pride when disappointed of success, less personality, less intrigue, cabal, management, or cunning than I ever saw in a public assembly." [29]

CHAPTER 16

★

July 1789

President Washington Wears Uniform
Military Marks Independence Day

Despite weakness from his recent emergency surgery and slow recovery, on July 4 President George Washington stood stiffly at attention in the doorway of the Presidential residence, wearing his old military uniform, and received the salute of marching military units stepping smartly to fife and drum. Cheering crowds lined the narrow New York City streets to celebrate the July 4, 1776, independence from Great Britain.[1]

The President began the day by signing a bill that had been hotly debated line by line last month in both the House and the Senate, establishing duties on "goods, wares and merchandizes imported into the United States." The President's signature making the measure law on the thirteenth anniversary of American political independence is the first tangible step for the new government to establish fiscal independence.[2]

Later President Washington received a delegation from the Society of the Cincinnati, an organization of former military officers who served under him during the Revolution. Only a few years ago, Congressman Elbridge Gerry of Massachusetts and others had assailed the proposal of a peacetime militia out of concern that the Cincinnati would join it in an attempt to influence the executive. They believed the combination posed a danger that could "exchange a British Administration for one that could be equally tyrannical, perhaps much more so."[3]

As the first President-General of the organization, Washington fought off efforts to have the Cincinnati disbanded because it was perceived as a conspiracy to create in America an aristocratic elite on the European model. Prussian-born Baron Friedrich von Steuben, president of the New York branch, was singled out by critics, who assailed him rather than attack General Washington directly.[4]

"Under your conduct, sir, " Baron von Steuben said in his thick Prussian accent to President Washington at the brief July 4 ceremony, "this band of soldiers was led to glory and to conquest, and we feel confident that under your administration our country will speedily arrive at an enviable state of prosperity and happiness."[5]

Appointment of Former Military Aides

A few years ago, such open expressions of support of civil government by the Cincinnati might have set off a political firestorm. However, the military theme of the July 4 celebration this year is due as much to the hero of the War of Independence who is now President as to the fact that he will very likely govern as he did as a military commander: by relying on subordinates. In fact, the three executive departments to be created by Congress will probably be filled by former high ranking military officers who are firm Federalists. Minor appointments are also likely to go to veteran officers. Many of the immediate problems facing the new national government, such as domestic and foreign debt, are direct results of the War.

Colonel Alexander Hamilton, this correspondent has learned, is being seriously considered to head the Treasury, the department directly responsible for dealing with the swollen debt. Colonel Hamilton not only is a former military aide to General Washington, but also gave the principal July 4 address for the Society of the Cincinnati at New York's St. Paul's Chapel, attended by Mrs. Washington (representing the recovering President), Vice President John Adams, and members of Congress.[6]

Colonel Hamilton took as his theme the heroism of the late General Nathanael Greene, who died three years ago at age 44 after a military career that earned him a reputation second only to that of General Washington.[7]

"The sudden termination of his life," Colonel Hamilton said in his lengthy eulogy to the hushed audience, "cut him off from those scenes, which the progress of a new immense and unsettled empire could not fail to open to the complete exertion of that universal and pervading genius, which qualified him not less for the senate, than for the field."[8]

Power in Control of the Purse

Friends have pressed Colonel Hamilton, 34, to stand for election to the Senate from New York or to indicate a willingness to serve as Chief Justice of the United States. However, according to one reliable source, the handsome lawyer has purposely made himself available for the post of Secretary of the Treasury.[9]

Most officials view the current $50 million debt as an albatross around the neck of the new government. Colonel Hamilton considers it a potentially powerful sword to subordinate the States to a strong national government. He is privately convinced, according to one source, that import duties would produce almost enough revenue to secure the debt and also pay the operating expenses of the government.[10]

When the House this month began debate on creation of a single secretary of the Treasury, tempers flared. Congressman Gerry and others expressed alarm at the enormous power of a single secretary. The debate revived long buried bitter feelings about Robert Morris, who was the Confederation government's superintendent of finance between 1781 and 1784. He resigned after repeated attacks on his financial policies, and was replaced by a three-member treasury board. Congressman Gerry proposed to render the power of the purse safe by the creation of a similar three-member treasury board.[11]

Senate Sustains Appointment Power

Fear of power in the hands of a single individual was also behind spirited Senate opposition this month to allowing the President sole power to remove appointments. Last month, the House upheld the power by only six or seven votes when debating bills that were to establish the Department of Foreign Affairs. It was argued, as President Washington fell ill in June, that he would not live forever. Checking Presidential power by Senate sanction both of appointments and of dismissals would avoid a dangerous concentration of power in the uncertain future.[12]

For three days this month the Senate debated the issue behind closed doors. One source described the debate as "fierce," resulting in a tie that was broken by Vice President John Adams. His vote upheld the right of the President to remove an appointee without consultation with the Senate.[13]

Senator Richard Henry Lee of Virginia argued that although the Constitution created a powerful office of the President, the same document limited the new national government. ". . . the Legislative Power of it is limited, and therefore the Executive and judicial must be limited," Senator Lee urged.[14]

Senator Oliver Ellsworth of Connecticut, a member of the Constitutional Convention in Philadelphia, boldly argued that the powers of the President should be increased. Americans in 1775 objected not to the powers of the King, he asserted, but to the powers of Parliament. "The areas of presidential action must not be intruded upon. Once started, there would be no stopping place and the legislative would in time devour the executive branch," he warned.[15]

Vice President Adams took great satisfaction, one source reports, in casting his tie-breaking vote in the matter of the President's power to remove an appointee, and believes it was the most important issue the Senate has yet faced.[16]

Virginia Senator William Grayson angrily declared that the vote was the fulfillment of a prophecy. "The matter predicted by Mr. [Patrick] Henry is now coming to pass; consolidation is the object of the new Government," Senator Grayson said, jumping to his feet after the tie vote was announced, "and the first attempt will be to destroy the Senate, as they are the representative of the State Legislatures." [17]

Bill of Rights Debate Delayed

Senator Grayson is keeping former Virginia Governor Henry informed about the efforts of Congressman James Madison to gain passage of a series of amendments to the Constitution. Cynically, both Senator Grayson and Patrick Henry regard Mr. Madison's efforts as a ploy to "break the spirit of the party by divisions," in proposing a bill of rights covering personal liberties, while side-stepping amendments they favor that would curb the power of the government to tax and the power of the judiciary.[18]

Nevertheless, six weeks after he first introduced the amendment issue, Congressman Madison on July 21 was defeated in his effort to convene a full House debate on amendments. He "begged the House" for a debate, but it voted to send his proposals, along with recommendations for amendments from the States, to a special Committee of Eleven, composed of one representative from each State.[19]

Roger Sherman of Connecticut joined with James Jackson of Georgia in opposing any amendment debate. Mr. Sherman told the House that "experience should point out" the necessity for amendments. "Consequently we shall lose our labor and had better decline having any thing further to do with it for the present." Mr. Jackson was more direct when he said a debate would be "a mere waste of time."[20]

As a member of the select Committee of Eleven, Congressman Madison was relieved on July 28 when it reported back to the full House with no substantial changes. The committee's version is a virtual restatement of the amendments proposed by Mr. Madison, with certain stylistic changes and two consolidated with others, but it refused to set a time for a full House debate.[21]

The amendments provide the following:

- There shall be one representative for every 30,000 until the number shall amount to one hundred, after which the proportion shall be regulated by Congress;
- No law shall take effect until an election of Representatives shall have taken place;
- No religion shall be established by law, nor shall the equal rights of conscience be infringed;
- Freedom of speech, of the press, right of the people peaceably to assemble and consult for their common good, and to apply to the government for redress of grievances, shall not be infringed;

- A well-regulated militia, composed of the body of the people, being the best security of a free State, the right of the people to keep and bear arms shall not be infringed, but no person religiously scrupulous shall be compelled to bear arms;
- No soldier shall in time of peace be quartered in any house without the consent of the owner, nor in time of war but in a manner to be prescribed by law;
- No person shall be subject, except in case of impeachment, to more than one trial or one punishment for the same offence; nor shall be compelled to be a witness against himself, nor be deprived of life, liberty, or property without due process of law; nor shall private property be taken for public use without just compensation;
- Excessive bail shall not be required, nor excessive fines imposed, nor cruel and unusual punishments inflicted;
- The right of the people to be secure in their person, houses, papers, and effects, shall not be violated by warrants issuing, without probable cause supported by oath or affirmation, and not particularly describing the places to be searched, and the persons or things to be seized;
- The enumeration in this Constitution of certain rights shall not be construed to deny or disparage others retained by the people;
- No State shall infringe the equal rights of conscience, nor the freedom of speech, or of the press, nor of the right of trial by jury in criminal cases;
- But no appeal to such court shall be allowed where the value in controversy does not amount to one thousand dollars;
- In all criminal prosecutions the accused shall enjoy the right to a speedy and public trial, to be informed of the nature and cause of the accusation, to be confronted with the witnesses against him, to have compulsory process for obtaining witnesses in his favor, and to have the assistance of counsel for his defence;
- The trial of all crimes (except in cases of impeachment, and in cases arising in the land or naval forces, or in the militia, when in actual service in time of war or public danger) shall

be by an impartial jury...; and no person shall be held to answer for a capital, or otherwise infamous crime, unless on a presentment or indictment by a Grand Jury...;

- In suits at common law the right of trial by jury shall be preserved;
- The powers delegated by this Constitution to the government of the United States, shall be exercised so that the Legislative shall never exercise the powers vested in the Executive or the Judicial; nor the Executive the powers vested in the Legislative or Judicial, nor the Judicial the powers vested in the Legislative or Executive.
- The powers not delegated by this Constitution, nor prohibited by it to the States, are reserved to the States respectively.[22]

Most Congressmen do not share Mr. Madison's urgency for amendments, believing that the national Legislature must devote its time to more important issues. A few others believe passage of amendments or a bill of rights might induce Rhode Island and North Carolina to ratify the Constitution, thus creating a sense of national unity now lacking in the national Congress.[23]

Washington Watches the West

Mr. Madison, according to one source, has concluded that Congress does not comprehend the importance of the western frontier settlements, particularly the Kentucky territory, which is part of Virginia. Spain's current efforts to detach the territory from the American Union would have been less explosive had the Confederation Congress granted the frontier province the stature of statehood.

"It is a misfortune," Mr. Madison wrote in a letter dated July 5, a copy having been obtained by this correspondent, "that the Western Country is not represented in the Senate. The speedy erection of Kentucky into a State is a desirable event in order to supply that defect as well as on other accounts."[24]

Mr. Madison's reference to "other accounts" may be related to President Washington's desire to re-establish secret diplomatic discussions with Spain about reopening the Mississippi River to American trade. In confidential notes to Acting Secretary of Foreign Affairs John Jay and Congressman Madison, the President sought advice about whether he needed to inform the Senate about his intent to renew negotiations which had been suspended in September 1788.[25]

Spanish and British intrigues against American frontier settlements and their use of Indian tribes as surrogates are potentially explosive issues the President hopes to deal with through diplomacy, since the government lacks money and military power.

It is significant that the first department of the executive to be approved by Congress and signed into law by the President on July 27 was the Department of Foreign Affairs. One observer points out that the President is likely to be his own foreign secretary and war secretary.[26]

The President may also be his own Post Master General. Despite a deluge of dispatches descending on him while he is recovering from surgery, the President on July 17 wrote the acting Post Master General wanting to know the whereabouts of $39,995 in postal service profits.

"As it is not shewn, by any of the documents which you have sent me," the President inquired of Ebenezer Hazard, "whether this ballance has been lodged in the Treasury of the United States, or appropriated to the use of the Post Office Department, I shall therefore thank you for early and satisfactory information on this head."[27]

CHAPTER 17

★

August 1789

House Approves Bill of Rights
President Gives Priority to Indian Problem

After weeks of persistent political plodding, on August 24 Congressman James Madison engineered House passage of a Federal Bill of Rights consisting of seventeen amendments, which principally protect civil liberties.[1]

The measure, which still faces a fight in the Senate, was subjected to ten days of House debate that Mr. Madison privately described to a friend as "extremely difficult and fatiguing."[2] With considerable skill, he fought off efforts by critics of the new Constitution to "defeat by delaying" action on the amendments.

"... It has been absolutely necessary," he confided to another friend, "in order to effect any thing, to abbreviate debate, and exclude every proposition of a doubtful & unimportant nature.... Two or three contentious additions would even now frustrate the whole project."[3]

Fight over Form of Amendments

When the House debate opened on August 13, Mr. Madison was confronted by a half-dozen colleagues arguing that "there were several matters before them of more importance" than amendments. Another argument was that "the discussion would take up more time than the House could now spare."[4]

139

Surmounting this patent indifference, Mr. Madison was immediately confronted with a challenge from Congressman Roger Sherman. The former shoemaker and self-educated lawmaker opposed the proposal for weaving amendments into the main text of the Constitution, instead of adding them as supplemental articles at the end of the document.

"We ought not," the former delegate to the Constitutional Convention said, "to interweave our propositions into the work itself, because it will be destructive to the whole fabric. We might as well endeavor to mix brass, iron, and clay, as to incorporate such heterogeneous articles; the one contradictory to the other...."[5]

Clearly nettled by the challenge, Mr. Madison insisted the Constitution will be more neat when "the amendments are interwoven into those parts to which they naturally belong, than it will if they consist of separate and distinct parts. We shall then be able to determine its meaning without references or comparison...."[6]

Congressman Samuel Livermore of New Hampshire reminded the House of the well-established supplemental law precedents of the British Parliament and the State Legislatures throughout America. It is questionable, he said, whether Congress can be true to its oath to defend and protect the Constitution if Mr. Madison's view prevails.

"It is by virtue of the present constitution, I presume," observed the former Chief Justice of the New Hampshire Supreme Court, "that we attempt to make another; now, if we proceed to the repeal of this, I cannot see upon what authority we shall erect another; if we destroy the base, the superstructure falls of course."[7]

Madison's Political Tactics

Mr. Madison's position of desiring alterations in the main text of the Constitution prevailed and Mr. Sherman's supplemental proposal was defeated. However, after six days of intense debate on the seventeen amendments, two-thirds of the House on August 19 reversed themselves and approved Mr. Sherman's proposal to make all amendments supplemental.[8]

It has not been made entirely clear to this correspondent why the House reversed itself. One observer maintains that Mr. Madison realized how "tenacious" Mr. Sherman had become, and gave in on the form he favored to ensure the necessary votes for final passage.[9]

As a political defense against delay and defeat, Mr. Madison favored a debate conducted with dispatch, while his Anti-Federalist House foes complained that full debate was being denied. Congressman Elbridge Gerry, for example, rose and, taking aim at Mr. Madison, complained that he seemed "in a great hurry to get this business through." Mr. Gerry took exception to Mr. Madison's assertion that some members were delaying matters by insisting on discussion of "doubtful propositions."

"... It is natural, sir," Mr. Gerry said with sarcasm, "for us to be fond of our own work. We do not like to see it disfigured by other hands. That honorable gentleman brought forward a string of propositions ... he is no doubt ready for the question, and determined not to admit what we think an improvement...."[10]

Stung by the charge, Mr. Madison was not willing to remain silent while he and the House Committee of Eleven, which debated and approved the amendments he had drafted, were charged with not acting with candor and refusing to consider amendments offered by other members.

"I appeal to the gentlemen who have heard the voice of their country," Mr. Madison said with an edge to his voice, "to those who have attended the debates of the State conventions, whether the amendments now proposed are not those most strenuously required by opponents to the Constitution? It was wished that some security should be given for those great and essential rights which they had been taught to believe were in danger."[11]

Moment of Victory ... and Defeat

The amendments guaranteeing individual rights of speech, of religion, right to petition, and a free press — the core of the seventeen amendments — provoked less debate than those that appeared to retain or enlarge the powers of the national government.

Congressman Thomas Tucker of South Carolina tried but failed to have deleted the amendment that prevented State governments from infringing the right of conscience, free speech, a free press, and trial by jury. The States had already been "excessively weakened," he argued.[12]

In reply Congressman Madison said he considered "this to be the most valuable amendment on the whole list; if there was any reason to restrain the government of the United States from infringing upon these essential rights, it was equally necessary that they should be secured against the state governments. . . ."[13]

As savage as grape shot was the exchange over proposals for apportioning representation and fixing the pay of legislators. Equally explosive was the failed effort of Anti-Federalist House members to secure the adoption of amendments that would restrict the power of Congress over elections and that would forbid direct taxes.[14]

The most critical moment for both sides came on August 18 when the House by a 34 to 16 vote refused to allow consideration of amendments submitted by the States that had been excluded by Mr. Madison and the Committee of Eleven. Further debates were confined to precise phrasing, Mr. Gerry proposing, for instance, that the word "expressly" be inserted so as to read "the powers not expressly delegated by the constitution. . . ." Nevertheless, the weary House members left Mr. Madison's original of the seventeen amendments largely unaltered.[15]

Sent to the Senate on August 24, the proposed bill of rights immediately ran into hostile opposition and an effort to postpone consideration until the next congressional session in January 1790. One source revealed that some Senators viewed the amendments with contempt and warned against hasty approval. One motion was defeated that would have delayed consideration until "a little experience" might prove that a bill of rights was necessary.

"As if experience," scornfully replied Virginia Senator Richard Henry Lee, "were not necessary to prove the propriety of those great principles of Civil liberty which the wisdom of the Ages has found to be necessary barriers against the encroachments of power in the hand of frail Man!"[16]

The Senate finally set debate for August 31, but it was postponed for two more days so that the members could finish a lengthy consideration of rates of daily pay for Senate and House members and compensation for the Senate staff.[17]

War Department and Warpath

All these details have been supplied to this correspondent by sources close to the Senate, which, unlike the House, has been conducting its business behind closed doors. This correspondent has learned that the Senate is not keeping full journals of its debates.[18] This same source reports that the Senate on August 7 quickly approved creation of the Department of War.[19]

Acting Secretary of War Henry Knox added urgency to Senate action when on the same day he delivered to the Senate and the House a message from President Washington. In the document, a copy having been obtained by this correspondent, the President asked Congress to authorize funds and a three-member commission to commence peace treaty talks with the Creek Indians in southern Georgia. The President noted that "hostilities which have in several instances been committed on the frontiers seem to require the immediate interposition of the general Government."[20]

Within the last two months, General Knox is reported to have made an extensive report to the President in which he warned that recent clashes between some Indian tribes and settlers could spread into a frontier-wide war in the South and West unless decisive action were taken. In recommending treaty talks, General Knox has conceded that the national government has neither the financial nor the manpower resources to mount a punitive military operation against Indian tribes on the warpath.[21]

Politics of Indian Protection

In his August 7 message to Congress, President Washington stressed treaty talks but also requested that Congress approve the establishment of a uniform militia drawn from the various States. The President said he was "particularly anxious it should receive an early attention" since he envisioned the militia would be composed of veteran officers and soldiers of the War of Independence.

"While the measures of Government ought to be calculated to protect its Citizens from all injury and violence," the President said, "a due regard should be extended to those Indians whose happiness in the course of events so materially depends on national justice and humanity of the United States."[22]

In choosing to initiate treaty talks with the Creeks and other tribes, estimated to number 14,000 in the South, the President hopes to deal with the greater danger since the Creeks are allied with, and supplied by, Spain.

At the same time, according to one observer, since June the infant unorganized government has been subjected to a steady stream of pleas for protection from Indian attacks in the Ohio Valley frontier. The pleas, mostly from Kentucky, are coming not just from settlers, but also from at least three eastern-based land companies with considerable political influence in the War Department and with Acting Secretary Knox.[23]

The President and Congressman Madison both see the future of the Republic in the West, with the sale of western lands by private for-profit companies to settlers as one way to pay off the huge foreign and domestic debt the government was saddled with as a result of the War of Independence. The Indian tribes who claim those lands present an implacable explosive challenge.

Preparing for Peace and for War

The urgency of the Indian challenge in the Ohio Valley with the Wabash Indians was underscored this month when Congress approved a statute that constitutionally adopts the existing Confederated military of 840 officers and enlisted men as a regular national army. Secretary Knox reported to Congress on August 10 that 596 of that total were serving in "various posts north-west of the River Ohio."[24]

According to one source, Congress has also given the executive authority to conduct military operations on the frontier as well as temporary authorization for the President to call out the militia of the States. The House limited the numbers the President could request from each State while the Senate amended the measure to give the President substantially more power to deal with the inflamed Northwest frontier. The President was reported to have made the request after receiving an urgent letter from the Northwest Territorial

Governor, Arthur St. Clair, pleading for the military means to calm the fears of settlers and to intimidate the Indians.[25]

The President put his personal prestige behind treaty talks with the Indian tribes in the South when on August 22 he appeared unannounced at the Senate, accompanied by General Knox, and asked the Door Keeper to inform the upper house of their presence. The Secretary of War handed a lengthy document to the President who in turn handed it to a nervous and surprised Vice President John Adams, presiding officer of the Senate. The paper spelled out the administration's proposals for treating with the southern Indian tribes and asked for Senate advice and consent as specified in the Constitution when it relates to treaties with foreign powers.

"The measure includes," the document said in part, "not only peace and security to the whole Southern frontier, but is calculated to form a barrier against the Colonies of an European power, which in the mutations of policy, may one day become the Enemy of the United States. The fate of the Southern States therefore, or the neighboring Colonies, may principally depend on the present measures of the Union towards the Southern Indians." [26]

A Comic Senate Confrontation

According to one source, the first effort of the President to seek the advice and consent of the Senate turned into a confrontation with comic overtones. President Washington, thinking of his wartime staff meetings with his generals, failed to realize that the Senators were concerned with a wide variety of subjects and would require time to make up their minds on matters presented them fresh and for the first time.[27]

As President of the Senate, Mr. Adams began to read aloud the lengthy document, but, according to one eyewitness, could not be heard by the members of the Senate above the rumble of carriages on the cobblestone streets outside. Senator Robert Morris of Pennsylvania requested that the Vice President read the treaty through a second time. When finished, Mr. Adams abruptly asked, "Do you advise and consent?" on the first of seven questions. There was a long uncomfortable silence.[28]

Pennsylvania Senator William Maclay insisted that since "the business is new to the Senate," the treaty be read again in full, as well as the documents relating to it. General Knox at one point was asked for a document he could not find. Eyewitnesses report that President Washington, still stiff and sore from his surgery, was clearly irritated as Senators discussed the treaty among themselves only to propose postponement or referral to a committee.[29]

"This defeats every purpose of my coming here," the President said, jumping to his feet with an anger in his voice that shocked the contentious Senate into stunned silence. He had brought General Knox to explain everything only to encounter delay. According to one eyewitness, the President's temper cooled "by degrees" and he agreed to a postponement, although he departed with "a discontented air" and "sullen dignity."[30]

On August 24 President Washington returned to the Senate well in control of himself and was "placid and serene and manifested a spirit of accommodation." The President was reported to have received from the Senate what he sought, with a few minor changes, although the price he had to pay was sitting silent for hour after hour listening to a boring Senate debate on other subjects. He was overheard to say when he departed that he would "be damned if [he] ever went there again."[31]

One informed source says that because of that first experience with the Senate, the President is not likely to repeat the process, and is more likely to formulate his own foreign policy and seek no advice; and to solicit consent from the Senate only when necessary.[32]

CHAPTER 18

★

September 1789

Successful First Congress Adjourns
Paris Mobs Imperil French Monarchy

The first session of the First Congress under the new Constitution adjourned on September 29, leaving behind a full catalogue of accomplishments and a highly pleased President George Washington, saying he was "satisfied with its success" as a fulfillment of the American Revolution of freedom.

"I have always believed," the President observed, "that an unequivocally free and equal Representation of the People in the Legislature, together with an efficient and responsible Executive, were the great Pillars on which the preservation of American Freedom must depend."[1]

Nevertheless, while the President considers it "next to a Miracle"[2] that organization of the new national government has gone so well, he is troubled by incomplete reports from Paris, first published in New York on September 16, describing the swift disintegration of the French monarchy, which had played so crucial a military and monetary role in winning American independence. One observer notes that the President regards any political disaster in France as one that also involves danger to the infant Republic of the United States.[3]

First reports from France about six weeks old described how on July 14 a Paris mob stormed the ancient fortress prison known as the Bastille, resulting in 100 deaths. As disorders spread, a mob blamed bread shortages on government officials and aristocrats, some of whom were seized and murdered, their heads cut off and impaled on pikes and paraded through Paris streets. One observer states that both the King and the old government have lost control of not just Paris but cities throughout France.[4]

Jefferson Is Eyewitness

U.S. Minister to France Thomas Jefferson, in a July 22 letter to Congressman James Madison — a copy was obtained by this correspondent after its receipt in early September — provides an eyewitness account of the Paris mobs. He predicted that the violent events in France "will ever be memorable in history." He wrote that the King had refused to use his troops against the mobs, and that when word of the beheadings spread, every minister resigned and fled in the face of a Paris mob said to number 60,000 "armed with guns, pistols, swords, pikes, pruning hooks, scythes, & whatever they could lay hold of. . . ."[5]

Earlier, before the explosion of the Paris mobs, Minister Jefferson had requested permission for a six-month leave of absence from his diplomatic post, which he had held for five years without leave. He gave as his reasons the need to look after his Monticello plantation, to bring his two daughters back to Virginia and leave them there, and, this correspondent has learned, to deal directly with his serious financial problems.[6]

Mr. Jefferson is expected to arrive in Norfolk, Virginia, in late November. In the meantime, on September 25 President Washington nominated Mr. Jefferson for the newly renamed post of Secretary of State; the Senate confirmed the appointment the following day. The common delay of at least six weeks in communications means that Mr. Jefferson was en route to the United States even as his new post was being approved — without his knowledge.[7]

Third Branch of Government Created

John Jay, acting Secretary of Foreign Affairs — before Congress this month changed the department's name — was President Washington's first choice for Secretary of State. Mr. Jay made it clear that he preferred the post of Chief Justice of the Supreme Court of the United States. Hence, he was nominated and confirmed by the Senate two days after Congress approved, and the President signed, on September 24, the Federal Judiciary Act. The measure creates the third branch of the government, establishing a single Supreme Court, a Chief Justice, five associates, as well as thirteen district courts and three circuit courts, and it establishes the office of the Attorney General.[8]

President Washington made certain that each geographic section of the Republic is represented in his appointments. This is illustrated by his Supreme Court selections: John Jay of New York, John Rutledge of South Carolina, James Iredell of North Carolina, John Blair of Virginia, James Wilson of Pennsylvania, and William Cushing of Massachusetts. Relying on the advice of Congressman Madison and others for the 1,000 appointive posts, but avoiding partisanship, the President has, according to one source, refused to appoint anyone who is a known enemy — an Anti-Federalist — of the Constitution.[9]

The President has made it clear to his appointees to the Supreme Court that "the administration of justice is the strongest cement of good Government" and the "first organization of the federal judiciary is essential to the happiness of our Country, and to the stability of our political system."[10]

State vs. Individual Rights

Fellow Virginian Senator Richard Henry Lee regards the Federal judiciary as a potentially powerful instrument for destruction of the individual States. When the Senate on September 2 took up the constitutional amendments passed by the House last month, he sought unsuccessfully to have adopted the amendments drafted by Patrick Henry but not approved by the House. The amendments would have curbed the powers of the judiciary, as well as the powers of the national government to impose direct taxation and to create a standing army.

"We might as well have attempted to move Mount Atlas upon our shoulders," Senator Lee bitterly observed of the Senate debate.

"...Some valuable rights are indeed declared, but the power to violate them to all intents and purposes remains unchanged."[11]

Although the Senate debate was secret, a source has revealed that a majority of twenty-two members were convinced that some amendments, in the form of a bill of rights, must be passed before adjournment to ensure domestic political tranquility. Senator Lee was concerned about the rights of the States and the tendency toward a consolidated government, but a majority of the Senate favored only those amendments originally drafted by Congressman James Madison guaranteeing personal and legal rights of individuals.[12]

Critics Reconciled by Bill of Rights

When the Senate concluded its secret debate on September 9, it had reduced the seventeen House amendments to twelve by incorporating several amendments into one. By September 25, a Senate and House conference had worked out the minor differences in wording. Besides safeguarding personal rights of individual citizens, the dozen amendments sent to the President for forwarding to the States for ratification contain a provision for reserving State powers not granted to the national government, and two articles calling for apportionment of the legislators and fixing the pay of Congressmen.[13]

Congressional approval of a bill of rights has defused an explosive domestic issue and calmed the most vocal critics of the Constitution. Rhode Island, for example, is reported to have told President Washington this month that congressional action on amendments is likely to lead to the hold-out New England State now joining the new Union.[14]

Another example is Colonel George Mason of Virginia, who refused to sign the Constitution at the Philadelphia Convention in 1787 because it lacked a bill of rights. He was the first delegate to propose a bill of rights, similar to the one he authored for Virginia in 1776. Now, according to one source, he has expressed great satisfaction, with a qualification, that Congress has moved to approve twelve amendments. He remarked upon hearing the news, "I could cheerfully put my Hand and Heart to the New Government," if Congress included two or three additional amendments.[15]

Public Credit Still of Concern

The question of amendments having been settled in Congress, there is still the unsettling problem of the government's public debt. The chaotic finances of the old Confederated government, especially the inaction on the swollen domestic and foreign debts incurred during the War, have yet to be addressed by the new government. On August 21 several prominent public creditors in Pennsylvania warned the new Congress in a public document that it would be subjected to public scorn if action were not taken on a long-term debt-funding formula before the first session concluded.[16]

Colonel Alexander Hamilton, who was appointed as Secretary of the Treasury on September 11 by President Washington and confirmed the same day by the Senate, was directed by the House on September 21 to prepare a plan for support of public credit "as a matter of high importance to the national honor and prosperity."[17]

Secretary Hamilton has only until the start of the second session of the First Congress in January 1790 to gather information on the actual extent of foreign and domestic debt and to devise a plan for servicing it. One observer reports that Secretary Hamilton sees no alternative but to emulate the British system of finance by creating a national bank and issuing government bonds as the basis for the new nation's money supply. The political risks in this proposal are explosive, given the anti-British attitude of Americans ever since the Declaration of Independence.[18]

At the present time, Secretary Hamilton must borrow money from existing private banks to fund the first administration's projects authorized by Congress. Among them is Treasury Department Warrant No. 1 signed by the Secretary, dated September 13, and made out to the Bank of New York in the amount of $20,000 to be paid to the Secretary of War. The amount was authorized by Congress last month to pay for the negotiation of treaties and the expenses of three commissioners appointed by the President to seek peace with the Creek Indians.[19]

Congress Divided over the West

Although the First Congress went along with President Washington's Indian and military initiatives related to the southern and western frontier, it remains divided over the importance of the West to the future of the infant Republic. One observer has told this correspondent that the West would have played a much smaller role in the just-concluded first session of Congress had the executive not submitted substantive messages and proposals to the legislature. In fact, over 80 percent of all the proposals and messages sent from the President to Congress in its first session relate to western issues.[20]

Besides authorizing on September 29 a 1,000-man regular army, Congress also authorized a western land office, surveys for public lands, surveys for estimating the amount of unclaimed public lands, and settlement of the claims of settlers in Vincennes, Indiana.[21]

The most important action taken this month relates to the West: Congress approved legislation declaring the Northwest Ordinance to be Federal law under the Constitution. The act had originally been passed by the Confederated Congress in July 1787, but since it allowed new States to be admitted on an equal footing with the original thirteen states, the Philadelphia Convention, struggling over the problems of sectionalism (North versus South), did not include any mention of it in the Constitution. President Washington considers the western lands of great importance to the new Union and to its prosperity, and therefore signed the Northwest Territory Act, which reaffirms the Northwest Ordinance under the new Constitution. It allows new States to be admitted to the Union on the same basis of equality of representation in the Congress as the original thirteen, all of which are on the Atlantic Coast, yet it also prohibits slavery in new States north of the Ohio River. The Northwest Territory Act is the first national effort to establish a framework for new State representation in the Union, and at the same time it comes to grips with the slavery issue by outlawing it in new States north of the Ohio River. It is expected that Kentucky (considered southern since it is part of Virginia) and Vermont (northern) will petition to join the Union under this new act.[22]

Sectional Differences Remain in Congress

The Federal government is being plagued with the same problems of sectional jealousies as was the Confederated Congress. They have contributed to the longest and most acrimonious debate of the First Congress, namely, that over the location of the permanent capital.[23]

Congressman Madison favors a site on the Potomac River between Maryland and his native Virginia, but northwest of the President's home, Mount Vernon, so as to be easily accessible to the West. His impassioned plea for a Potomac location farther inland, citing mileage and other advantages, fell on deaf ears. A majority in the House and Senate appear to favor a mid-Atlantic site near Philadelphia, which would accommodate both North and South and, they believe, be closer to the growing West, which may represent the future of the American Union.

Mr. Madison admits, "The seat of government is of great importance; if you consider the diffusion of wealth, that proceeds from this source...."[24] But he believes that it should be placed in the center of the Union, for there was every inducement, "both of interest and of prudence, to fix on the Potowmack, as most satisfactory to our western brethren.

"It is impossible," Mr. Madison continued in his lengthy September 4 argument before the House, "to reflect a moment on the possible severance of that branch of the union, without seeing the mischiefs which such an event must create. The area of the United States, divided into two equal parts, will leave, perhaps, one half on the west side of the Allegany mountains: From the fertility of soil, the fineness of climate, and every thing that can favor a growing population, we may suppose the settlement will go on with every degree of rapidity which our imagination can conceive...."[25]

A bill establishing a permanent seat of government that was in favor of the Susquehanna River finally passed the House.[26] Mr. Madison believes it may not pass the Senate in its present form, for the Susquehanna River is considered either too far south, or too far north; but southern members felt they could not do any better.[27] The Senate has postponed the issue until the second session, which opens in January 1790.

CHAPTER 19

★

October 1789

Washington Tours New England
Secret Opening to England Sought

His triumphal April tour to New York after his election still warm in his memory, President Washington this month visited New England. While greeting official delegations, he wore his Continental Army uniform, astride a white horse with a silver-mounted saddle resting on a leopardskin. His striking appearance during the tour is part of his plan to dramatize personally to the people the reality of the new centralized government, which to many, if not most, people in the outlying States seems remote and shadowy. He is not; his name is known and loved by nearly everyone. And he is the symbol against which the government can be measured.[1]

The President departed New York in the early morning hours of October 15 in a carriage drawn by four white horses, accompanied by two personal secretaries and six servants. Mrs. Washington remained in New York with her grandchildren. Before his departure, the President is reported to have told his sister that he viewed the tour as "relaxation from business and reestablishment of my health after the long and tedeous complaint with which I have been afflicted."[2]

Only in the last ten days has the President fully recovered from the emergency surgery in late June to control a life-threatening infection in his left thigh. Although still in considerable pain and discomfort, the President worked throughout the summer and right up to the September 29 adjournment of Congress. The President now regards the national government as organized and, in his words, "to the satisfaction of all parties."[3]

As part of this optimistic outlook, the President on October 3 issued a proclamation, recommended by the House and the Senate, designating Thursday, November 26 next, as a day of prayer and thanksgiving, "acknowledging with grateful hearts the many signal favors of Almighty God, especially by affording them an opportunity peaceably to establish a form of government for their safety and happiness."[4]

Secret Overtures to Former Foe

Securing such safety and happiness will depend in some measure on the Washington administration's ability to expand the United States' future trade with foreign nations.

Before his departure for New England, according to one source, President Washington on October 7 suggested that a private agent be employed to explore secretly with Great Britain the prospects for concluding a commercial treaty without reprisal or discrimination. The President discussed the proposal with several trusted advisers and then decided to act on the advice of Treasury Secretary Alexander Hamilton. He urged the President to ask his close personal friend and wealthy lawyer-financier Gouverneur Morris, already in France, to explore with the ministers of George III the feasibility of improving relations. The President has not been able to solicit advice from his Secretary of State-designate since Thomas Jefferson is aboard a ship returning to the United States from France.[5]

This correspondent has learned from reliable sources that Treasury Secretary Hamilton has already approached the British, without the President's knowledge. According to this source, Secretary Hamilton has held secret talks in New York with British agent Major George Beckwith without informing President Washington. Major Beckwith warned the Secretary that the British are likely to retaliate, however, because of the recent congressional passage of discriminatory trade legislation.[6]

It is difficult to determine whether Secretary Hamilton's secret discussions with Major Beckwith will undermine Mr. Morris's proposed mission in Great Britain. A transcript of a conversation between the gentlemen, obtained by this correspondent, indicates that Secretary Hamilton and Congressman James Madison may be on a collision course. Mr. Madison was the principal author of the discriminatory trade legislation, which Major Beckwith described as "decidedly hostile." The transcript indicates that Secretary Hamilton concurred with this conclusion.

"The truth is," Secretary Hamilton told Major Beckwith, "that although this gentleman [Mr. Madison] is a clever man, he is very little Acquainted with the world. That he is Uncorrupted and incorruptible I have not a doubt; he has the same End in view that I have."[7]

Causes for Future Conflict

As Secretary Hamilton expressed to Major Beckwith, "I have always preferred a Connexion with you, to that of any other Country. *We think in English*, and have a similarity of prejudices, and of predilections. . . ."[8]

One observer points out that Congressman Madison does not share this view. He and Secretary of State-designate Thomas Jefferson want more political independence from, not more reliance upon, Great Britain. If Mr. Madison were aware of the secret discussions being conducted, he would doubtless be alarmed and, given his powerful political position with President Washington, voice his vigorous opposition directly to the President.[9]

Mr. Hamilton has given indications that he would not only emulate the British system of finances, but also favor Great Britain over France since, as he informed Major Beckwith, the latter "is by no means so Essential or so suited to us as Your productions, nor do our raw Materials suit her so well as they do you."[10]

Nevertheless, he has assured Marquis de Lafayette in Paris that the $9 million owed to France for the finances provided during the American War of Independence would be "the first objects of my attention." On the other hand, he has grave doubts about the current upheavals in France, while rejoicing in the Marquis' efforts to effect a revolution of liberty in France.

As he wrote on October 6 to the nobleman, ". . . I dread the reveries of your Philosophic politicians who appear in the moment to have great influence and who being mere speculatists may aim at more refinement than suits either with human nature or the composition of your Nation." [11]

Jefferson's Enmity for English

Privately, Secretary Hamilton has made known his views of Congressman Madison and Secretary of State-designate Jefferson, both of whom he regards as speculative politicians who harbor hostility for Great Britain while being enthusiastic about the revolution that is engulfing France. Mr. Jefferson, in a letter received mid-October by Mr. Madison, a copy having been obtained by this correspondent, reported from Paris on August 28 that the new revolutionary government in Paris intends to emulate the American political experiment in every way, regarding it "like that of the bible, open to explanation but not to question." [12]

Mr. Jefferson clearly opposes placing Great Britain and the new French revolutionary regime on the same footing, pointing out that France "spent her blood & money to save us" while England "has moved heaven, earth & hell to exterminate us in war, has insulted us in all her councils in peace. . . ." [13]

Revolutionary Reefs

Minister Jefferson is not the only American, however, who has been an eyewitness to the sweeping revolutionary changes in France. Perhaps his views have been tempered because he left shortly after the revolution began, and has been traveling since, so has not yet had a full perspective. Gouverneur Morris witnessed the July 14 storming of the Bastille and the mob violence that led to beheadings. He penned his opinions to President Washington on July 31 and is far more pessimistic than Thomas Jefferson.

"You may consider the revolution as complete," writes the former delegate to the Philadelphia Convention and stylistic penman of the Constitution. "The authority of the king and of the nobility is completely subdued; yet I tremble for the [French] constitution. They have all the romantic spirit and all the romantic ideas of government, which, happily for America, we were cured of before it was too late." [14]

Concerned about his old French comrades in arms, President Washington wrote several letters to Frenchmen, including Marquis de Lafayette, before his departure for New England. He expressed his prayerful hope that the "consequences" of the revolution would prove "happy to a nation, in whose fate we have much cause to be interested and that its influence may be felt with pleasure by future generations." [15]

The President is not blinded to the possible results, and was much more candid in a series of three letters addressed to Mr. Morris, in which he spelled out his instructions for Mr. Morris's diplomatic mission in London. Terming the revolution in France "wonderful," meaning to be viewed with amazement and awe, he expressed hope that the optimistic accounts would prove accurate. Nevertheless, he expressed in his October 13 letter, a copy having been obtained by this correspondent, his belief that the revolution is far from over and faces in the future dangerous reefs.

"... In a word, the revolution is of too great magnitude to be effected in so short a space, and with the loss of so little blood," added the judicious and experienced General and politician. "The mortification of the King, the intrigues of the Queen, and the discontents of the Princes and the Noblesse will foment divisions, if possible, in the national assembly.... Great temperance, firmness, and foresight are necessary in the movements of that Body. To forebear running from one extreme to another is no easy matter, and, should this be the case, rocks and shelves not visible at present may wreck the vessel." [16]

Bill of Rights Sent to States

According to Minister Jefferson, the French National Assembly has emulated the United States by drawing up a Declaration of Rights. Congressman Madison had sent Mr. Jefferson a copy of the proposed U.S. Bill of Rights.

"I like it [the American Bill of Rights] as far as it goes; but I should have been for going further," the author of the Declaration of Independence declared from Paris. [17]

According to one source, Mr. Jefferson wants more precise wording in the twelve amendments passed by Congress and transmitted to the States by President Washington on October 2. He is still opposed to the new government's granting monopolies and he fears a standing army, especially one that might employ mercenaries.[18] During the War of Independence, Great Britain employed German mercenaries who were regarded by the Americans as barbaric.

Virginia became the first State this month to take up consideration of the Bill of Rights when its Assembly met on October 19. The Assembly also had read to it a letter sent it by U.S. Senators Richard Henry Lee and William Grayson; the missive warned that despite the amendments, dangers still exist for civil liberties and the States. The sheer physical size of the United States, the two concerned Virginians said, will compel a distant national government to command obedience from citizens not by informed consent but by "a resort to fear resulting from great force and excessive power in Government."[19]

Patrick Henry Looks to Other States

Former Virginia Governor Patrick Henry, according to one source, has abandoned all hope that a second convention of the States can be called to pass those amendments that were rejected last month by the new Congress. Those amendments would curb the powers of the national government. He is reported to be looking now to North Carolina and Rhode Island to withhold joining the Union until further amendments are accepted as the price for ratification. Because of this, he will seek a delay by the Virginia Legislature on the Federal Bill of Rights until both States hold ratification conventions.[20]

Although he served five terms as Virginia's Governor, Mr. Henry no longer has the absolute influence over the Virginia Legislature that he once exercised. Federalists in the body have become more numerous and they have the support of former Governor Edmund Randolph — considered by one observer as the most powerful person in the Legislature next to Mr. Henry.[21]

Mr. Randolph, who refused to sign the Constitution at the conclusion of the Philadelphia Convention, was once regarded as an ally of the Anti-Federalists. He later defected to the Federalists and played a pivotal role in securing Virginia's narrow ratification of the document. The former Governors came close to fighting a pistol duel during the State Ratifying Convention in June 1788. The incident erupted when Mr. Henry taunted Governor Randolph for an explanation of why he was renouncing his earlier reservations about the Constitution. Mr. Randolph, sensitive to private whispers that his motivation was due more to personal ambition than to principle, exploded with anger and their quarrel eventually extended to seconds arranging a duel. Cooler heads prevailed and Mr. Henry decided that ballots were preferable to pistol balls.[22]

President Washington has nominated Governor Randolph for the post of Attorney General and the Senate confirmed his appointment on September 26. However, Mr. Randolph has hesitated to accept because of financial problems. The President tried to reassure Mr. Randolph that after his service, he could expect a lucrative private practice.[23] One observer points out that the prudent, cautious President gave no indication that he offered the appointment as a reward for Mr. Randolph's key role in Virginia's ratification, although at the time the outcome greatly worried General Washington.[24]

Governor Randolph told Congressman Madison that he wished it were in his power "actually to *refuse* an office" in order to refute the repeated calumny "poured upon me" that he could not secure elective or appointive office because of his conduct during the struggle to ratify the Constitution.[25]

State vs. Presidential Supremacy

During his tour of Massachusetts this month, President Washington in a skillful but diplomatic way sought to drive home to the advocates of States rights the lesson of Presidential supremacy over a State Governor.

Governor John Hancock, a militant advocate of State supremacy, had invited the President to stay at his Boston home. President Washington declined because of what one observer says was an effort by the Governor to establish the principle that the President shall visit States as a guest of a local administration, not as a supreme executive. The President is not without tact and consideration. When he and his party arrived on October 24 at Cambridge, just outside the town of Boston — the place where in 1775 he first took command of the Continental Army — Governor Hancock was not on hand to greet him. The President, as a courtesy, refused to review the Cambridge militia, which he knows to be under State control.[26]

President Washington sent word ahead to Boston that he would be pleased to dine with Governor Hancock, although he expected as the nation's President a courtesy call at his tavern quarters before dinner at the Governor's mansion. Governor Hancock sent word that he was too "indisposed" to make the first call upon the President. Aware of the Governor's past use of illnesses for political purposes and delay, President Washington canceled his dinner date and, instead, had his evening meal with Vice President John Adams.[27]

Realizing the potential political damage of not receiving the nation's President, who was also a national hero of the American Revolution, Governor Hancock reconsidered his position. Two days later, at noon on Sunday, October 26, he sent a note to the President in which he apologized for not having called before. He inquired whether he might do so in half an hour. The President replied, tongue-in-cheek, according to one source, that he would derive much pleasure at seeing him, but begged him not to do anything that might hazard his health.[28]

It must have been with warm satisfaction, and an inner smile, one source surmises, that the President received Governor Hancock, whose feet were swathed in bandages to relieve his nonexistent gout, as husky servants lifted him from his coach and carried him into the drawing room of the President's quarters.[29] The incident set a clear precedent whereby the President is to be regarded as the official superior to every State Governor in the fledgling Union. President Washington, who understood during the War how men are governed largely by impressions, has settled once and for all in the public's mind that the nation is to come first.[30]

CHAPTER 20

★

November 1789

North Carolina Joins Union
Bill of Rights Stalled in Virginia

Faced with the threat of an Indian war on its frontier and with economic isolation by its sister States, North Carolina on November 21 voted 194 to 77 to become the twelfth State to ratify the new Constitution.[1]

One observer tells this correspondent that the successful efforts of Congressman James Madison to floor-manage a bill of rights in the Congress to final approval, eased the anxiety of Anti-Federalists in North Carolina and gave them a reason for accepting defeat "like sportsmen."[2]

Last year, in August 1788, an Anti-Federalist-controlled convention in North Carolina refused to ratify the new Constitution in the belief that its action would shock the country into calling a second convention that would adopt amendments curbing the powers of the national government. But in the ensuing fifteen months, Anti-Federalists in North Carolina and Virginia have been sorely disappointed as they watched the second convention movement fade like fog in the morning sunlight of Federalist political success.[3]

In a concession to their defeated foes, North Carolina Federalist leaders did agree this month to recommend key amendments that would have been considered at a second convention. They are: a ban on direct taxes, no Federal interference with paper money already in circulation, and a prohibition on a standing army.[4]

Rhode Island Likely to Ratify

The sole State remaining outside the Union is now tiny Rhode Island. President Washington, as if to underscore its isolation, excluded Rhode Island from his just-concluded tour of the New England States. The head of Rhode Island College, Jabez Bowen, has written the President, saying that North Carolina's action "will have some weight with the opposition with us, but I am afraid not sufficient to Insure a Convention."[5]

Anti-Federalist Rhode Island has steadfastly refused to convene a ratification convention (the only State not to do so) for fear that the new national government would be the instrument of its economic ruin with its power to levy taxes and to control domestic and foreign commerce. In addition, the State's large Quaker population is united in its opposition to the Constitution's extension of slavery until 1808. Two years ago, Rhode Island banned all its citizens from engaging in the slave trade.[6]

One obstacle to Rhode Island's joining the Union may have been removed, one source tells this correspondent. Last month the State Legislature repealed its legal tender laws, which allowed the State to operate a paper-money system that was the scorn and censure of sister States. It has also "retired" its debt by repudiating 90 percent of it and paying off the remaining 10 percent with paper currency. Rhode Island now believes that with this action, its economy — of which paper money was a key component — will not be destroyed by the provisions in the Constitution prohibiting States from printing paper currency and requiring that debts be paid in gold and silver coin.[7]

Patrick Henry's Power Declines

New Jersey, with swift action on November 20, became the first State to ratify the Bill of Rights. Meanwhile, in Richmond, Virginia, Patrick Henry received a cold rejection from the House of Delegates when he moved to postpone consideration of the twelve amendments until the next session. He argued that the delay would allow time to test popular sentiment on the subject. The lack of support by the

House may have so dismayed the once powerful former Governor, and signaled certain defeat, that he surprised everyone by departing for home without even calling for a vote on his resolution.[8]

Another former Virginia Governor, Edmund Randolph, also a member of the Virginia House of Delegates, wrote President Washington on November 22, describing Mr. Henry's departure as a product of political "discontent" with the growth of Federalist strength in the State Legislature.[9]

President Washington had once described Mr. Henry's power over the Virginia Legislature as absolute, comparable to that of a monarch of Europe. Admiration for him throughout the colonies is second only to that for General Washington. However, the North Carolina ratification and the failure of other States to agree to a second convention, a source close to Mr. Henry says, lead him "in the business of the lately proposed amendments [to where] I see no ground to hope for good...."[10]

Deadlock Leads to Delay

Although lacking Patrick Henry's leadership, his allies in the Virginia House of Delegates were given an unexpected opportunity at deadlock and delay on November 30 after they had approved ten of the twelve amendments article by article. To everyone's surprise, Governor Randolph mounted a strong attack on the final two amendments. He insisted that it would be safer to enact amendments that explicitly prevented Congress from extending the powers of the Federal government than to try and protect vague terms of "rights" and "powers" that were to be "retained" by the people or "reserved" to the States.[11]

Fellow Federalists in the House were thrown into confusion, thus providing Anti-Federalists with an opportunity to propose a resolution demanding that the Federal Congress approve amendments that Patrick Henry had drafted during the Virginia Ratifying Convention. Their measure failed by only one vote of 125 recorded. The House Federalists managed to gain approval of the two amendments disputed by Governor Randolph. Then the Anti-Federals in the Virginia Senate successfully used Governor Randolph's argument in objecting to the two amendments and they were not passed. Thus a deadlock in the Assembly was created, with no room for compromise and with neither branch retreating. As a result, consideration in Virginia of the Bill of Rights, with its twelve amendments, is now believed delayed until next year.[12]

U.S. Congressman Madison, at his Virginia plantation in Orange, is reported to have been angry when he learned details of how his friend Governor Randolph, by his objections to the two amendments, ended up "furnishing a handle to the disaffected."[13] A close associate told Mr. Madison that had Patrick Henry foreseen the opportunity provided by Mr. Randolph, "he would not have left us."[14]

Jefferson Arrives in America

Thomas Jefferson, U.S. Minister to France, landed at Norfolk on November 23, then traveled to Richmond where he received a warm welcome and congratulations from both houses of the Virginia Legislature. According to one observer, the cordiality extended to him was due less to his appointment as Secretary of State than to his once serving as Governor of Virginia and his presence once again among political associates and friends.[15]

On disembarking from the *Clermont*, Mr. Jefferson was surprised to read in the Norfolk newspapers that not only had President Washington appointed him Secretary of State a month ago while he was sailing home, but also the Senate had confirmed his nomination the following day (September 26). Before he pushed on to his home, Monticello, with his two daughters, his servants, and his dogs, an October 13 letter from the President caught up with him asking him to accept the post. Friends report that his initial reaction was negative.[16]

While in Richmond, he had an opportunity to inspect firsthand the new capitol that he had a part in designing. He also learned about the Virginia Legislature's debate over the Bill of Rights and the surprise departure of Patrick Henry. Mr. Jefferson predicts that Mr. Henry will not return "unless an opportunity offers to overturn the new constitution."[17]

Ironically, the Bill of Rights would not now be within reach of ratification had it not been for pressure from Colonel George Mason, Patrick Henry, and the vocal campaign of the Anti-Federalists.[18]

Washington — A Polar Star

The single most significant obstacle for the Anti-Federalists has been the enormous popularity and hero status of George Washington, freshly illustrated by his just-concluded triumphal Presidential tour of New England.

The President arrived back in New York on November 13, having been gone twenty-nine days. Eleven of those were taken up with travel over roads that he called "intolerable" and in overnight accommodations at inns and taverns that were "indifferent" to the point of being extremely annoying.[19]

The President rejected all invitations to stay at private homes during the tour, choosing instead only public inns or taverns despite discomfort and often poor meals. This allowed for greater flexibility in scheduling while avoiding partisanship and offending those officials who would have had their eager invitations rejected.[20]

One source reports that the President was much more confident and relaxed during his New England tour than he was during his April trip from Mount Vernon to New York. The emotional tidal wave that swept over him earlier made him fear that the people's expectations were so unrealistic that the new government would suffer a catastrophic loss of confidence when it failed to fulfill them.

Now, the cheering crowds, military escorts, artillery salutes, dinner speeches, and effusive praise in the form of songs sung and poems published in New England newspapers suggest to the President that the people are supportive of the new government.[21] For example, on his arrival at the State-house in Boston, the President was greeted by a sign over a temporary archway that read "To THE MAN WHO UNITES ALL HEARTS" and a choir that sang, in part:

> When th' impending storm of War,
> Thick clouds and darkness hid our way,

Great WASHINGTON our Polar Star
Arose; and all was light as day![22]

The President observed with pleasure that the archway that greeted him was twenty feet high, topped with an American Eagle, and crowned with a wreath of laurels bearing the inscription "Boston Relieved March 17, 1776." It must have revived memories of when the British evacuated Boston after an eight-month siege that he had directed as Commander-in-Chief.

From the balcony of the State-house he acknowledged the "three cheers... given by a vast concourse of people" who had assembled at the arch. During the procession of "different Professions and Mechanics,..." the President observed that "The Streets, the Doors, windows and tops of the Houses were crowded with well dressed Ladies and Gentlemen." [23]

Farms, Factories, Fishing

The President patiently endured the cheering crowds, dinners, speeches, fireworks, military escorts, and thirteen-gun salutes at his every stop. He also found time to enjoy chatting with farmers about crops, visiting cotton, woolen, and sail-making factories, viewing Revolutionary War sites, and fishing for cod off Portsmouth, New Hampshire.

He found less pleasurable, a source revealed, sitting for a portrait. And he accepted with grace the fact that traveling on the Sabbath is illegal in some New England States and frowned on in all. The President, therefore, attended church services twice each Sunday, once in the morning and again in the afternoon.[24]

While in Boston bad weather had prevented President Washington from visiting Lexington. But upon his return from Portsmouth, the President on November 5 "viewed the spot on which the first blood was spilt in the dispute with Great Britain, on the 19th of April, 1775." [25]

Illustrating his high spirits perhaps as a result of his successful tour, the President, while viewing the spot where the Massachusetts Minute Men stood on the Lexington green, related a story told to him by Dr. Benjamin Franklin. When the news of the Battle of Lexington reached London, British critics protested that it was unfair for the Americans to hide behind stone walls and to fire on the King's soldiers. Dr. Franklin, who was then in London, asked with impish innocence whether it was not true that there were two sides to a wall.[26]

Crooked Roads and Lost Lodgings

When leaving Lexington the next day, the President and his party went the wrong way. Instead of going south to Watertown, they took the wrong road, losing valuable time.

"The roads in every part of this State," the President is reported to have observed with annoyance, "are amazingly crooked, to suit the convenience of every man's fields; and the directions you receive from the people equally blind and ignorant;..."[27]

To compound their annoyance that same day, the President and his party arrived in Uxbridge only to be turned away at the only public lodging. The wife of the owner of the local tavern said she was sick and her husband away, and, therefore, "we could not gain admittance; which was the reason of my coming on to Taft's; where, though the people were obliging, the entertainment was not very inviting."[28]

Samuel Taft, a farmer with two sons and two daughters, offered his home and a dinner. He told the President that he had named one of his sons after him, and the other after Mrs. Washington's family. Touched by the gesture and the hospitality, the President during a stopover in Hartford a few days later sent the Taft girls a piece of brightly colored chintz and five guineas for Patty Taft, who had served the President his dinner.

"As I do not give these things," the President wrote to Mr. Taft, "with a view to having it talked of, or even to its being known, the less there is said about the matter the better you will please me, but that I may be sure the chintz and money have got safe to hand, let Patty, who I dare say is equal to it, write me a line informing me thereof directed to 'The President of the United States at New York.'"[29]

A Coin for an Old Comrade

During his New England tour of four major cities (New Haven, Hartford, Boston, and Portsmouth) and a dozen or more small towns, the outpouring of adulation that greeted the President was as much for his past military leadership in the War of Independence as for the high expectations that his new national civil administration would be crowned with similar success. Meeting many former officers who served with him, or under his command, revived a flood of memories of the long struggle.

In Newbury-Port, the President was carried back beyond the Revolution to 1755, when he was a 23-year-old Virginia militia officer serving under British General Edward Braddock. Lieutenant Colonel Washington survived the disastrous ambush of General Braddock's troops on the banks of the Ohio by a French and Indian force, even though two horses were shot out from under him and four musket balls pierced his tunic without drawing blood.

During a reception at Newbury-Port on October 31, the President was introduced to a poor old soldier by the name of "Cotton," commonly called "Colonel," who was in the same 1755 battle. Immediately "recollecting his person," the President took his hand and asked of his life since that time thirty-four years ago.

"I thank God," Cotton replied, "that I have an opportunity of seeing my old Commander once more. I have seen him in adversity, and now seeing him in glory, I can go home and die contented." The President gave the old soldier a guinea, which Cotton promised to wear as a pendant, "as a token of remembrance" of his former Commander."[30]

Indian Negotiations Fail

When he arrived back in New York on November 13, the glow of his triumphal tour, notwithstanding roads and rooms, quickly became clouded by news from the three Indian commissioners he had sent South. Their efforts at peace talks with the Creek Indians in southern Georgia had failed. One source reported that the President was puzzled and disappointed, but nevertheless willing to try to induce the chief of the Creeks to come to New York so that he might, face to face, persuade the chief that the Creeks had more to gain from an American than from a Spanish alliance.[31]

More bad news followed. On November 20 he received a letter from Congressman James Madison saying that the Spanish have "finally put an entire stop to the trade of our Citizens" down the Mississippi.[32]

The Spanish Minister to the United States is about to leave New York to return to Madrid, but a source has told this correspondent the President is worried for fear that a private talk with him, without first consulting the Senate, might violate the Constitution. Meanwhile, the President, a seasoned military and Indian veteran, is reported to have drawn up a plan for a national militia and has asked Secretary of War Henry Knox to draft a bill to be submitted to Congress when it returns from recess.[33]

First Thanksgiving Protested by Some

Before his election, President Washington conceded the value of the Anti-Federalist opposition, forcing the Federalists to defend the Constitution with greater energy and crystallizing many of the crucial issues. However, it is not known whether he was amused or annoyed when an Anti-Federalist newspaper in Boston and in New York objected to his Proclamation that set aside November 26 as the day of National Thanksgiving. Both papers complained that the President's message should have been directed to the governors of the individual States so they could proclaim the day.[34] The objection may seem trivial, but it illustrates the strong current facing the national government from States' rights advocates.

To mark the day of National Thanksgiving, the President attended chapel services at St. Paul's in New York. The words in his Proclamation appear to have a deep personal meaning, made more so by the fact that he has just returned from New England and his tour of Cambridge, Boston, Lexington, and Concord where he had assumed command of the citizens' army in 1775 that most observers concluded at the time had no hope of succeeding against the most powerful army and navy in the world.

President Washington's Thanksgiving Proclamation said in part:

> That we may then all unite in rendering unto him our sincere and humble thanks, for his kind care and protection of the People of this country previous to their becoming a Nation, for the signal and manifold mercies, and the favorable interpositions of his providence, which we experienced in the course and conclusion of the late war, for the great degree of tranquility, union, and plenty, which we have since enjoyed, for the peaceable and rational manner in which we have been enabled to establish constitutions of government for our safety and happiness, and particularly the national One now lately instituted. . . .[35]

CHAPTER 21

★

December 1789

Paris Mobs Directed by Agitators
French Royal Family Hostages

President George Washington has received information from a reliable source that recent riots in Paris have been fanned by agitators financed by a wealthy French nobleman who is ambitious and wants to replace Louis XVI as King of France.[1]

Colonel John Trumbull, a former wartime aide to General Washington and now a portrait painter, has just returned from Paris and personally briefed the President at the direct request of the Marquis de Lafayette. The briefing took place shortly after the President returned to New York from his New England tour.[2]

Colonel Trumbull advised the President that General Lafayette is certain the Duke of Orleans is using his considerable wealth to hire "discontented artisans and laborers" from the south of France to mingle among the Paris mobs for the purpose of "exciting the passions of the people to frenzy...."

"Every city and town," Colonel Trumbull related to the President, "has young men eminent for abilities, particularly in the law — ardent in character, eloquent, ambitious of distinction, but poor. These are the instruments which the Duke may command by money, and they will do his bidding. His hatred of the royal family can be satiated only by their ruin; his ambition, probably, leads him to aspire to the throne."[3]

King Is Reported Hostage of Mobs

In Paris with U.S. Minister Thomas Jefferson, whom he sketched for a projected painting depicting the signing of the Declaration of Independence, Colonel Trumbull witnessed mobs surging through the streets in July and storming the Bastille, the ancient fortress prison. He and Mr. Jefferson left for America before the October 6 outbreak of mob violence and the bloodshed at the King and Queen's palace at Versailles.[4]

Reports now reaching New York by ship place the Duke of Orleans at Versailles on October 6 encouraging a rampaging mob to seek out and kill the French King and Queen. The Marquis de Lafayette, as commander of the National Guard, was reported to have saved the royal couple and convinced them to leave for Paris under his protection, but they were also escorted by a threatening mob.[5]

One eyewitness reports that as the procession left the smashed and looted Versailles palace, the heads of two of the King's bodyguards were impaled on pikes and served as an escort for the royal couple. This same eyewitness reports that when their heads were first severed, the mob set up a great cry of approval, some bathing their hands in the blood and smearing it on their faces.[6]

One observer believes that despite the Paris mobs' hailing the King as a great benefactor of the people, he is now in fact a hostage, prisoner of a revolution that has been gaining violent momentum since early summer.[7]

Ambivalent Anxious Administration

President Washington, while concerned for the safety of the Marquis de Lafayette, is also worried about what effect these developments might have on future relations between the United States and its former wartime ally to which it owes some $9 million. The President states that although he welcomes the influence of the American Revolution on France, his greatest fear is "that the nation would not be sufficiently cool and moderate in making arrangements for the security of that liberty, of which it seems to be fully possessed."[8]

Vice President John Adams, who returned this month to New York from his home in Massachusetts to prepare for the opening of Congress on January 5, 1790, views the recent events in France from the perspective of his long diplomatic career and personal experience in Europe. He has written to friends saying that French philosophers like Voltaire and Rousseau have contributed more to the events in France than English theorists like John Locke, who, to a degree, influenced major participants in the American Revolution. He has also told friends that unless France emulates America and chooses a government of balanced and divided powers, the revolution will involve the country "in great and lasting calamities. . . .

"I own to you I know not what to make of a republic of thirty million atheists," the Vice President told one friend. He added that his experience has taught him that in revolutions "the most fiery spirits and flighty geniuses frequently obtain more influence than men of sense and judgment; and the weakest man may carry foolish measures in opposition to wise ones proposed by the ablest. France is in great danger from this quarter." [9]

Master of Monticello Returns

Secretary of State-designate Thomas Jefferson is much more optimistic about the events in France than Vice President Adams. He fears the violent disorders less than does President Washington or Congressman James Madison, and worries far less about the turbulence of democracy than Treasury Secretary Alexander Hamilton. One observer reports that Minister Jefferson regards the disorders and decapitations as inevitable and that he is interested more in the direction of the French Revolution than in the immediate forms it assumes. He has rejoiced, for example, in the fact that in late August France emulated America and adopted a Declaration of Rights that declared, among other things: "Men are born and remain free and equal in rights." [10]

On December 25 Mr. Jefferson and his two daughters arrived at their Albemarle County plantation, four weeks after landing in Norfolk from France. According to Martha Jefferson, her father was

surprised at the joyous reception he received from his Monticello
slaves after a five-year absence.

"Such a scene I never witnessed in my life,..." she related.
"When the door of the carriage was opened they received him in
their arms and bore him to the house, crowding round and kissing
his hands and feet — some blubbering and crying — others laugh-
ing. It seemed impossible to satisfy their anxiety to touch and kiss
the very earth which bore him." [11]

Jefferson Meets with Madison

Since his arrival back in America, Mr. Jefferson has been under
mounting pressure to accept the post of Secretary of State. On
December 15 he wrote President Washington saying that he would
prefer to return to France unless the President insisted on his
accepting the secretarial post. [12]

Congressman Madison traveled to Monticello near the end of
December in an effort to persuade his long-time friend and neigh-
bor, according to one source, that his hopes for the success of the
French Revolution could be effectively realized more as a member
of the Washington administration in New York than as a mere U.S.
Minister in Paris. [13]

Mr. Madison confidently left the meeting and prepared to return
to New York and the convening of Congress next month, believing,
according to one source, that he and Mr. Jefferson would be working
together, although the latter might not be able to assume the post of
Secretary of State until March. Mr. Madison wrote the President,
advising that he would persist in his effort to obtain Mr. Jefferson's
acceptance, observing that "all whom I have heard speak on the subject are remarkably solicitous for his acceptance...." [14]

Mr. Jefferson is likely to accept the appointment of Secretary of
State, according to one source, primarily because he fears what
President Washington and others might think were he to turn it
down and return to France. This same observer believes that Mr.
Jefferson's sensitiveness to the opinions of others is his chief tem-
peramental weakness and might prove to be a source of personal

unhappiness should he clash with others while serving in the highly visible position of Secretary of State.[15]

Credit Plan Source of Conflict

A potentially immediate source of conflict within the new administration could be Treasury Secretary Alexander Hamilton's Report on the Public Credit, which he is expected to submit next month to a reconvened Congress. When news of the plan becomes public it is likely to trigger a speculative stampede in government certificates issued to simple soldiers as payment for their wartime service. One reliable source reports that speculators are likely to send agents north and south by boat and horse to buy up those remaining certificates for a few cents on the dollar in the anticipation that some may be redeemed for their face value. This would allow speculators to reap huge profits while simple soldiers would not receive their deserved benefits.[16]

Congressman Madison is known to believe that justice requires that some payment be made to the original certificate holders and he is likely to demand payment to them when the House considers the credit plan. He is certain to oppose Secretary Hamilton's plan for the new national government to assume the Revolutionary War debts of the individual States. The Treasury Secretary estimates the total Federal debt at over $54 million, with an additional estimated $25 million as war debts of the thirteen States.[17]

The fate of the Constitution itself and the very existence of the infant Republic depend, one observer maintains, on how the financial obligations of the new government are handled. Of all the problems facing the Washington administration, none is as complex as, or more urgent and less understood than, the national debt. The political effect of Secretary Hamilton's expected financial proposals could be that State creditors would be folded into the national government along with national creditors, thus creating a powerful national government, assuming all debts, and all control over methods of payment, thus supreme over the individual States.[18]

President Prepares for War

It is not entirely clear whether President Washington realizes the potential political firestorm that Secretary Hamilton's proposals are likely to ignite in the Congress. If opposition is led by his trusted adviser James Madison and joined by Secretary of State-designate Thomas Jefferson, it could defeat his desire for domestic political tranquility. Only in recent months with congressional passage of the Bill of Rights, and ratification by the States counted on, has the campaign against the perceived dangers of the Constitution and the national government subsided.

The President has appeared more preoccupied with the growing danger of a generalized frontier war with various Indian tribes. The failure of talks with Creek Indians has apparently moved the President to propose that Congress adopt "A Plan for the Militia of the United States." Secretary of War Henry Knox this month drew up the plan, which calls for compulsory military training for all males and for summer training camps in locations distant from city vices. Secretary Knox perceives a national militia as a way to shape the moral and patriotic fiber of the nation and encourage republican virtue.[19]

When the President addresses both houses of Congress on January 8 he is expected to link his proposal for a national militia to the failure of peace talks with the Creek Indians. An advance draft copy of his speech, obtained by this correspondent, makes clear that the President believes the new national government should be prepared "to punish aggressors" in order to provide protection for frontier settlers.

"To be prepared for War is one of the most effectual means of preserving Peace," President Washington is expected to tell the First Congress.[20]

Privately the President is considering writing the Governor of South Carolina that he believes the talks with the Creek Indians failed because of the influence of Spain. He believes, a source reveals, that although his Indian policy will be one based on national justice, faith, and honor, should "every reasonable pacific measure" fail, the national government will be obliged "to have a recourse to arms" and it will be "a prompt and decisive effort, rather than... defensive and lingering operations." [21]

As the President prepares to greet the new year of 1790, his worries are centered mostly on external dangers: Spain's inciting a frontier Indian war, the apparent collapse of the French monarchy, and the economic need to re-establish trade ties with the British. He has more reason to be pleased with internal matters: the establishment of the Federal government has gone smoothly, the opposition by Anti-Federalists has diminished with the Bill of Rights sent to the States for ratification, the harvests have been good, commerce is visible in every American port, and manufacturing introduced in the past year is "astonishing."

"The establishment of our new Government seemed to be the last great experiment for promoting human happiness by reasonable compact in civil Society," President Washington observes in summing up this historic year. "It must be, in the first instance, in a considerable degree a government of accommodation, as well as a government of Laws. Much was to be done by *prudence*, much by *conciliation*, much by *firmness*." [22]

CHAPTER 22

★

January 1790

A Reporter's Reflections

As the First Congress reconvenes in New York for its second session, reports from Philadelphia indicate that 84-year-old Dr. Benjamin Franklin is near death. His once powerful frame has been reduced to what he himself describes as "a skeleton covered with a skin." Confined to bed during the last year with a painful bladder stone condition, he is reported to have eased the unrelenting physical agony with opium, which in turn has sapped his appetite.

"I grow thinner and weaker, so that I can not expect to hold out much longer," he confided to a friend seven weeks ago.

Although he has abandoned his autobiography, Dr. Franklin published a public paper on November 9, 1789, advocating his lifetime goal of abolishing slavery. The paper will be submitted to Congress next month. As early as 1751, he was the first to point out the economic weakness of the institution, which had been established in the American Colonies by the British. He was also the first to propose, in 1754, a plan for uniting the Colonies. That effort in Albany, New York, thirty-six years ago is now regarded as the first step toward establishment of the new American Union. He also played a part in saving the Union from the possibility of failure at the deadlocked Philadelphia Convention during the summer of 1787.

Dr. Franklin wrote President Washington last September that he would have died shortly after the Philadelphia Convention if that summer of statecraft had ended in failure. He went on to write that the last two years "spent in excruciating pain" were a small price for witnessing the Constitution's ratification, its implementation, and the "growing strength of our New Government under your administration."

The American Revolution vs. the French Revolution

The anticipated passing of Dr. Franklin from the American and the world scene comes at the moment when the era of the American Revolution is nearing an end. The uncertain era of the American Republic is just beginning now that the first elections have been held and the new national government is in place and functioning. Dr. Franklin is one of only a handful of Americans who have been influential participants in the American Revolution from its beginning to its successful conclusion.

After years in England and after his participation in drafting the Declaration of Independence, Dr. Franklin was based in Paris during the War of Independence and through his fame and political finesse obtained France's aid during the eight-year struggle. It was Dr. Franklin, for example, who was instrumental in concluding the French Alliance in Paris that involved money, men, and ships, all of which proved crucial to the military defeat of Great Britain. Imbued with the spirit of the victorious War of Independence, many of the French officers who fought in that conflict returned to Paris and are now active participants in the revolution that has been sweeping France since last summer.

Like President Washington and others, Dr. Franklin is deeply troubled by the reports of mob violence and decapitations in Paris, fueled by a burning hatred for the aristocracy. This type of savagery was almost totally absent during the American Revolution. And in the last two years it has been demonstrated to a disbelieving world that it is possible, on this side of the Atlantic, to effect revolutionary political reform without recourse to mob violence and internal bloodshed. Even during the long War of Independence, the conflict was governed within specific codes of conduct that prevented it from degenerating into a savage civil conflict between people of the same cultural traditions.

Ingrained Fear of Disorder

President Washington, Dr. Franklin, and other American leaders always assumed that the American Revolution would influence Europe, which might eventually follow its example. Now that a revolution has erupted in France, brought on in large part by the huge debt resulting from the sums spent by the Paris monarchy during the American War, her most ardent friends in America have welcomed the revolution. Yet, they are deeply disturbed that the nation appears in danger of losing its humanity and high culture, descending into anarchy and barbarism.

An ingrained fear by Americans of civil disorder manifested itself in the shock waves that coursed throughout the separate States when the Massachusetts-based Shays's Rebellion erupted in 1786. Brief and bloodless as the mass protest was by debt-ridden farmers laying siege to the State courts to protest foreclosures and the collection of taxes, the widespread dread it produced played a role in the decision to convene the Philadelphia Convention of 1787. Although the conclave was motivated by economic and political reform, it was also viewed as an opportunity to frame an instrument (or by many to adapt the Articles of Confederation) to inoculate the new American Republic against plagues of political anarchy and barbaric disorders that in ancient and contemporary nations had consumed life, liberties, and property.

The alarm of the American leaders over what they fervently hope are only isolated incidents of savagery in the streets of Paris is also explained in part by their own experience. For over a century the European settler culture and the warrior-hunting culture of the native North American tribes have been in continuous conflict. The use by the competing European powers of Indian tribes as surrogates in, for instance, the French and Indian Wars, in which President Washington fought, produced countless massacres and acts of mutilation. Although such savagery might be an unfortunate fact of life on the American frontier, its appearance on the supposedly civilized streets of Paris has shocked and stunned American political leaders.

Foreign Affairs and the Frontiers

The French upheaval foreshadows an abrupt change in the delicate power relationships in Europe as France struggles to reform its internal political institutions and come to terms with its fiscal crisis. The weakening, even displacement, of the French monarchy almost certainly means a period of an internal struggle for power among various groups. This, in turn, means that the Washington administration will find France less cooperative in the matter of the tremendous war debt it owes to the French monarchy and brings into question the anticipated trade assistance.

Commercial relations with other countries, especially with France and Great Britain, remain for the new national government the most pressing foreign affairs problem, now complicated and made uncertain by the French upheaval and by what moves London might make worldwide to profit from the political paralysis in Paris.

France has long been allied with Spain against England. It may now be unable to support its old ally should the British seek to seize Spain's possession in North America. President Washington is privately predicting that the British in Canada may contemplate seizing Spanish New Orleans to gain control of the vital Mississippi River commerce. The British would have to cross American territory if they decided to move against the Spanish in the South. If this happened, the President worries that such a conflict would trigger a frontier war, and result in the infant nation's being surrounded on all sides by the British, including a blockade from the seas by their naval power. As a strong ally, France would make this prospect less likely.

Even without an immediate war between England and Spain on American frontiers, which are ill defined and disputed, the Washington administration must find a way to induce Spain to reopen the Mississippi to American trade while keeping peace on the southern frontiers with Indian tribes used by the Spanish government to wage violence against American settlers. The objects of the Spanish in closing the Mississippi River to American trade in

1785 were to stem the swelling tide of settlers, and to strangle the American frontier economically.

Two Cultures in Collision

During the past five years, American settlers in growing numbers have continued to move into the South and the Northwest, lured by the promise of cheap land and a new life principally through the efforts of land speculators. Currently, land in New England is selling for $20 to $30 an acre, while western lands can be purchased in installment payments of 20 cents to 30 cents an acre. Since the end of the War of Independence, speculation in western lands has coursed throughout the former Colonies like a fever, involving many prominent leaders, including George Washington.

The Washington administration fully supports a policy of western land sales for settlement for much the same reason that the old Confederation government did: western lands are a certain national asset and developed would be a source of revenue to help retire the Revolutionary War debt. Although the President considers foreign trade essential to the survival of the new Union, as a former surveyor he views the wilderness West as the foundation for future national wealth and greatness.

This was patently indicated by the fact that a majority of initiatives from the President to the First Congress last year dealt with western problems. The President has made it clear that he desires to treat the Indians peacefully, fairly, and humanely, but he is prepared to use military force against those tribes that continue to attack American frontier settlements. This collision of cultures dates back to the establishment of the first permanent English settlements.

Dr. David Ramsay, a South Carolina physician and historian, points out in his just-published *The History of the American Revolution* (October 1789) that most Indian tribes sided with Great Britain during the War of Independence. Dr. Ramsay blames the British colonization policy since 1607 for the massive loss of Indian lands and national existence, terming it "an event scarcely to be paralleled in the history of the world."

Old Attitudes, New Era

Just as the evil institution of slavery was inherited from the British and has caused much heat and debate in the new Union of States, the English legacy regarding the Indian tribes will not be easy to erase. Many settlers who have moved to the frontier continue to harbor bitter hatred and fear of all Indians, although only specific tribes acting as British surrogates massacred and mutilated Americans during the War. Use of Indian tribes by the Spanish against American settlers in the southern frontier areas reinforces American fears and is likely to frustrate efforts of the Washington administration to persuade settlers and their political representatives to honor existing and future tribal treaties.

Dr. Ramsay argues in his published history that the attitude of Great Britain and other European powers toward native North Americans was one in which "right to the soil was disregarded" and their land "looked upon as a waste, which was open to occupancy and use," while the "right and interests of the native proprietors" were "deemed of no account." Nevertheless, this attitude did not prevent the British from using the Indian tribes against the Americans who wished independence.

Most Americans continue to accept the old view, even though the Washington administration has committed itself to a new era of equity toward the Indian tribes. The President has, for example, invited Indian tribes to make use of the new Federal court system to settle their disputes, although the process is as alien to the Indian as it would be for the frontiersman to seek justice from a tribal council of chiefs.

The profound gulf between the cultures of the European settler and the American Indian will doubtless prove a greater frustration to the Washington administration than the designs of either the British or the Spanish. Acceptance by the Indian of the white man's civilization would mean rejection of the Indian brave's creed that his manhood is achieved and maintained as a hunter and warrior. Any other pursuit would bring disgrace on himself, his tribe, and his ancestors, and turn him into a woman. Thus, most tribes find little to emulate in the white settler culture of yeoman farming.

Influence of Frontier on Future Politics

Beyond the problem of Indian tribes serving as Spanish and British surrogates, the frontier West is likely to influence the domestic politics of the new American Republic for decades. Consideration of the application of Kentucky, the western portion of Virginia, to become the fourteenth State has been delayed because eastern States fear that its admission will affect the balance of political power in Congress between the northern and the southern States.

Under the Articles of Confederation, States like tiny Rhode Island had the same number of votes in the Confederated Congress as the territorially expansive and populous Virginia. Under the Constitution, the number of House seats for each State is based on population. Fear that the large States would dominate the small ones in the Congress was resolved by making the Senate equal in State representation: each State Legislature now elects two Senators with one vote each. This is a new and novel system of representation and has yet to be tested by time and experience.

Kentucky is more likely to favor an alliance with southern States than one with the Middle Atlantic or New England States. Southerners see the West and new States as allies for controlling the new national government.

Vermont is also seeking admission to the new Union. But the growth of population is certain to be in the West, and new States are certain to be developed in the West and Southwest. At the end of the War, for example, the Kentucky and Tennessee frontier had only a few thousand settlers. When the first census, mandated by the new Constitution, is completed in 1790, the new Union is likely to show a population of approximately four million, 120,000 of that number in the Kentucky-Tennessee region. In 1788 alone, 967 boats containing 18,370 men, women, and children from the eastern States floated down the Ohio River seeking new lands in the West, while an equal number made their way through the Cumberland Gap on the Virginia-Tennessee Territory border.

The Emerging American Empire

Many of these emigrants are from the original thirteen States, raising concerns in Congress that continued western migration will leave the New England and Middle Atlantic States weakened economically and politically. Federalists and southerners like Congressman James Madison have raised the British and Spanish danger on the frontier to gain support for the administration's policies that offer military and political protection to frontier settlers.

The American frontier, extending west to the Mississippi and south to Georgia, is now being viewed as the gateway to a future American republican empire, the largest in the history of the world. Just last year Jedidiah Morse predicted in his popular *American Geography* that the time will come "when the AMERICAN EMPIRE will comprehend millions of souls, West of the Mississippi."

Nevertheless, both the Congress and President Washington have moved with caution on the frontier issues from concern that requests for increases in the regular army and for the formation of a national militia will ignite a furor over authorizing a standing army in peacetime. Senator William Maclay of Pennsylvania has bluntly insisted that "the Constitution certainly never contemplated a Standing Army in time of peace."

Senator Maclay is one of only a handful of Anti-Federalist lawmakers in the First Congress. But the Anti-Federalists believe that the evolution of an American empire under a consolidated national government is certain to end in replacing hard-won freedoms with force because so vast a geographical area will prove ungovernable. Senator Richard Henry Lee of Virginia, another Anti-Federalist, argues that "the history of the world, and reason concur in proving that so extensive a territory as the United States comprehend, never was, or can be governed in freedom."

Congressman James Madison has countered that the infant Republic, composed of the national and state governments, can accommodate the problems of distance and geography because power is not concentrated "in the hands of one body of men" but "lodged in separate and dissimilar bodies" requiring their approval of "every public act."

The Untried Third Branch

While Anti-Federalists Senator Lee and former Governor Patrick Henry and others have assailed the powers of Congress to impose taxes, their greatest concern for the future is the influence of the still untried third branch of the new government — the Federal judiciary. In fact, no other part of the Constitution is so vague as, or has been subjected to more criticism during the long ratification debates than, Article III, which begins: "The judicial power of the United States, shall be vested in one supreme Court, and in such inferior Courts as the Congress may from time to time ordain and establish."

At the Virginia Ratification Convention, Patrick Henry vigorously attacked Article III of the Constitution because of his concern that the Federal judiciary would dominate and effectively extinguish the State courts. "The [State] judiciary," he said, "are the sole protection against a tyrannical execution of the laws. But if by this system we lose our judiciary, and they cannot help us, we must sit down quietly, and be oppressed." Young John Marshall responded that the Federal judiciary was, in fact, an essential bulwark against Federal tyranny, eventually to give meaning to the Bill of Rights: "To what quarter will you look for protection from an infringement on the Constitution, if you will not give the power to the judiciary?"

In framing the powers of the legislative and executive branches, the delegates to the Philadelphia Convention drew on their past experiences at the State level. With respect to the judiciary, the Confederation government's legal jurisdiction was confined to cases arising on the high seas; all other judicial functions were left to the individual States. The idea of a single national Supreme Court is new. Supreme over what? Supreme by what process?

Neither friends nor foes of the third branch were able to answer these questions during the heated debate in Congress last July and

September over the National Judiciary Act, which created the Federal court system as the third branch of the national government. Although the first session of the Court is scheduled for February 1, it may be several years before it decides its first case.

Rough Roads of the Republic

In the meantime, the six justices appointed to the Supreme Court are likely to be kept busy fulfilling a provision of the Judiciary Act that requires them to hold court twice a year in each of the three designated circuits (Eastern, Middle, and Southern) in the company of District Judges. Travel from New York to these locations, and between them, whether by horse or carriage, is likely to be frustrating, time-consuming, and even dangerous for the older justices, just as it was for members of the Confederation Congress. Even President Washington barely escaped injury or death when his horse carriage broke through rotten planks spanning a raging river. Future appointees might decline to serve on the Court because of the ordeal of traveling between the various sections of a still semi-wilderness nation.

President Washington complained after his New England tour late last year that the roads were "intolerable" and the accommodations of local taverns "indifferent." The President undertook his tour to establish in the public mind the reality of the new national government. He believes, similarly, as do the authors of the Judiciary Act, that justices "riding the Circuit" are the best way to acquaint Americans at the local level with the third branch of the new national government.

The President has told Chief Justice John Jay that he has been persuaded that "the stability and success of the National Government, and consequently the happiness of the people of the United States, will depend in a considerable degree on the interpretation and execution of its laws."

The Politics of Federal vs. State Power

Chief Justice Jay has acknowledged that the Court he now heads has never existed before and has "no light of experience" on which it can rely for guidance. Each existing State court system, he adds, is different, accommodating itself to local policy. He admits that in the future it will be an "arduous" task to prevent "discord" from developing between the existing State courts and the new Federal courts. What is needed, the Chief Justice explains, is "to render them auxiliary instead of hostile to each other, and so to connect both as to leave each sufficiently independent and yet sufficiently combined.... Institutions formed under such circumstances should therefore be received with candor and tried with temper and prudence."[1]

The unrelenting Anti-Federalist opposition to the ratification and implementation of the Constitution is almost certain to continue and may mature into a permanent political opposition championing the rights of the States against the policies of the national government, especially against the new Federal judiciary.

During the Judiciary Act debate in the House and Senate last year, Anti-Federalists in both houses restated arguments that had first been raised during the Constitution ratification debates, with predictions that the power of the State courts would be diminished and ultimately destroyed. Senator William Maclay of Pennsylvania insisted that the Judiciary Act is the "gunpowder plot of the Constitution" created by a "knot of lawyers." The document, he argued, is designed not only to swallow up "the State Constitutions by degrees," but also "to swallow, by degrees, all the State Judiciaries."

Forecast of Future Factionalism

Another debate just beginning this month in Congress is already developing as a Federal versus State power struggle and is also one that pits countryside farmers against city merchants. The subject is Treasury Alexander Hamilton's package of proposals to fund the $54 million war debt. During the Constitution ratification debates in the States, city merchants favored adoption of the document, believing it would aid their economic interests. Whereas the frontiersmen and farmers advocated rejection from fear that the outlawing of paper money would result in their economic ruin.

Secretary Hamilton's proposal that $25 million of the States' war debts be assumed by the new national government clearly favors the commercial and financial interests in the cities and seaports. As of 1789 the bulk of the domestic war debt was in the hands of the city-based commercial speculators who acquired wartime-issued government certificates from former soldiers for as little as fifteen cents on the dollar. The proposal to "fund" the certificates — that is, pledge semi-permanent revenues to meet annual interest payments — at a hundred cents on the dollar will realize for speculators a huge windfall profit while simultaneously doubling the national debt.

However financially feasible, and even visionary, Secretary Hamilton's proposals might be, they do not directly benefit the mass of Americans who till the soil, and they are open to attack as having come from the privileged commercial aristocracy. Patrick Henry of Virginia denounced the debt assumption in just those terms. He warned that they would create one of two evils: either "the prostration of agriculture at the feet of commerce," or a change in the form of the Federal government "fatal to the existence of American liberty." Former Governor Henry argues that he can find "no clause in the Constitution authorizing Congress to assume the debts of the States."

Washington's Support

There are only a handful of Anti-Federalists in the First Congress, and Secretary Hamilton is counting on eventually passing his proposals because President Washington supports them. There is little doubt, nonetheless, that the debate over his debt assumption policy will be lengthy and bitter, and may leave what Secretary Hamilton predicts will be the foundation "for the great schism" in the politics of the newly formed Republic, with the States and the agricultural South opposing Federal power and the commercial North.

"This is the first symptom," Alexander Hamilton wrote of Patrick Henry's attack on his debt assumption policies, "of a spirit which must either be killed, or will kill the Constitution of the United States."

Although President Washington does not completely understand Secretary Hamilton's proposals, he does understand that resolving the war debt issue is a matter of personal as well as national honor. As military Commander-in-Chief, he persuaded near-mutinous soldiers and officers to go home at the War's end carrying certificates of indebtedness instead of back pay in hard money. Repudiation of that debt, as suggested by some, would have made a mockery of the assurances he had given and would penalize those who had patriotically loaned money to the wartime government.

President Washington also understands that the debt issue must be resolved, no matter what it costs in domestic political discord, in order to demonstrate to the world that the independent United States is prepared to honor its past obligations and therefore can be counted on to honor future obligations.

Beyond a Wall of Words

Assumption of the States' war debts by the national government is, for President Washington, the first bold policy effort to forge a union based on deeds rather than on merely the words contained in the Constitution. As the first national measure concerning the entire thirteen States, which acted in a common cause for national independence only fourteen years ago, assumption of the States' war debts is as much the first firm act of union as a hoped-for act of bonding the States to the central government.

It is profoundly symbolic that the man who headed the armies that militarily secured independence should also have been crucial in convening the Constitutional Convention; have been influential in resolving delegates' differences, helping to ensure the Constitution's narrow ratification; and now be serving as its principal agent of implementation. The new national government's first elections and the first steps of organization would certainly have been crowned with less success had George Washington been taken ill, or died. Little wonder that before he became President and after his election George Washington should again and again ascribe his role in this epochal train of events since 1776 to Divine inspiration and guidance.

The General has been mindful that all that has been secured still hangs in the balance if those men entrusted with the management of the new government are moved by a lust for power. If that lust meets with an indifference in the people, such men will o'erleap the barriers of the Constitution. The General has warned that "no wall of words," "no mound of parchment" can stand against "the sweeping torrent of boundless ambition on the one side, aided with the sapping current of corrupted morals on the other."

Like President Washington, Dr. Franklin has reason to look back with satisfaction on so much that has been achieved in so short a time. As members of a graying Revolutionary generation, both have demonstrated to a still disbelieving world that it is possible to break with the past and construct for the future a new political framework based on consent, consensus, and compromise.

"Our new Constitution is now established," Dr. Franklin wrote to a friend in Paris, "and has an appearance that promises permanency; but in this world nothing can be said to be certain, except death and taxes."[2] *

---

* At eleven o'clock on April 17, 1790, Dr. Benjamin Franklin died quietly at 84 years, 3 months. His funeral in Philadelphia was attended by no less than 20,000, said to have been the largest funeral for a single person in the history of the city of 70,000. When the news reached France, three days of mourning were declared, and throughout Europe Franklin's passing was mourned as a loss for the cause of liberty.

READER'S GUIDE TO THE APPENDICES

★

Space and style limitations in the body of this book highlighting the debate and passage of the Bill of Rights did not allow a full exposition of the more than one hundred amendments proposed by members of the first Federal Congress and five of the thirteen States: Massachusetts, South Carolina, New Hampshire, Virginia, and New York.

Appendices* 1, 2, and 3 contain the text of the U.S. Constitution, the ten amendments ratified by a majority of thirteen States in 1791, and subsequent amendments up to and including the twenty-sixth, adopted in 1971.

Appendix 4 contains the twelve amendments approved by Congress on September 28, 1791, and sent to President George Washington for his signature. He then forwarded them to the separate States for ratification. The first two as presented in the text failed to win approval.

The original first amendment stipulated one Representative for every 30,000 citizens up to 100,000, and one Representative for every 40,000 thereafter until 200 Representatives was reached. Above 200, one Representative would be added for every 60,000 citizens.

The original second amendment prohibited members of Congress from voting on their own salaries and compensation until after an election had been held. It is significant that 200 years later the issue of Congress granting itself pay raises remains a politically volatile and emotional issue.

---

* Irwin Glusker and Richard M. Ketchum, eds., *American Testament: Fifty Great Documents of American History* (New York: American Heritage Publishing Co., 1971).

In Appendix 5 are the original seventeen amendments submitted by Congressman James Madison. After extensive debate and minor changes, they were approved by the House and sent to the Senate. By consolidating the wording of several amendments and deleting others, the Senate reduced the number to the twelve sent to the President.

The Senate's deletion that most angered James Madison was the one that applied the Bill of Rights to the individual States and specifically prohibited them from interfering with criminal jury trials, with rights of individual conscience, and with freedom of the press and speech.

Also deleted by the Senate from what is today the second amendment (the right to keep and bear arms) was a concluding phrase that permitted anyone to refuse to bear arms or to serve in the military if that person's religion prohibited such service. Not until the twentieth century was the conscientious objector status, on religious or moral grounds, recognized by the Federal government.

Appendix 6 provides the full text of the amendments — with similarities and duplications — submitted by each of the five States to the first Federal Congress. They were not considered or debated in their entirety. However, all of the amendments that formed the Federal Bill of Rights had in one form or another been submitted by a majority of the five States. All of the five States sought both to limit the power of Congress to engage in direct taxation and to curb the power of the judiciary; the latter restriction is still a goal sought by many Americans two centuries later. All of the five States advocated limitations on the power of the Federal government to interfere with the power of the States (in contemporary terms, States rights).

New Hampshire and Massachusetts specifically sought to prevent Congress from creating a privileged monopoly for commercial interests, an issue that is still debated in the context of free trade versus protectionism.

Virginia's amendments, largely the work of Patrick Henry, numbered forty. Significantly, Henry proposed an amendment that would have made the separation of powers concept among the three branches of the Federal government explicit rather than implied, as it is interpreted today. Congressman Madison had included this amendment in the seventeen passed by the House but it was deleted by the Senate.

An amendment proposed by Virginia and several other States, term limitations on members of the Senate (twelve years) and a two-term limit on the President, is being debated anew today. Virginia also sought to put limits on a standing army in peacetime by requiring a two-thirds vote of Congress and a limitation of four years for individual enlistments.

New York was perhaps, next to Virginia, the most militant of the States when it came to distrusting the Federal judiciary and the new and novel Supreme Court. It proposed an amendment that would have limited the power of Congress to create lower courts, except those concerned with appeals, and stated that the powers of the Supreme Court were not "in any case to be increased enlarged or extended by any Fiction Collusion or mere suggestion."

APPENDIX 1

★

The Constitution
of the United States, 1787

WE THE PEOPLE of the United States, in Order to form a more perfect Union, establish Justice, insure domestic Tranquility, provide for the common defence, promote the general Welfare, and secure the Blessings of Liberty to ourselves and our Posterity, do ordain and establish this Constitution for the United States of America.

ART. I

Sec. 1. All legislative Powers herein granted shall be vested in a Congress of the United States, which shall consist of a Senate and House of Representatives.

Sec. 2. The House of Representatives shall be composed of Members chosen every second Year by the People of the several States, and the Electors in each State shall have [the] Qualifications requisite for Electors of the most numerous Branch of the State Legislature.

No Person shall be a Representative who shall not have attained to the Age of twenty five Years, and been seven Years a Citizen of the United States, and who shall not, when elected, be an Inhabitant of that State in which he shall be chosen.

Representatives and direct Taxes shall be apportioned among the several States which may be included within this Union, according to their respective Numbers, which shall be determined by adding to the whole Number of free Persons, including those bound to Service for a Term of Years, and excluding Indians not taxed, three fifths of all other Persons. The actual Enumeration shall be made within three Years after the first Meeting of the Congress of the United States, and within every subsequent Term of ten Years, in such Manner as they shall by Law direct. The Number of Representatives shall not exceed one for every thirty Thousand, but each State shall have at Least one Representative; and until such enumeration shall be made, the State of New Hampshire shall be entitled to chuse three, Massachusetts eight, Rhode-Island and Providence Plantations one, Connecticut five, New-York six, New Jersey four, Pennsylvania eight, Delaware one, Maryland six, Virginia ten, North Carolina five, South Carolina five, and Georgia three.

When vacancies happen in the Representation from any State, the Executive Authority thereof shall issue Writs of Election to fill such Vacancies.

The House of Representatives shall chuse their Speaker and other Officers; and shall have the sole Power of Impeachment.

Sec. 3. The Senate of the United States shall be composed of two Senators from each State, chosen by the Legislature thereof, for six Years; and each Senator shall have one Vote.

Immediately after they shall be assembled in Consequence of the first Election, they shall be divided as equally as may be into three Classes. The Seats of the Senators of the first Class shall be vacated at the Expiration of the second Year, of the second Class at the Expiration of the fourth Year, and of the third Class at the Expiration of the sixth Year, so that one third may be chosen every second Year; and if Vacancies happen by Resignation, or otherwise, during the Recess of the Legislature of any State, the Executive thereof may make temporary Appointments until the next Meeting of the Legislature, which shall then fill such Vacancies.

No Person shall be a Senator who shall not have attained to the Age of thirty Years, and been nine Years a Citizen of the United States, and who shall not, when elected, be an Inhabitant of that State for which he shall be chosen.

The Vice President of the United States shall be President of the Senate, but shall have no Vote, unless they be equally divided.

The Senate shall chuse their other Officers. and also a President pro tempore, in the Absence of the Vice President, or when he shall exercise the Office of President of the United States.

The Senate shall have the sole Power to try all Impeachments. When sitting for that Purpose, they shall be on Oath or Affirmation. When the President of the United States is tried, the Chief Justice shall preside: And no person shall be convicted without the Concurrence of two thirds of the Members present.

Judgment in Cases of Impeachment shall not extend further than to removal from Office, and disqualification to hold and enjoy any Office of honor, Trust or Profit under the United States: but the Party convicted shall nevertheless be liable and subject to Indictment, Trial, Judgment and Punishment, according to Law.

Sec. 4. The Times, Places and Manner of holding Elections for Senators and Representatives, shall be prescribed in each State by the Legislature thereof; but the Congress may at any time by Law make or alter such Regulations, except as to the Places of chusing Senators.

The Congress shall assemble at least once in every Year, and such Meeting shall be on the first Monday in December, unless they shall by Law appoint a different Day.

Sec. 5. Each House shall be the Judge of the Elections, Returns and Qualifications of its own Members, and a Majority of each shall constitute a Quorum to do Business; but a smaller Number may adjourn from day to day, and may be authorized to compel the Attendance of absent Members, in such Manner, and under such Penalties as each House may provide.

Each House may determine the Rules of its Proceedings, punish its Members for disorderly Behaviour, and, with the Concurrence of two thirds, expel a Member.

Each House shall keep a Journal of its Proceedings, and from time to time publish the same, excepting such Parts as may in their Judgment require Secrecy; and the Yeas and Nays of the Members of either House on any question shall, at the Desire of one fifth of those Present, be entered on the Journal.

Neither House, during the Session of Congress, shall, without the Consent of the other, adjourn for more than three days, nor to any other Place than that in which the two Houses shall be sitting.

Sec. 6. The Senators and Representatives shall receive a Compensation for their Services, to be ascertained by Law, and paid out of the Treasury of the United States. They shall in all Cases, except Treason, Felony and Breach of the Peace, be privileged from Arrest during their Attendance at the Session of their respective Houses, and in going to and returning from the same; and for any Speech or Debate in either House, they shall not be questioned in any other Place.

No Senator or Representative shall, during the Time for which he was elected, be appointed to any civil Office under the Authority of the United States which shall have been created, or the Emoluments whereof shall have been encreased during such time; and no Person holding any Office under the United States, shall be a Member of either House during his Continuance in Office.

Sec. 7. All Bills for raising Revenue shall originate in the House of Representatives; but the Senate may propose or concur with Amendments as on other Bills.

Every Bill which shall have passed the House of Representatives and the Senate, shall, before it become a Law, be presented to the President of the United States; If he approve he shall sign it, but if not he shall return it, with his Objections to that House in which it shall have originated, who shall enter the Objections at large on their Journal, and proceed to reconsider it. If after such Reconsideration two thirds of that House shall agree to pass the Bill, it shall be sent, together with the Objections, to the other House, by which it shall likewise be reconsidered, and if approved by two thirds of that House, it shall become a Law. But in all such Cases the Votes of both Houses shall be determined by Yeas and Nays, and the Names of the Persons voting for and against the Bill shall be entered on the Journal of each House respectively. If any Bill shall not be returned by the President within ten Days (Sundays excepted) after it shall have been presented to him, the Same shall be a Law, in like Manner as if he had signed it, unless the Congress by their Adjournment prevent its Return, in which Case it shall not be a Law.

Every Order, Resolution, or Vote to which the Concurrence of the Senate and House of Representatives may be necessary (except on a question of Adjournment) shall be presented to the President of the United States; and before the Same shall take Effect, shall be approved by him, or being disapproved by him, shall be repassed by two thirds of the Senate and House of Representatives, according the Rules and Limitations prescribed in the Case of a Bill.

Sec. 8. The Congress shall have Power To lay and collect Taxes, Duties, Imposts and Excises, to pay the Debts and provide for the common Defence and general Welfare of the United States; but all Duties, Imposts and Excises shall be uniform throughout the United States;

To borrow Money on the credit of the United States;

To regulate Commerce with foreign Nations, and among the several States, and with the Indian Tribes;

To establish an uniform Rule of Naturalization, and uniform Laws on the subject of Bankruptcies throughout the United States;

To coin Money, regulate the Value thereof, and of foreign Coin, and fix the Standard of Weights and Measures;

To provide for the Punishment of counterfeiting the Securities and current Coin of the United States;

To establish Post Offices and post Roads;

To promote the Progress of Science and useful Arts, by securing for limited Times to Authors and Inventors the exclusive Right to their respective Writings and Discoveries;

To constitute Tribunals inferior to the supreme Court;

To define and punish Piracies and Felonies committed on the high Seas, and Offences against the Law of Nations;

To declare War, grant Letters of Marque and Reprisal, and make Rules concerning Captures on Land and Water;

To raise and support Armies, but no Appropriation of Money to that Use shall be for a longer Term than two Years;

To provide and maintain a Navy;

To make Rules for the Government and Regulation of the land and naval Forces;

To provide for calling forth the Militia to execute the Laws of the Union, suppress Insurrections and repel Invasions;

To provide for organizing, arming, and disciplining the Militia, and for governing such Part of them as may be employed in the Service of the United States, reserving to the States respectively, the Appointment of the Officers, and the Authority of training the Militia according to the discipline prescribed by Congress;

To exercise exclusive Legislation in all Cases whatsoever, over such District (not exceeding ten Miles square) as may, by Cession of particular States, and the Acceptance of Congress, become the Seat of the Government of the United States, and to exercise like Authority over all Places purchased by the Consent of the Legislature of the State in which the Same shall be, for the Erection of Forts, Magazines, Arsenals, dock-Yards, and other needful Buildings;—And

To make all Laws which shall be necessary and proper for carrying into Execution the foregoing Powers, and all other Powers vested by this Constitution in the Government of the United States, or in any Department or Officer thereof.

Sec. 9. The Migration or Importation of such Persons as any of the States now existing shall think proper to admit, shall not be prohibited by the Congress prior to the Year one thousand eight hundred and eight, but a Tax or duty may be imposed on such Importation, not exceeding ten dollars for each Person.

The Privilege of the Writ of Habeas Corpus shall not be suspended, unless when in Cases of Rebellion or Invasion the public Safety may require it.

No Bill of Attainder or ex post facto Law shall be passed.

No Capitation, or other direct, Tax shall be laid, unless in Proportion to the Census or Enumeration herein before directed to be taken.

No Tax or Duty shall be laid on Articles exported from any State.

No Preference shall be given by any Regulation of Commerce or Revenue to the Ports of one State over those of another: nor shall Vessels bound to, or from, one State, be obliged to enter, clear, or pay Duties in another.

No Money shall be drawn from the Treasury, but in Consequence of Appropriations made by Law; and a regular Statement and

Account of the Receipts and Expenditures of all public Money shall be published from time to time.

No Title of Nobility shall be granted by the United States: And no Person holding any Office of Profit or Trust under them, shall, without the Consent of the Congress, accept of any present, Emolument, Office, or Title, of any kind whatever, from any King, Prince or foreign State.

Sec. 10. No State shall enter into any Treaty, Alliance, or Confederation; grant Letters of Marque and Reprisal; coin Money; emit Bills of Credit; make any Thing but gold and silver Coin a Tender in Payment of Debts; pass any Bill of Attainder, ex post facto Law, or Law impairing the Obligation of Contracts, or grant any Title of Nobility.

No State shall, without the Consent of the Congress, lay any Imposts or Duties on Imports or Exports, except what may be absolutely necessary for executing its inspection Laws: and the net Produce of all Duties and Imposts, laid by any State on Imports or Exports, shall be for the Use of the Treasury of the United States; and all such Laws shall be subject to the Revision and Controul of the Congress.

No State shall, without the Consent of Congress, lay any Duty of Tonnage, keep Troops, or Ships of War in time of Peace, enter into any Agreement or Compact with another State, or with a foreign Power, or engage in War, unless actually invaded, or in such imminent Danger as will not admit of delay.

ART. II

Sec. 1. The executive Power shall be vested in a President of the United States of America. He shall hold his Office during the Term of four Years, and, together with the Vice President, chosen for the same Term, be elected, as follows:

Each State shall appoint, in such Manner as the Legislature thereof may direct, a Number of Electors, equal to the whole Number of Senators and Representatives to which the State may be entitled in the Congress: but no Senator or Representative, or Person holding an Office of Trust or Profit under the United States, shall be appointed an Elector.

The Electors shall meet in their respective States, and vote by Ballot for two Persons, of whom one at least shall not be an Inhabitant of the same State with themselves. And they shall make a List of all the Persons voted for, and of the Number of Votes for each; which List they shall sign and certify, and transmit sealed to the Seat of the Government of the United States, directed to the President of the Senate. The President of the Senate shall, in the Presence of the Senate and House of Representatives, open all the Certificates, and the Votes shall then be counted. The Person having the greatest Number of Votes shall be the President, if such Number be a Majority of the whole Number of Electors appointed; and if there be more than one who have such Majority, and have an equal Number of Votes, then the House of Representatives shall immediately chuse by Ballot one of them for President; and if no person have a Majority, then from the five highest on the List the said House shall in like Manner chuse the President. But in chusing the President, the Votes shall be taken by States, the Representation from each State having one Vote; A quorum for this Purpose shall consist of a Member or Members from two thirds of the States, and a Majority of all the States shall be necessary to a Choice. In every Case, after the Choice of the President, the Person having the greatest Number of Votes of the Electors shall be the Vice President. But if there should remain two or more who have equal Votes, the Senate shall chuse from them by Ballot the Vice President.

The Congress may determine the Time of chusing the Electors, and the Day on which they shall give their Votes; which Day shall be the same throughout the United States.

No Person except a natural born Citizen, or a Citizen of the United States, at the time of the Adoption of this Constitution, shall be eligible to the Office of President; neither shall any Person be eligible to the Office who shall not have attained to the Age of thirty five Years, and been fourteen Years a Resident within the United States.

In Case of the Removal of the President from Office, or of his Death, Resignation, or Inability to discharge the Powers and Duties of the said Office, the Same shall devolve on the Vice President, and the Congress may by Law provide for the Case of Removal, Death, Resignation or Inability, both of the President and Vice President, declaring what Officer shall then act as President, and such Officer shall act accordingly, until the Disability be removed, or a President shall be elected.

The President shall, at stated Times, receive for his Services, a Compensation, which shall neither be encreased nor diminished during the Period for which he shall have been elected, and he shall not receive within that Period any other Emolument from the United States, or any of them.

Before he enter on the Execution of his Office, he shall take the following Oath or Affirmation:—"I do solemnly swear (or affirm) that I will faithfully execute the Office of President of the United States, and will to the best of my Ability, preserve, protect and defend the Constitution of the United States."

Sec. 2. The President shall be Commander in Chief of the Army and Navy of the United States, and of the Militia of the several States, when called into the actual Service of the United States; he may require the Opinion, in writing, of the principal Officer in each of the executive Departments, upon any Subject relating to the Duties of their respective Offices, and he shall have Power to grant Reprieves and Pardons for Offences against the United States, except in Cases of Impeachment.

He shall have Power, by and with the Advice and Consent of the Senate, to make Treaties, provided two thirds of the Senators present concur; and he shall nominate, and by and with the Advice and Consent of the Senate, shall appoint Ambassadors, other public Ministers and Consuls, Judges of the supreme Court, and all other Officers of the United States, whose Appointments are not herein otherwise provided for, and which shall be established by Law: but the Congress may by Law vest the Appointment of such inferior Officers, as they think proper, in the President alone, in the Courts of Law, or in the Heads of Departments.

The President shall have Power to fill up all Vacancies that may happen during the Recess of the Senate, by granting Commissions which shall expire at the End of their next Session.

Sec. 3. He shall from time to time give to the Congress Information of the State of the Union, and recommend to their Consideration such Measures as he shall judge necessary and expedient; he may, on extraordinary Occasions, convene both Houses, or either of them, and in Case of Disagreement between them, with Respect to the Time of Adjournment, he may adjourn them to such Time as he shall think proper; he shall receive Ambassadors and other public Ministers; he shall take Care that the Laws be faithfully executed, and shall Commission all the Officers of the United States.

Sec. 4. The President, Vice President and all civil Officers of the United States, shall be removed from Office on Impeachment for, and Conviction of, Treason, Bribery, or other high Crimes and Misdemeanors.

ART. III

Sec. 1. The judicial Power of the United States, shall be vested in one supreme Court, and in such inferior Courts as the Congress may from time to time ordain and establish. The Judges, both of the supreme and inferior Courts, shall hold their Offices during good Behaviour, and shall, at stated Times, receive for their Services, a Compensation, which shall not be diminished during their Continuance in Office.

Sec. 2. The judicial Power shall extend to all Cases, in Law and Equity, arising under this Constitution, the Laws of the United States, and Treaties made, or which shall be made, under their Authority;—to all Cases affecting Ambassadors, other public Ministers and Consuls;—to all Cases of admiralty and maritime Jurisdiction;—to Controversies to which the United States shall be a Party;—to Controversies between two or more States;—between a State and Citizens of another State;—between Citizens of different States;—between Citizens of the same State claiming Lands under Grants of different States, and between a State, or the Citizens thereof, and foreign States, Citizens or Subjects.

In all Cases affecting Ambassadors, other public Ministers and Consuls, and those in which a State shall be Party, the supreme Court shall have original Jurisdiction. In all the other cases before mentioned, the supreme Court shall have appellate Jurisdiction, both as to Law and Fact, with such Exceptions, and under such Regulations as the Congress shall make.

The Trial of all Crimes, except in Cases of Impeachment, shall be by Jury; and such Trial shall be held in the State where the said Crimes shall have been committed; but when not committed within any State, the Trial shall be at such Place or Places as the Congress may by Law have directed.

Sec. 3. Treason against the United States, shall consist only in levying War against them, or in adhering to their Enemies, giving them Aid and Comfort. No Person shall be convicted of Treason unless on the Testimony of two Witnesses to the same overt Act, or on Confession in open Court.

The Congress shall have Power to declare the Punishment of Treason, but no Attainder of Treason shall work Corruption of Blood, or Forfeiture except during the Life of the Person attainted.

ART. IV

Sec. 1. Full Faith and Credit shall be given in each State to the Public Acts, Records, and judicial Proceedings of every other State. And the Congress may by general Laws prescribe the Manner in which such Acts, Records and Proceedings shall be proved, and the Effect thereof.

Sec. 2. The Citizens of each State shall be entitled to all Privileges and Immunities of Citizens in the Several States.

A Person charged in any State with Treason, Felony, or other Crime, who shall flee from Justice, and be found in another State, shall on Demand of the executive Authority of the State from which he fled, be delivered up, to be removed to the State having Jurisdiction of the Crime.

No Person held to Service or Labour in one State, under the Laws thereof, escaping into another, shall, in Consequence of any Law or Regulation therein, be discharged from such Service or Labour, but shall be delivered up on Claim of the Party to whom such Service or Labour may be due.

Sec. 3. New States may be admitted by the Congress into this Union; but no new States shall be formed or erected within the Jurisdiction of any other State; nor any State be formed by the Junction of two or more States, or Parts of States, without the

Consent of the Legislatures of the States concerned as well as of the Congress.

The Congress shall have Power to dispose of and make all needful Rules and Regulations respecting the Territory or other Property belonging to the United States; and nothing in this Constitution shall be so construed as to Prejudice any Claims of the United States, or of any particular State.

Sec. 4. The United States shall guarantee to every State in this Union a Republican Form of Government, and shall protect each of them against Invasion; and on Application of the Legislature, or of the Executive (when the Legislature cannot be convened) against domestic Violence.

ART. V

The Congress, whenever two thirds of both Houses shall deem it necessary, shall propose Amendments to this Constitution, or, on the Application of the Legislatures of two thirds of the several States, shall call a Convention for proposing Amendments, which, in either Case, shall be valid to all Intents and Purposes, as Part of this Constitution, when ratified by the Legislatures of three fourths of the several States, or by Conventions in three fourths thereof, as the one or the other Mode of Ratification may be proposed by the Congress; Provided that no Amendment which may be made prior to the Year One thousand eight hundred and eight shall in any Manner affect the first and fourth Clauses in the Ninth Section of the first Article; and that no State, without its Consent, shall be deprived of its equal Suffrage in the Senate.

ART. VI

All Debts contracted and Engagements entered into, before the Adoption of this Constitution, shall be as valid against the United States under this Constitution, as under the Confederation.

This Constitution, and the Laws of the United States which shall be made in Pursuance thereof; and all Treaties made, or which shall be made, under the Authority of the United States, shall be the supreme Law of the Land; and the Judges in every State shall be bound thereby, any Thing in the Constitution or Laws of any State to the Contrary notwithstanding.

The Senators and Representatives before mentioned, and the Members of the several State Legislatures, and all executive and judicial Officers, both of the United States and of the several States, shall be bound by Oath or Affirmation, to support this Constitution; but no religious Test shall ever be required as a Qualification to any Office or public Trust under the United States.

ART. VII

The Ratification of the Conventions of nine States, shall be sufficient for the Establishment of this Constitution between the States so ratifying the Same.

Done in Convention by the Unanimous Consent of the States present the Seventeenth Day of September in the Year of our Lord one thousand seven hundred and Eighty seven and of the Independence of the United States of America the Twelfth. In witness whereof We have hereunto subscribed our Names,

G⁰ WASHINGTON—Presid^t
and deputy from Virginia

Delaware	RICHARD BASSETT
	GUNNING BEDFORD JUN
	JACO: BROOM
	JOHN DICKINSON
	GEO: READ
Maryland	DAN^L CARROLL
	DAN OF S^T THO^s JENIFER
	JAMES M^{C}HENRY
Virginia	JOHN BLAIR
	JAMES MADISON JR.
North Carolina	W^M BLOUNT
	RICH^D DOBBS SPAIGHT
	HU WILLIAMSON

South Carolina	PIERCE BUTLER
	CHARLES COTESWORTH PINCKNEY
	CHARLES PINCKNEY
	J. RUTLEDGE
Georgia	ABR BALDWIN
	WILLIAM FEW
New Hampshire	NICHOLAS GILMAN
	JOHN LANGDON
Massachusetts	NATHANIEL GORHAM
	RUFUS KING
Connecticut	W^M SAM^L JOHNSON
	ROGER SHERMAN
New York	ALEXANDER HAMILTON
New Jersey	DAVID BREARLEY
	JONA: DAYTON
	WIL: LIVINGSTON
	W^M PATERSON
Pennsylvania	GEO. CLYMER
	THO^S FITZSIMONS
	B FRANKLIN
	JARED INGERSOLL
	THOMAS MIFFLIN
	GOUV MORRIS
	ROB^T MORRIS
	JAMES WILSON

APPENDIX 2

★

The Bill of Rights
December 15, 1791

ART. I

Congress shall make no law respecting an establishment of religion, or prohibiting the free exercise thereof; or abridging the freedom of speech, or of the press; or the right of the people peaceably to assemble, and to petition the government for a redress of grievances.

ART. II

A well regulated Militia, being necessary to the Security of a free State, the right of the people to keep and bear Arms, shall not be infringed.

ART. III

No soldier shall, in time of peace be quartered in any house, without the consent of the Owner, nor in time of war, but in a manner to be prescribed by law.

ART. IV

The right of the people to be secure in their persons, houses, papers, and effects, against unreasonable searches and seizures, shall not be violated, and no Warrants shall issue, but upon probable cause, supported by Oath or affirmation, and particularly describing the place to be searched, and the persons or things to be seized.

ART. V

No person shall be held to answer for a capital, or otherwise infamous crime, unless on a presentment or indictment of a Grand Jury, except in cases arising in the land or naval forces, or in the Militia, when in actual service in time of War or public danger; nor shall any person be subject for the same offence to be twice put in jeopardy of life or limb; nor shall be compelled in any criminal case to be a witness against himself, nor be deprived of life, liberty, or property, without due process of law; nor shall private property be taken for public use, without just compensation.

ART. VI

In all criminal prosecutions, the accused shall enjoy the right to a speedy and public trial, by an impartial jury of the State and district wherein the crime shall have been committed, which district shall have been previously ascertained by law, and to be informed of the nature and cause of the accusation; to be confronted with the witnesses against him; to have compulsory process for obtaining witnesses in his favor, and to have the Assistance of Counsel for his defence.

ART. VII

In Suits at common law, where the value in controversy shall exceed twenty dollars, the right of trial by jury shall be preserved, and no fact tried by a jury, shall be otherwise re-examined in any Court of the United States, than according to the rules of the common law.

ART. VIII

Excessive bail shall not be required, nor excessive fines imposed, nor cruel and unusual punishments inflicted.

ART. IX

The enumeration in the Constitution, of certain rights, shall not be construed to deny or disparage others retained by the people.

ART. X

The powers not delegated to the United States by the Constitution, nor prohibited by it to the States, are reserved to the States respectively, or to the people.

APPENDIX 3

★

Amendments to the Constitution
1798–1971

ART. XI
JANUARY 8, 1798

The judicial power of the United States shall not be construed to extend to any suit in law or equity, commenced or prosecuted against one of the United States by Citizens of another State, or by Citizens or Subjects of any Foreign State.

ART. XII
SEPTEMBER 25, 1804

The Electors shall meet in their respective states, and vote by ballot for President and Vice-President, one of whom, at least, shall not be an inhabitant of the same state with themselves; they shall name in their ballots the person voted for as President, and in distinct ballots the person voted for as Vice-President, and they shall make distinct lists of all persons voted for as President, and of all persons voted for as Vice-President, and of the number of votes for each, which lists they shall sign and certify, and transmit sealed to the seat of the government of the United States, directed to the President of the Senate; — The President of the Senate shall, in the presence of the Senate and House of Representatives, open all the certificates and the votes shall then be counted; — The person having the greatest number of votes for President, shall be the President, if such number be a majority of the whole number of Electors appointed; and if no person have such majority, then from the persons having the highest numbers not exceeding three on the list of those voted for as President, the House of Representatives shall choose immediately, by ballot, the President. But in choosing the President, the votes shall be taken by states, the representation from each state having one vote; a quorum for this purpose shall consist of a member or members from two-thirds of the states, and a majority of all the states shall be necessary to a choice. And if the House of Representatives shall not choose a President whenever the right of choice shall devolve upon them, before the fourth day of March next following, then the Vice-President shall act as President, as in the case of the death or other constitutional disability of the President. — The person having the greatest number of votes as Vice-President, shall be the Vice-President, if such number be a majority of the whole number of Electors appointed, and if no person have a majority, then from the two highest numbers on the list, the Senate shall choose the Vice-President; a quorum for the purpose shall consist of two-thirds of the whole number of Senators, and a majority of the whole number shall be necessary to a choice. But no person constitutionally ineligible to the office of President shall be eligible to that of Vice-President of the United States.

ART. XIII
DECEMBER 18, 1865

Sec. 1. Neither slavery nor involuntary servitude, except as punishment for crime whereof the party shall have been duly convicted, shall exist within the United States, or any place subject to their jurisdiction.

Sec. 2. Congress shall have power to enforce this article by appropriate legislation.

ART. XIV
JULY 9, 1868

Sec. 1. All persons born or naturalized in the United States, and subject to the jurisdiction thereof, are citizens of the United States and of the State wherein they reside. No State shall make or enforce any law which shall abridge the privileges or immunities of citizens of the United States; nor shall any State deprive any person of life, liberty, or property, without due process of law; nor deny to any person within its jurisdiction the equal protection of the laws.

Sec. 2. Representatives shall be apportioned among the several States according to their respective numbers, counting the whole number of persons in each State, excluding Indians not taxed. But when the right to vote in any election for the choice of electors for President and Vice President of the United States, Representatives in Congress, the Executive and Judicial officers of a State, or the members of the Legislature thereof, is denied to any of the male inhabitants of such State, being twenty-one years of age, and citizens of the United States, or in any way abridged, except for participation in rebellion, or other crime, the basis of representation therein shall be reduced in the proportion which the number of such male citizens shall bear to the whole number of male citizens twenty-one years of age in such State.

Sec. 3. No person shall be a Senator or Representative in Congress, or elector of President and Vice President, or hold any office, civil or military, under the United States, or under any State, who, having previously taken an oath, as a member of Congress, or as an officer of the United States, or as a member of any State legislature, or as an executive or judicial officer of any State, to support the Constitution of the United States, shall have engaged in insurrection or rebellion against the same, or given aid or comfort to the enemies thereof. But Congress may by a vote of two-thirds of each House, remove such disability.

Sec. 4. The validity of the public debt of the United States, authorized by law, including debts incurred for payment of pensions and bounties for services in suppressing insurrection or rebellion, shall not be questioned. But neither the United States nor any State shall assume or pay any debt or obligation incurred in aid of insurrection or rebellion against the United States, or any claim for the loss or emancipation of any slave; but all such debts, obligations and claims shall be held illegal and void.

Sec. 5. The Congress shall have the power to enforce, by appropriate legislation, the provisions of this article.

ART. XV
MARCH 30, 1870

Sec. 1. The right of citizens of the United States to vote shall not be denied or abridged by the United States or by any State on account of race, color, or previous condition of servitude —

Sec. 2. The Congress shall have power to enforce this article by appropriate legislation —

ART. XVI
FEBRUARY 25, 1913

The Congress shall have power to lay and collect taxes on incomes, from whatever source derived, without apportionment among the several States and without regard to any census or enumeration.

ART. XVII
MAY 31, 1913

The Senate of the United States shall be composed of two Senators from each State, elected by the people thereof, for six years; and each Senator shall have one vote. The electors in each State shall have the qualifications requisite for electors of the most numerous branch of the State legislature.

When vacancies happen in the representation of any State in the Senate, the executive authority of such State shall issue writs of election to fill such vacancies: *Provided,* That the legislature of any State may empower the executive thereof to make temporary appointments until the people fill the vacancies by election as the legislature may direct.

This amendment shall not be so construed as to affect the election or term of any Senator chosen before it becomes valid as part of the Constitution.

ART. XVIII
JANUARY 29, 1919

After one year from the ratification of this article, the manufacture, sale, or transportation of intoxicating liquors within, the importation thereof into, or the exportation thereof from the United States and all territory subject to the jurisdiction thereof for beverage purposes is hereby prohibited.

The Congress and the several States shall have concurrent power to enforce this article by appropriate legislation.

This article shall be inoperative unless it shall have been ratified as an amendment to the Constitution by the legislatures of the several States, as provided in the Constitution, within seven years from the date of the submission hereof to the States by Congress.

ART. XIX
AUGUST 26, 1920

The right of citizens of the United States to vote shall not be denied or abridged by the United States or by any States on account of sex.

The Congress shall have power by appropriate legislation to enforce the provisions of this article.

ART. XX
FEBRUARY 6, 1933

Sec. 1. The terms of the President and Vice-President shall end at noon on the twentieth day of January, and the terms of Senators and Representatives at noon on the third day of January, of the years in which such terms would have ended if this article had not been ratified; and the terms of their successors shall then begin.

Sec. 2. The Congress shall assemble at least once in every year, and such meeting shall begin at noon on the third day of January, unless they shall by law appoint a different day.

Sec. 3. If, at the time fixed for the beginning of the term of the President, the President-elect shall have died, the Vice-President-elect shall become President. If a President shall not have been chosen before the time fixed for the beginning of his term, or if the President-elect shall have failed to qualify, then the Vice-President-elect shall act as President until a President shall have qualified; and the Congress may by law provide for the case wherein neither a President-elect nor a Vice-President-elect shall have qualified, declaring who shall then act as President, or the manner in which one who is to act shall be selected, and such person shall act accordingly until a President or Vice-President shall have qualified.

Sec. 4. The Congress may by law provide for the case of the death of any of the persons from whom the House of Representatives may choose a President whenever the right of choice shall have devolved upon them, and for the case of the death of any of the persons from whom the Senate may choose a Vice-President whenever the right of choice shall have devolved upon them.

Sec. 5. Sections 1 and 2 shall take effect on the 15th day of October following the ratification of this article.

Sec. 6. This article shall be inoperative unless it shall have been ratified as an amendment to the Constitution by the legislatures of three-fourths of the several States within seven years from the date of its submission.

ART. XXI
DECEMBER 5, 1933

Sec. 1. The eighteenth article of amendment to the Constitution of the United States is hereby repealed.

[Sections 2 and 3 repeat most of Article XVIII.]

ART. XXII
FEBRUARY 26, 1951

Sec. 1. No person shall be elected to the office of the President more than twice, and no person who has held the office of President, or acted as President for more than two years of a term to which some other person was elected President shall be elected to the office of the President more than once. But this Article shall not apply to any person holding the office of President when this Article was proposed by the Congress, and shall not prevent any person who may be holding the office of President, or acting as President, during the term within which this Article becomes operative from holding the office of President or acting as President during the remainder of such term.

Sec. 2. The Congress shall have power to enforce this article by appropriate legislation.

ART. XXIII
MARCH 29, 1961

Sec. 1. The District constituting the seat of Government of the United States shall appoint in such manner as the Congress may direct:

A number of electors of President and Vice-President equal to the whole number of Senators and Representatives in Congress to which the District would be entitled if it were a State, but in no event more than the least populous state; they shall be in addition to those appointed by the states, but they shall be considered, for the purposes of the election of President and Vice-President, to be electors appointed by a state; and they shall meet in the District and perform such duties as provided by the twelfth article of amendment.

Sec. 2. The Congress shall have power to enforce this article by appropriate legislation.

ART. XXIV
JANUARY 24, 1964

Sec. 1. The right of citizens of the United States to vote in any primary or other election for President or Vice-President, for electors for President or Vice-President, or for Senator or Representative in Congress, shall not be denied or abridged by the United States or any state by reason of failure to pay any poll tax or other tax.

Sec. 2. The Congress shall have power to enforce this article by appropriate legislation.

ART. XXV
FEBRUARY 10, 1967

Sec. 1. In case of the removal of the President from office or his death or resignation, the Vice-President shall become President.

Sec. 2. Whenever there is a vacancy in the office of the Vice-President, the President shall nominate a Vice-President who shall take the office upon confirmation by a majority vote of both houses of Congress.

Sec. 3. Whenever the President transmits to the President pro tempore of the Senate and the Speaker of the House of Representatives his written declaration that he is unable to discharge the powers and duties of his office, and until he transmits to them a written declaration to the contrary, such powers and duties shall be discharged by the Vice-President as Acting President.

Sec. 4. Whenever the Vice-President and a majority of either the principal officers of the executive departments, or of such other body as Congress may by law provide, transmit to the President pro tempore of the Senate and the Speaker of the House of Representatives their written declaration that the President is unable to discharge the powers and duties of his office, the Vice-President shall immediately assume the powers and duties of the office as Acting President.

Thereafter, when the President transmits to the President pro tempore of the Senate and the Speaker of the House of Representatives his written declaration that no inability exists, he shall resume the powers and duties of his office unless the Vice-President and a majority of either the principal officers of the executive department, or of such other body as Congress may by law provide, transmit within four days to the President pro tempore of the Senate and the Speaker of the House of Representatives their written declaration that the President is unable to discharge the powers and duties of his office. Thereupon Congress shall decide the issue, assembling within 48 hours for that purpose if not in session. If the Congress, within 21 days after receipt of the latter written declaration, or, if Congress is not in session, within 21 days after Congress is required to assemble, determines by two-thirds vote of both houses that the President is unable to discharge the powers and duties of his office, the Vice-President shall continue to discharge the same as Acting President; otherwise, the President shall resume the powers and duties of his office.

ART. XXVI
JUNE 30, 1971

Sec. 1. The right of citizens of the United States, who are 18 years of age or older, to vote shall not be denied or abridged by the United States or any state on account of age.

Sec. 2. The Congress shall have the power to enforce this article by appropriate legislation.

APPENDIX 4

★

Amendments to the Constitution
Sent to the States for Ratification

THE Conventions of a number of the States, having at the time of their adopting the Constitution, expressed a desire, in order to prevent misconstruction or abuse of its powers, that further declaratory and restrictive clauses should be added: And as extending the ground of public confidence in the Government, will best ensure the beneficent ends of its institution.

RESOLVED by the Senate and House of Representatives of the United States of America, in Congress assembled, two thirds of both Houses concurring, that the following Articles be proposed to the Legislatures of the several States, as amendments to the Constitution of the United States, all or any of which Articles, when ratified by three fourths of the said Legislatures, to be valid to all intents and purposes, as part of the said Constitution; vizt.

ARTICLES in addition to, and amendment of the Constitution of the United States of America, proposed by Congress, and ratified by the Legislatures of the several States, pursuant to the fifth Article of the original Constitution.

ARTICLE THE FIRST. After the first enumeration required by the first Article of the Constitution, there shall be one Representative for every thirty thousand, until the number shall amount to one hundred, after which, the proportion shall be so regulated by Congress, that there shall be not less than one hundred Representatives, nor less than one Representative for every forty thousand persons, until the number of Representatives shall amount to two hundred, after which the proportion shall be so regulated by Congress, that there shall not be less than two hundred Representatives, nor more than one Representative for every fifty thousand persons.

ARTICLE THE SECOND. No law, varying the compensation for the services of the Senators and Representatives, shall take effect, until an election of Representatives shall have intervened.

ARTICLE THE THIRD. Congress shall make no law respecting an establishment of religion, or prohibiting the free exercise thereof; or abridging the freedom of speech, or of the press, or the right of the people peaceably to assemble, and to petition the Government for a redress of grievances.

ARTICLE THE FOURTH. A well regulated militia, being necessary to the security of a free State, the right of the people to keep and bear arms, shall not be infringed.

ARTICLE THE FIFTH. No Soldier shall, in time of peace be quartered in any House, without the consent of the owner, nor in time of war, but in a manner to be prescribed by law.

ARTICLE THE SIXTH. The right of the people to be secure in their persons, houses, papers, and effects, against unreasonable searches and seizures, shall not be violated, and no warrants shall issue, but upon probable cause, supported by oath or affirmation, and particularly describing the place to be searched and the persons or things to be seized.

ARTICLE THE SEVENTH. No person shall be held to answer for a capital, or otherwise infamous crime, unless on a presentment or indictment of [a] Grand Jury, except in cases arising in the land or naval forces, or in the militia, when in actual service in time of war or public danger; nor shall any person be subject for the same offence to be twice put in jeopardy of life or limb; nor shall be compelled in any criminal case to be a witness against himself, nor be deprived of life, liberty, or property, without due process of law; nor shall private property be taken for public use, without just compensation.

ARTICLE THE EIGHTH. In all criminal prosecutions, the accused shall enjoy the right to a speedy and public trial, by an impartial jury of the State and district wherein the crime shall have been committed; which district shall have been previously ascertained by law, and to be informed of the nature and cause of the accusation; to be confronted with the witnesses against him; to have compulsory process for obtaining witnesses in his favor, and to have the assistance of counsel for his defence.

ARTICLE THE NINTH. In suits at common law, where the value in controversy shall exceed twenty dollars, the right of trial by jury shall be preserved, and no fact tried by a jury, shall be otherwise re-examined in any Court of the United States, than according to the rules of the common law.

ARTICLE THE TENTH. Excessive bail shall not be required, nor excessive fines imposed, nor cruel and unusual punishments inflicted.

ARTICLE THE ELEVENTH. The enumeration in the Constitution, of certain rights, shall not be construed to deny or disparage others retained by the people

ARTICLE THE TWELFTH. The powers not delegated to the United States by the Constitution, nor prohibited by it to the States, are reserved to the States respectively, or to the people.

> FREDERICK AUGUSTUS MUHLENBERG
> Speaker of the House of Representatives
> JOHN ADAMS
> Vice-President of the United States, and
> President of the Senate

ATTEST,
JOHN BECKLEY, Clerk of the House of Representatives
SAM A. OTIS, Secretary of the Senate

APPENDIX 5

★

House Resolution and Articles of Amendment
August 24, 1789

CONGRESS OF THE UNITED STATES
In the House of Representatives,
Monday, 24th *August,* 1789,

RESOLVED, BY THE SENATE AND HOUSE OF REPRESENTATIVES OF THE UNITED STATES OF AMERICA IN CONGRESS ASSEMBLED, two thirds of both Houses deeming it necessary, That the following Articles be proposed to the Legislatures of the several States, as Amendments to the Constitution of the United States, all or any of which Articles, when ratified by three fourths of the said Legislatures, to be valid to all intents and purposes as part of the said Constitution—Viz.

ARTICLES in addition to, and amendment of, the Constitution of the United States of America, proposed by Congress, and ratified by the Legislatures of the several States, pursuant to the fifth Article of the original Constitution.

ARTICLE THE FIRST.

After the first enumeration, required by the first Article of the Constitution, there shall be one Representative for every thirty thousand, until the number shall amount to one hundred, after which the proportion shall be so regulated by Congress, that there shall be not less than one hundred Representatives, nor less than one Representative for every forty thousand persons, until the number of Representatives shall amount to two hundred, after which the proportion shall be so regulated by Congress, that there shall not be less than two hundred Representatives, nor less than one Representative for every fifty thousand persons.

ARTICLE THE SECOND.

No law varying the compensation to the members of Congress, shall take effect, until an election of Representatives shall have intervened.

ARTICLE THE THIRD.

Congress shall make no law establishing religion or prohibiting the free exercise thereof, nor shall the rights of Conscience be infringed.

ARTICLE THE FOURTH.

The Freedom of Speech, and of the Press, and the right of the People peaceably to assemble, and consult for their common good, and to apply to the Government for a redress of grievances, shall not be infringed.

ARTICLE THE FIFTH.

A well regulated militia, composed of the body of the People, being the best security of a free State, the right of the People to keep and bear arms, shall not be infringed, but no one religiously scrupulous of bearing arms, shall be compelled to render military service in person.

ARTICLE THE SIXTH.

No soldier shall, in time of peace, be quartered in any house without the consent of the owner, nor in time of war, but in a manner to be prescribed by law.

ARTICLE THE SEVENTH.

The right of the People to be secure in their persons, houses, papers and effects, against unreasonable searches and seizures, shall not be violated, and no warrants shall issue, but upon probable cause supported by oath or affirmation, and particularly describing the place to be searched , and the persons or things to be seized.

ARTICLE THE EIGHTH.

No person shall be subject, except in case of impeachment, to more than one trial, or one punishment for the same offence, nor shall be compelled in any criminal case, to be a witness against himself, nor be deprived of life, liberty or property, without due process of law; nor shall private property be taken for public use without just compensation.

ARTICLE THE NINTH.

In all criminal prosecutions, the accused shall enjoy the right to a speedy and public trial, to be informed of the nature and cause of the accusation, to be confronted with the witnesses against him, to have compulsory process for obtaining witnesses in his favor, and to have the assistance of counsel for his defence.

ARTICLE THE TENTH.

The trial of all crimes (except in cases of impeachment, and in cases arising in the land or naval forces, or in the militia when in actual service in time of War or public danger) shall be by an impartial Jury of the Vicinage, with the requisite of unanimity for conviction, the right of challenge, and other accustomed requisites; and no person shall be held to answer for a capital, or otherways infamous crime, unless on a presentment or indictment by a Grand Jury; but if a crime be committed in a place in the possession of an enemy, or in which an insurrection may prevail, the indictment and trial may by law be authorised in some other place within the same State.

ARTICLE THE ELEVENTH.

No appeal to the Supreme Court of the United States, shall be allowed, where the value in controversy shall not amount to one thousand dollars, nor shall any fact, triable by a Jury according to the course of the common law, be otherwise re-examinable, than according to the rules of common law.

ARTICLE THE TWELFTH.

In suits at common law, the right of trial by Jury shall be preserved.

ARTICLE THE THIRTEENTH.

Excessive bail shall not be required, nor excessive fines imposed, nor cruel and unusual punishments inflicted.

ARTICLE THE FOURTEENTH.

No State shall infringe the right of trial by Jury in criminal cases, nor the rights of conscience, nor the freedom of speech, or of the press.

ARTICLE THE FIFTEENTH.

The enumeration in the Constitution of certain rights, shall not be construed to deny or disparage others retained by the people.

ARTICLE THE SIXTEENTH.

The powers delegated by the Constitution to the government of the United States, shall be exercised as therein appropriated, so that the Legislative shall never exercise the powers vested in the Executive or Judicial; nor the Executive the powers vested in the Legislative or Judicial; nor the Judicial the powers vested in the Legislative or Executive.

ARTICLE THE SEVENTEENTH.

The powers not delegated by the Constitution, nor prohibited by it, to the States, are reserved to the States respectively.

Teste,

JOHN BECKLEY, CLERK

In SENATE, *August* 25, 1789

Read and ordered to be printed for the consideration of the Senate.

Attest, SAMUEL A. OTIS, Secretary

APPENDIX 6

★

Amendments Proposed by the States
June 8, 1789

[AMENDMENTS PROPOSED BY THE MASSACHUSETTS CONVENTION
FEBRUARY 6, 1788]

FIRST, That it be explicitly declared that all Powers not expressly delegated by the aforesaid Constitution are reserved to the several States to be by them exercised.

SECONDLY, That there shall be one representative to every thirty thousand persons according to the Census mentioned in the Constitution until the whole number of the Representatives amounts to Two hundred.

THIRDLY, That Congress do not exercise the powers vested in them by the fourth Section of the first article, but in cases when a State shall neglect or refuse to make the regulations therein mentioned or shall make regulations subversive of the rights of the People to a free & equal representation in Congress agreeably to the Constitution.

FOURTHLY, That Congress do not lay direct Taxes but when the Monies arising from the Impost & Excise are insufficient for the publick exigencies nor then until Congress shall have first made a requisition upon the States to assess levy & pay their respective proportions of such Requisition agreeably to the Census fixed in the said Constitution; in such way & manner as the Legislature of the States shall think best, & in such case if any State shall neglect or refuse to pay its proportion pursuant to such requisition then Congress may assess & levy such State's proportion together with interest thereon at the rate of Six per cent per annum from the time of payment prescribed in such requisition.

233

FIFTHLY, That Congress erect no Company of Merchants with exclusive advantages of commerce.

SIXTHLY, That no person shall be tried for any Crime by which he may incur an infamous punishment or loss of life until he be first indicted by a Grand Jury, except in such cases as may arise in the Government & regulation of the Land & Naval forces.

SEVENTHLY, The Supreme Judicial Federal Court shall have no jurisdiction of Causes between Citizens of different States unless the matter in dispute whether it concerns the realty or personalty be of the value of Three thousand dollars at the least, nor shall the Federal Judicial Powers extend to any actions between Citizens of different States where the matter in dispute whether it concerns the Realty or Personalty is not of the value of Fifteen hundred dollars at the least.

EIGHTHLY, In civil actions between Citizens of different States every issue of fact arising in Actions at common law shall be tried by a Jury if the parties or either of them request it.

NINTHLY, Congress shall at no time consent that any Person holding an office of trust or profit under the United States shall accept of a title of Nobility or any other title or office from any King, Prince or Foreign State.

[AMENDMENTS PROPOSED BY THE SOUTH CAROLINA CONVENTION
MAY 23, 1788]

AND WHEREAS it is essential to the preservation of the rights reserved to the several states, and the freedom of the people under the operations of a General government that the right of prescribing the manner time and places of holding the Elections to the Federal Legislature, should be for ever inseperably annexed to the sovereignty of the several states. This convention doth declare that the same ought to remain to all posterity a perpetual and fundamental right in the local, exclusive of the interference of the General Government except in cases where the Legislatures of the States, shall refuse or neglect to perform and fulfil the same according to the tenor of the said Constitution.

THIS CONVENTION doth also declare that no Section or paragraph of the said Constitution warrants a Construction that the states do not retain every power not expressly relinquished by them and vested in the General Government of the Union.

RESOLVED that the general Government of the United States ought never to impose direct taxes, *but* where the monies arising from the duties, imposts and excise are insufficient for the public exigencies *nor then until* Congress shall have made a requisition upon the states to Assess levy and pay their respective proportions of such requisitions And in case any state shall neglect or refuse to pay its proportion pursuant to such requisition then Congress may assess and levy such state's proportion together with Interest thereon at the rate of six per centum per annum from the time of payment prescribed by such requisition.

RESOLVED that the third section of the Sixth Article ought to be amended by inserting the word "*other*" between the words "*no*" and "*religious.*"

[AMENDMENTS PROPOSED BY THE NEW HAMPSHIRE CONVENTION]
JUNE 21, 1788]

FIRST, That it be Explicitly declared that all Powers not expressly & particularly Delegated by the aforesaid Constitution are reserved to the several States to be, by them Exercised.

SECONDLY, That there shall be one Representative to every Thirty thousand Persons according to the Census mentioned in the Constitution, untill the whole number of Representatives amount to Two hundred.

THIRDLY, That Congress do not Exercise the Powers vested in them, by the fourth Section of the first Article, but in Cases when a State shall neglect or refuse to make the Regulations therein mentioned, or shall make regulations Subversive of the rights of the People to a free and equal Representation in Congress. Nor shall Congress in any Case make regulations contrary to free and equal Representation.

FOURTHLY, That Congress do not lay direct Taxes but when the money arising from Impost, Excise and their other resources are insufficient for the Publick Exigencies; nor then, untill Congress shall have first made a Requisition upon the States, to Assess, Levy, & pay their respective proportions, of such requisition agreeably to the Census fixed in the said Constitution in such way &

manner as the Legislature of the State shall think best and in such Case [if any] State shall neglect, then Congress may Assess & Levy such States proportion together with the Interest thereon at the rate of six per Cent per Annum from the Time of payment prescribed in such requisition.

FIFTHLY, That Congress shall erect no Company of Merchants with exclusive advantages of Commerce.

SIXTHLY, That no Person shall be Tryed for any Crime by which he may incur an Infamous Punishment, or loss of Life, untill he first be indicted by a Grand Jury except in such Cases as may arise in the Government and regulation of the Land & Naval Forces.

SEVENTHLY, All Common Law Cases between Citizens of different States shall be commenced in the Common Law Courts of the respective States & no appeal shall be allowed to the Federal Court in such Cases unless the sum or value of the thing in Controversy amount to three Thousand Dollars.

EIGHTHLY, In Civil Actions between Citizens of different States every Issue of Fact arising in Actions at Common Law shall be Tryed by Jury, if the Parties, or either of them request it.

NINTHLY, Congress shall at no Time consent that any Person holding an Office of Trust or profit under the UNITED STATES shall accept any Title of Nobility or any other Title or Office from any King, Prince, or Foreign State.

TENTH, That no standing Army shall be Kept up in time of Peace unless with the consent of three fourths of the Members of each branch of Congress, nor shall Soldiers in Time of Peace be Quartered upon private Houses without the consent of the Owners.

ELEVENTH, Congress shall make no Laws touching Religion, or to infringe the rights of Conscience.

TWELFTH, Congress shall never disarm any Citizen unless such as are or have been in Actual Rebellion.

[AMENDMENTS PROPOSED BY THE VIRGINIA CONVENTION
JUNE 27, 1788]

That there be a Declaration or Bill of Rights asserting and securing from encroachment the essential and unalienable Rights of the People in some such manner as the following:

FIRST, That there are certain natural rights of which men, when they form a social compact cannot deprive or divest their posterity, among which are the enjoyment of life and liberty, with the means of acquiring, possessing and protecting property, and pursuing and obtaining happiness and safety. SECOND, That all power is naturally vested in and consequently derived from the People; that Magistrates, therefore, are their trustees and agents and at all times amenable to them. THIRD, That Government ought to be instituted for the common benefit, protection and security of the People; and that the doctrine of non-resistance against arbitrary power and oppression is absurd slavish, and destructive of the good and happiness of mankind. FOURTH, That no man or set of Men are entitled to exclusive or separate public emoluments or privileges from the community, but in consideration of public services; which not being descendible, neither ought the offices of Magistrate, Legislator or Judge, or any other public office to be hereditary. FIFTH, That the legislative, executive, and judiciary powers of Government should be separate and distinct, and that the members of the two first may be restrained from oppression by feeling and participating the public burthens, they should, at fixt periods be reduced to a private station, return into the mass of the people; and the vacancies be supplied by certain and regular elections; in which all or any part of the former members to be eligible or ineligible, as the rules of the Constitution of Government, and the laws shall direct. SIXTH, That elections of representatives in the legislature ought to be free and frequent, and all men having sufficient evidence of permanent common interest with and attachment to the community ought to have the right of suffrage: and no aid, charge, tax or fee can be set, rated, or levied upon the people without their own consent, or that of their representatives so elected, nor can they be bound by any law to which they have not in like manner assented for the public good. SEVENTH, That all power of suspending laws or the execution of laws by any authority, without the consent of the representatives of the people in the legislature is injurious to their rights, and ought not to be exercised. EIGHTH, That in all capital and criminal prosecutions, a man hath a right to demand the cause and nature of his accusation, to be confronted with the accusers and witnesses, to call for evidence and be allowed counsel in his favor, and to a fair and speedy trial by an impartial Jury of his vicinage, without whose unanimous consent he cannot be found guilty, (except in the government of the land and naval forces) nor can he be compelled to give evidence against himself. NINTH, That no freeman ought to be taken imprisoned, or disseised of his freehold, liberties, privileges or franchises, or outlawed or exiled, or in any manner destroyed or deprived of his life, liberty or property but by the law of the land. TENTH, That every freeman restrained of his liberty is entitled to a remedy to enquire into the lawfulness thereof, and to remove the same, if unlawful, and that such remedy ought not to be denied nor delayed. ELEVENTH, That in controversies respecting property, and in suits between man and man, the ancient trial by Jury is one of the greatest Securities to the rights of the people, and ought to remain sacred and inviolable. TWELFTH, That every freeman ought to find a certain remedy by recourse to the laws for all injuries and wrongs he may receive in his person, property or character. He ought to obtain right and justice freely without sale, compleatly and without denial, promptly and without delay, and that all establishments or regulations contravening these rights, are oppressive and unjust. THIRTEENTH, That excessive Bail ought not be required, nor excessive fines imposed, nor cruel and unusual punishments inflicted. FOURTEENTH, That every freeman has a right to be secure from all unreasonable searches and seizures of his person, his papers and his property; all warrants, therefore, to search suspected places, or seize any freeman, his papers or property, without information upon Oath (or affirmation of a person religiously scrupulous of taking an oath) of legal and sufficient cause, are grievous and oppressive; and all general Warrants to search suspected places, or to apprehend any suspected person, without specially naming or describing the place or person, are dangerous and ought not to be granted. FIFTEENTH, That the people have a right peaceably to assemble together to consult for the common good, or to instruct their Representatives; and that every freeman has a right to petition or apply to the legislature for redress of grievances. SIXTEENTH, That the people have a right to freedom of speech, and of writing and publishing their Sentiments; but the freedom of the press is one of the greatest bulwarks of liberty and ought not to be violated. SEVENTEENTH, That the people have a right to keep ard bear arms; that a well regulated Militia composed of the body of the people trained to arms is the proper, natural and safe defence of a free State. That standing armies in time of peace are dangerous to liberty, and therefore ought to be avoided, as far as the circumstances and protection of the Community will admit; and that in all cases the military should be under strict subordination to and governed by the Civil power. EIGHTEENTH, That no Soldier in time of peace ought to be quartered in any house without the consent of the owner, and in time of war in such manner only as the laws direct. NINETEENTH, That any person religiously scrupulous of bearing arms ought to be exempted upon payment of an equivalent to employ another to bear arms in his stead. TWENTIETH, That religion or the duty which we owe to our Creator, and the manner of discharging it can be directed only by reason and conviction, not by force or violence, and therefore all men have an equal, natural and unalienable right to the free exercise of religion according to the dictates of conscience, and that no particular religious sect or society ought to be favored or established by Law in preference to others.

AMENDMENTS TO THE BODY OF THE CONSTITUTION

FIRST, That each State in the Union shall respectively retain every power, jurisdiction and right which is not by this Constitution delegated to the Congress of the United States or to the departments of the Fœderal Government. SECOND, That there shall be one representative for every thirty thousand, according to the Enumeration or Census mentioned in the Constitution, until the whole number of representatives amounts to two hundred; after which that number shall be continued or encreased as the Congress shall direct, upon the principles fixed by the Constitution by apportioning the Representatives of each State to some greater number of people from time to time as population encreases. THIRD, When Congress shall lay direct taxes or excises, they shall immediately inform the Executive power of each State of the quota of such state according to the Census herein directed, which is proposed to be thereby raised; And if the Legislature of any State shall pass a law which shall be effectual for raising such quota at the time required by Congress, the taxes and excises laid by Congress shall not be collected, in such State.   FOURTH, That the members of the Senate and House of Representatives shall be ineligible to, and incapable of holding, any civil office under the authority of the United States, during the time for which they shall respectively be elected. FIFTH, That the Journals of the proceedings of the Senate and the House of Representatives shall be published at least once in every year, except such parts thereof relating to treaties, alliances or military operations, as in their judgment require secrecy.   SIXTH, That a regular statement and account of the receipts and expenditures of all public money shall be published at least once in every year.   SEVENTH, That no commercial treaty shall be ratified without the concurrence of two thirds of the whole number of the members of the Senate; and no Treaty ceding, contracting, restraining, or suspending the territorial rights or claims of the United States, or any of them or their, or any of their rights or claims to fishing in the American Seas, or navigating the American rivers shall be but in cases of the most urgent and extreme necessity, nor shall any such treaty be ratified without the concurrence of three fourths of the whole number of the members of both houses respectively. EIGHTH, That no navigation law, or law regulating Commerce shall be passed without the consent of two thirds of the members present in both houses.   NINTH, That no standing army or regular troops shall be raised or kept up in time of peace, without the consent of two thirds of the members present in both houses.   TENTH, That no soldier shall be inlisted for any longer term than four years, except in time of war, and then for no longer term than the continuance of the war.   ELEVENTH, That each State respectively shall have the power to provide for organizing, arming and disciplining its own Militia, whensoever Congress shall omit or neglect to provide for the same. That the Militia shall not be subject to Martial Law, except when in actual service in time of war, invasion, or rebellion; and when not in the actual service of the United States, shall be subject only to such fines, penalties and punishments as shall be directed or inflicted by the laws of its own State.   TWELFTH, That the exclusive power of legislation given to Congress over the Fœderal Town and its adjacent District and other places purchased or to be purchased by Congress of any of the States shall extend only to such regulations as respect the police and good government thereof. THIRTEENTH, That no person shall be capable of being President of the United States for more than eight years in any term of sixteen years. FOURTEENTH, That the judicial power of the United States shall be vested in one supreme Court, and in such courts of Admiralty as Congress may from time to time ordain and establish in any of the different States: The Judicial power shall extend to all cases in Law and Equity arising under treaties made, or which shall be made under the authority of the United States; to all cases affecting ambassadors other foreign ministers and consuls; to all cases of Admiralty and maritime jurisdiction; to controversies to which the United States shall be a party; to controversies between two or more States, and between parties claiming lands under the grants of different States. In all cases affecting ambassadors, other foreign ministers and Consuls, and those in which a State shall be a party, the supreme Court shall have original jurisdiction; in all other cases before mentioned the supreme Court shall have appellate jurisdiction as to matters of law only: except in cases of equity, and of admiralty and maritime jurisdiction, in which the supreme Court shall have appellate jurisdiction both as to law and fact, with such exceptions and under such regulations as the Congress shall make. But the judicial power of the United States shall extend to no case where the cause of action shall have originated before the ratification of this Constitution; except in disputes between States about their Territory, disputes between persons claiming lands under the grants of different States, and suits for debts due to the United States. FIFTEENTH, That in criminal prosecutions no man shall be restrained in the exercise of the usual and accustomed right of challenging or excepting to the Jury. SIXTEENTH, That Congress shall not alter, modify or interfere in the times, places, or manner of holding elections for Senators and Representatives or either of them, except when the legislature of any State shall neglect, refuse or be disabled by invasion or rebellion to prescribe the same. SEVENTEENTH, That those clauses which declare that Congress shall not exercise certain powers be not interpreted in any manner whatsoever to extend the powers of Congress. But that they may be construed either as making exceptions to the specified powers where this shall be the case, or otherwise as inserted merely for greater caution. EIGHTEENTH, That the laws ascertaining the compensation to Senators and Representatives for their services be postponed in their operation, until after the election of Representatives immediately succeeding the passing thereof; that excepted, which shall first be passed on the Subject. NINETEENTH, That some Tribunal other than the Senate be provided for trying impeachments of Senators. TWENTIETH, That the Salary of a Judge shall not be encreased or diminished during his continuance in Office, otherwise than by general regulations of Salary which may take place on a revision of the subject at stated periods of not less than seven years to commence from the time such Salaries shall be first ascertained by Congress.

[AMENDMENTS PROPOSED BY THE NEW YORK CONVENTION
JULY 26, 1788]

That all power is originally vested in and consequently derived from the People, and that Government is instituted by them for their common Interest, Protection and Security.

That the enjoyment of Life, Liberty and the pursuit of Happiness are essential rights which every Government ought to respect and preserve.

That the Powers of Government may be reassumed by the People, whensoever it shall become necessary to their Happiness; that every Power, Jurisdiction and Right, which is not by the said Constitution clearly delegated to the Congress of the United States, or the departments of the Government thereof, remains to the People of the several States, or to their respective State Governments to whom they may have granted the same; And that those Clauses in the said Constitution, which declare, that Congress shall not have or exercise certain Powers, do not imply that Congress is entitled to any Powers not given by the said Constitution; but such Clauses are to be construed either as exceptions to certain specified Powers, or as inserted merely for greater Caution.

That the People have an equal, natural and unalienable right, freely and peaceably to Exercise their Religion according to the dictates of Conscience, and that no Religious Sect or Society ought to be favoured or established by Law in preference of others.

That the People have a right to keep and bear Arms; that a well regulated Militia, including the body of the People *capable of bearing Arms*, is the proper, natural and safe defence of a free State;

That the Militia should not be subject to Martial Law, except in time of War, Rebellion or Insurrection.

That standing Armies in time of Peace are dangerous to Liberty, and ought not to be kept up, except in Cases of necessity; and that at all times, the Military should be under strict Subordination to the civil Power.

That in time of Peace no Soldier ought to be quartered in any House without the consent of the Owner, and in time of War only by the civil Magistrate in such manner as the Laws may direct.

That no Person ought to be taken imprisoned, or disseised of his freehold, or be exiled or deprived of his Privileges, Franchises, Life, Liberty or Property, but by due process of Law.

That no Person ought to be put twice in Jeopardy of Life or Limb for one and the same Offence, nor unless in case of impeachment, be punished more than once for the same Offence.

That every Person restrained of his Liberty is entitled to an enquiry into the lawfulness of such restraint, and to a removal thereof if unlawful, and that such enquiry and removal ought not to be denied or delayed, except when on account of Public Danger the Congress shall suspend the privilege of the Writ of Habeas Corpus.

That excessive Bail ought not to be required; nor excessive Fines imposed; nor Cruel or unusual Punishments inflicted.

That (except in the Government of the Land and Naval Forces, and of the Militia when in actual Service, and in cases of Impeachment) a Presentment or Indictment by a Grand Jury ought to be observed as a necessary preliminary to the trial of all Crimes cognizable by the Judiciary of the United States, and such Trial should be speedy, public, and by an impartial Jury of the County where the Crime was committed; and that no person can be found Guilty without the unanimous consent of such Jury. But in cases of Crimes not committed within any County of any of the United States, and in Cases of Crimes committed within any County in which a general

Insurrection may prevail, or which may be in the possession of a foreign Enemy, the enquiry and trial may be in such County as the Congress shall by Law direct; which County in the two Cases last mentioned should be as near as conveniently may be to that County in which the Crime may have been committed. And that in all Criminal Prosecutions, the Accused ought to be informed of the cause and nature of his Accusation, to be confronted with his accusers and the Witnesses against him, to have the means of producing his Witnesses, and the assistance of Council for his defence, and should not be compelled to give Evidence against himself.

That the trial by Jury in the extent that it obtains by the Common Law of England is one of the greatest securities to the rights of a free People, and ought to remain inviolate.

That every Freeman has a right to be secure from all unreasonable searches and seizures of his person, his papers or his property, and therefore, that all Warrants to search suspected places or seize any Freeman, his papers or property, without information upon Oath or Affirmation of sufficient cause, are grievous and oppressive; and that all general Warrants (or such in which the place or person suspected are not particularly designated) are dangerous and ought not to be granted.

That the People have a right peaceably to assemble together to consult for their common good, or to instruct their Representatives; and that every Person has a right to Petition or apply to the Legislature for redress of Grievances.

That the Freedom of the Press ought not to be violated or restrained.

That there should be once in four years an Election of the President and Vice President, so that no Officer who may be appointed by the Congress to act as President in case of the removal, death, resignation or inability of the President and Vice President can in any case continue to act beyond the termination of the period for which the last President and Vice President were elected.

That nothing contained in the said Constitution is to be construed to prevent the Legislature of any State from passing Laws at its discretion from time to time to divide such State into convenient Districts, and to apportion its Representatives to and amongst such Districts.

That the Prohibition contained in the said Constitution against *ex post facto* Laws, extends only to Laws concerning Crimes.

That all Appeals in Causes determinable according to the course of the common Law, ought to be by Writ of Error and not otherwise.

That the Judicial Power of the United States in cases in which a State may be a party, does not extend to criminal Prosecutions, or to authorize any Suit by any Person against a State.

That the Judicial Power of the United States as to Controversies between Citizens of the same State claiming Lands under Grants of different States is not to be construed to extend to any other Controversies between them, except those which relate to such Lands, so claimed under Grants of different States.

That the Jurisdiction of the Supreme Court of the United States, or of any other Court to be instituted by the Congress, is not in any case to be encreased, enlarged or extended by any Fiction, Collusion or mere suggestion; And

That no Treaty is to be construed so to operate as to alter the Constitution of any State.

UNDER these impressions and declaring that the rights aforesaid cannot be abridged or violated, and that the Explanations aforesaid are consistent with the said Constitution, And in confidence that the Amendments which shall have been proposed to the said Constitution will receive an early and mature Consideration: WE the said Delegates, in the Name and in the behalf of the People of the State of New York Do by these presents Assent to and Ratify the said Constitution. IN full Confidence nevertheless that until a Convention shall be called and convened for proposing Amendments to the said Constitution, the Militia of this State will not be continued in Service out of this State for a longer term than six weeks without the consent of the Legislature thereof; that the Congress will not make or alter any Regulation in this State respecting the times, places and manner of holding Elections for Senators or Representatives unless the Legislature of this State shall neglect or refuse to make Laws or regulations for the purpose, or from any circumstance be incapable of making the same, and that in those cases such power will only be exercised until the Legislature of this State shall make provision in the Premises; that no Excise will be imposed on any Article of the Growth, production or Manufacture of the United States, or any of them within this State, Ardent Spirits excepted; And that the Congress will not lay direct Taxes within this State, but when the Monies arising from the Impost and Excise shall be insufficient for the public Exigencies, nor then, until Congress shall first have made a Requisition upon this State to assess, levy and pay the Amount of such Requisition made agreeably to the Census fixed in the said Constitution in such way and manner as the Legislature of this State shall judge best, but that in such case, if the State shall neglect or refuse to pay its proportion pursuant to such Requisition, then the Congress may assess and levy this States proportion together with Interest at the Rate of six per Centum per Annum from the time at which the same was required to be paid.

AND the Convention do in the Name and Behalf of the People of the State of New York enjoin it upon their Representatives in the Congress, to Exert all their Influence, and use all reasonable means to Obtain a Ratification of the following Amendments to the said Constitution in the manner prescribed therein; and in all Laws to be passed by the Congress in the meantime to conform to the spirit of the said Amendments as far as the Constitution will admit.

That there shall be one Representative for every thirty thousand Inhabitants, according to the enumeration or Census mentioned in the Constitution, until the whole number of Representatives amounts to two hundred; after which that number shall be continued or encreased but not diminished, as Congress shall direct, and according to such ratio as the Congress shall fix, in conformity to the rule prescribed for the Apportionment of Representatives and direct Taxes.

That the Congress do not impose any Excise on any Article (except Ardent Spirits) of the Growth, production or Manufacture of the United States, or any of them.

That Congress do not lay direct Taxes but when the Monies arising from the Impost and Excise shall be insufficient for the Public Exigencies, nor then until Congress shall first have made a Requisition upon the States to assess, levy and pay their respective proportions of such Requisition, agreeably to the Census fixed in the said Constitution, in such way and manner as the Legislatures of the respective States shall judge best; and in such Case, if any State shall neglect or refuse to pay its proportion pursuant to such Requisition, then Congress may assess and levy such States proportion, together with Interest at the rate of six per Centum per Annum, from the time of Payment prescribed in such Requisition.

That the Congress shall not make or alter any Regulation in any State respecting the times, places and manner of holding Elections for Senators or Representatives, unless the Legislature of such State shall neglect or refuse to make Laws or Regulations for the purpose, or from any circumstance be incapable of making the same; and then only until the Legislature of such State shall make provision in the premises; provided that Congress may prescribe the time for the Election of Representatives.

That no Persons except natural born Citizens, or such as were Citizens on or before the fourth day of July one thousand seven hundred and seventy six, or such as held Commissions under the United States during the War, and have at any time since the fourth day of July one thousand seven hundred and seventy six become Citizens of one or other of the United States, and who shall be Freeholders, shall be eligible to the Places of President, Vice President, or Members of either House of the Congress of the United States.

That the Congress do not grant Monopolies or erect any Company with exclusive Advantages of Commerce.

That no standing Army or regular Troops shall be raised or kept up in time of peace, without the consent of two-thirds of the Senators and Representatives present, in each House.

That no Money be borrowed on the Credit of the United States without the Assent of two-thirds of the Senators and Representatives present in each House.

That the Congress shall not declare War without the concurrence of two-thirds of the Senators and Representatives present in each House.

That the Privilege of the *Habeas Corpus* shall not by any Law be suspended for a longer term than six Months, or until twenty days after the Meeting of the Congress next following the passing of the Act for such suspension.

That the Right of the Congress to exercise exclusive Legislation over such District, not exceeding ten Miles square, as may by cession of a particular State, and the acceptance of Congress, become the Seat of the Government of the United States, shall not be so exercised, as to exempt the Inhabitants of such District from paying the like Taxes Imposts Duties and Excises, as shall be imposed on the other Inhabitants of the State in which such District may be; and that no person shall be privileged within the said District from Arrest for Crimes committed, or Debts contracted out of the said District.

That the Right of exclusive Legislation with respect to such places as may be purchased for the Erection of Forts, Magazines, Arsenals, Dockyards and other needful Buildings, shall not authorize the Congress to make any Law to prevent the Laws of the States respectively in which they may be, from extending to such places in all civil and Criminal Matters, except as to such Persons as shall be in the Service of the United States; nor to them with respect to Crimes committed without such Places.

That the Compensation for the Senators and Representatives be ascertained by standing Laws; and that no alteration of the existing rate of Compensation shall operate for the Benefit of the Representatives, until after a subsequent Election shall have been had.

That the Journals of the Congress shall be published at least once a year, with the exception of such parts relating to Treaties or Military operations, as in the Judgment of either House shall require Secrecy; and that both Houses of Congress shall always keep their Doors Open during their Sessions, unless the Business may in their Opinion require Secrecy. That the yeas & nays shall be entered on the Journals whenever two Members in either House may require it.

That no Capitation Tax shall ever be laid by the Congress.

That no Person be eligible as a Senator for more than six years in any term of twelve years; and that the Legislatures of the respective States may recall their Senators or either of them, and elect others in their stead, to serve the remainder of the time for which the Senators so recalled were appointed.

That no Senator or Representative shall during the time for which he was elected be appointed to any Office under the Authority of the United States.

That the Authority given to the Executives of the States to fill the vacancies of Senators be abolished, and that such vacancies be filled by the respective Legislatures.

That the Power of Congress to pass uniform Laws concerning Bankruptcy shall only extend to Merchants and other Traders; and that the States respectively may pass Laws for the relief of other Insolvent Debtors.

That no Person shall be eligible to the Office of President of the United States a third time.

That the Executive shall not grant Pardons for Treason, unless with the Consent of the Congress; but may at his discretion grant Reprieves to persons convicted of Treason, until their Cases can be laid before the Congress.

That the President or person exercising his Powers for the time being, shall not command an Army in the Field in person, without the previous desire of the Congress.

That all Letters Patent, Commissions, Pardons, Writs and Process of the United States, shall run in the Name of *the People of the United States*, and be tested in the Name of the President of the United States, or the person exercising his powers for the time being, or the first Judge of the Court out of which the same shall issue, as the case may be.

That the Congress shall not constitute, ordain or establish any Tribunals or Inferior Courts, with any other than Appellate Jurisdiction, except such as may be necessary for the Trial of Causes of Admiralty and Maritime Jurisdiction, and for the Trial of Piracies and Felonies committed on the High Seas; and in all other Cases to which the Judicial Power of the United States extends, and in which the Supreme Court of the United States has not original Jurisdiction, the Causes shall be heard, tried, and determined in some one of the State Courts, with the right of Appeal to the Supreme Court of the United States, or other proper Tribunal to be established for that purpose by the Congress, with such exceptions, and under such regulations as the Congress shall make.

That the Court for the Trial of Impeachments shall consist of the Senate, the Judges of the Supreme Court of the United States, and the first or Senior Judge for the time being, of the highest Court of general and ordinary common Law Jurisdiction in each State; that the Congress shall by standing Laws designate the Courts in the respective States answering this Description, and in States having no Courts exactly answering this Description, shall designate some other Court, preferring such if any there be, whose Judge or Judges may hold their places during good Behaviour—Provided that no more than one Judge, other than Judges of the Supreme Court of the United States, shall come from one State—That the Congress be authorized to pass Laws for compensating the said Judges for such Services and for compelling their Attendance—and that a Majority at least of the said Judges shall be requisite to constitute the said Court—that no person impeached shall sit as a Member thereof. That each Member shall previous to the entering upon any Trial take an Oath or Affirmation, honestly and impartially to hear and determine the Cause—and that a Majority of the Members present shall be necessary to a Conviction.

That persons aggrieved by any Judgment, Sentence or Decree of the Supreme Court of the United States, in any Cause in which that Court has original Jurisdiction, with such exceptions and under such Regulations as the Congress shall make concerning the same, shall upon application, have a Commission to be issued by the President of the United States, to such Men learned in the Law as he shall nominate, and by and with the Advice and consent of the Senate appoint, not less than seven, authorizing such Commissioners, or any seven or more of them, to correct the Errors in such Judgment or to review such Sentence and Decree, as the case may be, and to do Justice to the parties in the Premises.

That no Judge of the Supreme Court of the United States shall hold any other Office under the United States, or any of them.

That the Judicial Power of the United States shall extend to no Controversies respecting Land, unless it relate to Claims of Territory or Jurisdiction between States, or to Claims of Land between Individuals, or between States and Individuals under the Grants of different States.

That the Militia of any State shall not be compelled to serve without the limits of the State for a longer term than six weeks, without the Consent of the Legislature thereof.

That the words *without the Consent of the Congress* in the seventh Clause of the ninth Section of the first Article of the Constitution, be expunged.

That the Senators and Representatives and all Executive and Judicial Officers of the United States shall be bound by Oath or Affirmation not to infringe or violate the Constitutions or Rights of the respective States.

That the Legislatures of the respective States may make Provision by Law, that the Electors of the Election Districts to be by them appointed shall chuse a Citizen of the United States who shall have been an Inhabitant of such District for the Term of one year immediately preceding the time of his Election, for one of the Representatives of such State.

NOTES

★

Chapter 1

1. Van Doren, *Great Rehearsal*, 242–43.
2. Ibid., 243.
3. *First Federal Elections*, 1:27–28.
4. Ibid., 1:241–42.
5. Van Doren, *Great Rehearsal*, 243.
6. Silverman, *Cultural History*, 582.
7. Ibid., 583.
8. Quoted in Silverman, *Cultural History*, 576.
9. McMaster, *History*, 1:493.
10. Ibid., 1:493–94.
11. Silverman, *Cultural History*, 583.
12. Bowen, *Miracle*, 309.
13. Silverman, *Cultural History*, 584–85.
14. Bowen, *Miracle*, 309.
15. Ibid.
16. Quoted in Silverman, *Cultural History*, 579.
17. *First Federal Elections*, 1:242.
18. Ibid., 1:16.
19. Ibid., 1:242.
20. Ibid., 1:243.
21. Ibid., 2:244.
22. Rutland, *Bill of Rights*, 158.
23. De Pauw, *Eleventh Pillar*, 217.
24. Rutland, *Ordeal*, 256.

Chapter 2

1. Brant, *Madison*, 227–28.
2. Grigsby, *Virginia Federal Convention*, 1:251.
3. Madison, *Papers*, 11:210. "To Tench Coxe. N.York July 30, 1788."
4. Rutland, *Ordeal*, 283.
5. Madison, *Papers*, 11:183. "To George Washington. Richmd. June 27, 1788."
6. Ibid., 11:183. "To Alexander Hamilton. Richd, June 27, [1788]."
7. Washington, *Writings*, 30:16. "To the Secretary for Foreign Affairs. Mount Vernon, July 18, 1788."

8. Rutland, *Ordeal*, 134.
9. *First Federal Elections*, 1:13.
10. De Pauw, *Eleventh Pillar*, 230.
11. Ibid., 237–38.
12. Van Doren, *Great Rehearsal*, 240–41.
13. De Pauw, *Eleventh Pillar*, 263.
14. Flexner, *Washington*, 155.
15. *First Federal Elections*, 1:13.
16. Ibid., 52. "Journal of Comte de Moustier, 28 July."
17. Ibid., 55.
18. Ibid.
19. Madison, *Papers*, 11:383. "To Thomas Jefferson. Philadelphia Decr. 8, 1788." Italicized words were written in code by James Madison.
20. *First Federal Elections*, 4:43. "John Adams to Abigail Smith. Braintree, Massachusetts, 16 July (excerpt)."
21. Ibid., "Abigail Smith to John Adams. Jamaica, New York, 27 July (excerpt)."

Chapter 3

1. Burnett, *Letters of... Continental Congress*, 8:662–63. "James Madison to Thomas Jefferson. New York. Octr. 24, 1787."
2. Madison, *Papers*, 11:239. "To Thomas Jefferson. New York Augst. 23. 1788."
3. Ibid., 11:239–40.
4. Ibid., 11:240 *fn*1.
5. Burnett, *Continental Congress*, 709–10.
6. Rakove, *Beginnings of National Politics*, 350.
7. *First Federal Elections*, 1:11–12.
8. Madison, *Papers*, 11:241–42. "To George Washington. New York Augst. 24, 1788."
9. Flexner, *Washington*, 138.
10. Bowen, *Miracle*, 179.
11. Madison, *Papers*, 11:46. "To George Nichols. Orange May 17th. 1788."
12. Washington, *Writings*, 30:62–63. "To Benjamin Lincoln. Mount Vernon, August 28, 1788."
13. Madison, *Papers*, 11:241. "To George Washington. New York Augst. 24. 1788."
14. *First Federal Elections*, 1:63 *fn*2.
15. Ibid., 1:75. "Journal of Comte de Moustier, 6 August."
16. Burnett, *Continental Congress*, 715.
17. *First Federal Elections* 1:112. "William Ellery to Benjamin Huntington, Newport, 31 August (excerpt)."
18. Rutland, *Ordeal*, 282–83.
19. Madison, *Papers*, 11:240. "To George Washington. New York Augst. 24. 1788."
20. Ibid., 11:237. "To Edmund Randolph. New York Aug. 22. 88."

Chapter 4

1. Burnett, *Letters of... Continental Congress*, 8:800. "John Swann to James Iredell. New York, Sept 21, 1788."
2. Ibid., 8:802. "George Thatcher to Nathan Dave. City of New York 2 October, 1788."
3. *First Federal Elections*, 1:133.
4. Madison, *Papers*, 11:254–55. "To George Washington. N.York Sepr. 14, 1788."
5. Ibid.
6. Washington, *Writings*, 30:62–63. "To Benjamin Lincoln. Mount Vernon, August 28, 1788."
7. Ibid., 30:100–101. "To James Madison. Mount Vernon, September 23, 1788."
8. Ibid., 30:96. "To Henry Lee. Mount Vernon, September 22, 1788."
9. *First Federal Elections*, 2:253.
10. Ibid., 1:140. "Antoine R. C. M. de la Forest to Comte de la Luzerne. New York, 14 September."
11. Rutland, *Ordeal*, 289.
12. *First Federal Elections*, 1:406. "William Petrikin to John Nicholson. Carlisle, 23 March."
13. Rutland, *Ordeal*, 289.
14. *First Federal Elections*, 1:279. "Observations by a Member of the Convention at Harrisburg. *Pittsburgh Gazette*, 20 September."
15. Flexner, *Washington*, 158–59.
16. Hamilton, *Papers*, 5:221. "To George Washington. New York September 1788."
17. Ibid.
18. Washington, *Writings*, 30:97–98. "To Henry Lee. Mount Vernon, September 22, 1788."
19. Ibid.
20. Ibid., 30:36. "To Doctor James Craik. Mount Vernon, August 4, 1788."
21. Harwell, *Washington*, 555.

Chapter 5

1. Van Doren, *Great Rehearsal*, 201–2.
2. *First Federal Elections*, 4:63. "Comte de Moustier Journal, 12 September."
3. Madison, *Papers*, 11:296. "To Thomas Jefferson. New York, 17 October."
4. Ibid. Italicized words were written in code.
5. *First Federal Elections*, 4:75. "James Madison to Thomas Jefferson. New York, 8 October (excerpt)."
6. Ibid., 4:292. "John Adams to Mercy Otis Warren, Quincy, Massachusetts, 20 July 1807 (excerpt)."
7. Ibid.

8. Flexner, *Washington*, 161.
9. Washington, *Writings*, 30:120. "To Benjamin Lincoln. Mount Vernon, October 26, 1788."
10. Ibid., 30:111. "To Alexander Hamilton. Mount Vernon, October 3, 1788."
11. *First Federal Elections*, 2:257.
12. Ibid., 2:260–61.
13. Ibid., 2:263. "Edward Carrington to James Madison, Fredericksburg, 22 October."
14. Brant, *Madison*, 236.
15. William Wirt Henry, *Patrick Henry*, 2:417.
16. Meade, *Patrick Henry*, 376.
17. Rutland, *Ordeal*, 293.
18. *First Federal Elections*, 2:262.
19. Reardon, *Edmund Randolph*, 169.
20. Rutland, *Ordeal*, 293.
21. William Wirt Henry, *Patrick Henry*, 2:420.
22. Ibid., 2:421.
23. Ibid., 2:422.

Chapter 6

1. Meade, *Patrick Henry*, 382.
2. Washington, *Writings*, 30:131. "To James Madison. Mount Vernon, November 17, 1788."
3. Madison, *Papers*, 11:356. "From Henry Lee. Alexa. Novr. 19h. 1788."
4. Ibid., 11:336. "From Edward Carrington. Richmond Nov 9, 1788."
5. Ibid., 11:344. "From George Lee Turberville. Richmond— Wednesday 13th. Novr. 1788."
6. Ibid., 11:369. "From Edward Carrington. Richmond Nov. 26. 1788."
7. Brant, *Madison*, 238.
8. Rutland, *Ordeal*, 295.
9. Hamilton, *Papers*, 5:356. "To James Madison [New York, November 23, 1788]."
10. Madison, *Papers*, 11:334–35. "To George Washington. N. York Novr. 5th, 1788."
11. *First Federal Elections*, 1:148.
12. Ibid.
13. Ibid., 1:181.
14. Ibid., 1:187. Apparently for campaign purposes, Ramsay was less than honest. In January 1785 he had written to Benjamin Rush in Philadelphia that "I trust the day will arrive when the test laws and slavery will both be abolished." *First Federal Elections*, 1:188 *fn*2.
15. Ibid., 1:173–76, 195 *fn*2.
16. Madison, *Papers*, 11:331–32. "To George Lee Turberville. N.York Novr. 2, 1788."
17. Ibid., 11:333. "To James Monroe. N York. Novr. 5. 88."
18. Meade, *Patrick Henry*, 381.

19. *First Federal Elections*, 1:339. "To the German Inhabitants of the State of Pennsylvania, Philadelphia, 13 November."
20. Ibid., 1:363. "A German, *Pennsylvania Packet*, 25 November."
21. Ibid., 1:233.
22. Ibid., 1:352. "Centinel XXIII, *Independent Gazetteer*, 20 November."
23. Ibid., 1:354. "Robert Morris to the Printer, 21 November." Printed in *Independent Gazetteer*, 22 November.
24. Ibid., 4:86. "*Pennsylvania Gazette* (Philadelphia), 5 November."
25. Ibid., 4:91.
26. De Pauw, *Eleventh Pillar*, 271–72.
27. Spaulding, *Clinton*, 185.
28. Smith, *Adams*, 740.
29. Hamilton, *Papers*, 5:236. "To James Madison [New York, November 23, 1788]."

Chapter 7

1. Rutland, *Ordeal*, 295.
2. *First Federal Elections*, 1:373.
3. Meade, *Patrick Henry*, 384–85.
4. Spaulding, *Clinton*, 185.
5. Ibid.
6. *First Federal Elections*, 3:197.
7. Ibid., 3:217. "Assembly and Senate Proceedings, Thursday, A.M., 11 December 1788."
8. Rutland, *Ordeal*, 295–96.
9. *First Federal Elections*, 3:214. "A Federal Republican, *New York Journal*, 11 December (excerpt)."
10. Madison, *Papers* 11:381. "To Thomas Jefferson. Philadelphia Decr. 8. 1788."
11. Brant, *Madison*, 238.
12. Rutland, *Ordeal*, 294.
13. Madison, *Papers*, 11:392. "From Richard Bland Lee. Richmond Decr. 12, 1788."
14. Ibid., 11:377. "To George Washington. Philada. Decr. 2d. 1788."
15. Washington, *Writings*, 30:146–47. "To David Stuart. Mount Vernon, December 2, 1788."
16. Spaulding, *Clinton*, 121. Also Boatner, *Encyclopedia*, 1137.
17. Freeman, *Washington*, 6:154.
18. Washington, *Writings*, 30:149. "To Jonathan Trumbull. Mount Vernon, December 4, 1788."
19. *First Federal Elections*, 2:169.
20. Freeman, *Washington*, 6:156.
21. Washington, *Writings*, 30:71. "To Benjamin Fishbourn. Mount Vernon, December 23, 1788."
22. Ibid., 30:169. "To Reverend William Gordon. Mount Vernon, December 23, 1788."

Chapter 8

1. Flexner, *Washington*, 161–62.
2. *First Federal Elections*, 3:197.
3. Hamilton, *Papers*, 5:245. "To Samuel Jones. [New York, January 21, 1789]."
4. Ibid.
5. Hamilton, *Papers*, 5:248. "To James Wilson. New York Jany 25, 1789."
6. Ibid.
7. Ibid., 5:249.
8. *First Federal Elections*, 1:381.
9. Ibid., 2:87. "Cato, *Delaware Gazette* (Wilmington), 10 January 1789."
10. Ibid., 2:90–91. "Delawarensis, *Delaware Gazette* (Wilmington), 31 January."
11. Washington, *Writings*, 30:183–84. "To the Secretary At War. Mount Vernon, January 29, 1789."
12. Freeman, *Washington*, 6:158.
13. Washington, *Writings*, 30:187. "To Marquis de Lafayette. Mount Vernon, January 29, 1789."
14. Ibid., 30:185–86.
15. Ibid., 30:190. "To Benjamin Lincoln. Mount Vernon, January 31, 1789."
16. *First Federal Elections*, 1:554–55. "Constitutionalist, *Massachusetts Centinel*, 13 December."
17. Ibid., 1:647. "Elbridge Gerry to the Electors of Middlesex, 22 January." This letter appeared, first, in the *Independent Chronicle*, Boston, and then in other newspapers.
18. Brant, *Madison*, 242–43.
19. Flexner, *Washington*, 164.
20. Washington, *Writings*, 30:301–2.
21. Brant, *Madison*, 240.
22. Madison, *Papers*, 11:405. "To George Eve. January 2d. 1789."
23. Brant, *Madison*, 241–42.

Chapter 9

1. Flexner, *Washington*, 171.
2. Ibid.
3. *First Federal Elections*, 1:xxvii–xxix. "Presidential Electors and Their Votes, 4 February 1789."
4. Ibid.
5. Ibid.
6. Ibid., 4:181. "Benjamin Rush to John Adams. Philadelphia. 21 February (excerpt)."
7. *First Federal Elections*, 2:47.
8. Hamilton, *Papers*, 5:247–48. "To James Wilson. [New York, January 25, 1789]."
9. *First Federal Elections*, 1:401. "Benjamin Rush to Tench Coxe, Philadelphia, 5 February (excerpt)."

10. Ibid., 4:203. "John Adams to Elbridge Gerry, Braintree, Massachusetts, 20 March."
11. Ibid., 4:402 *fn*2.
12. Ibid., 2:176. "Comte de Moustier to Comte de Montmorin. New York. 12 February." Also Freeman, *Washington*, 6:232.
13. Madison, *Papers*, 11:296. "To Thomas Jefferson. New York Oct. 17, 1788."
14. Morse, *Adams*, 242. Also Freeman, *Washington*, 6:232.
15. Morse, *Adams*, 242.
16. Ibid., 243.
17. *First Federal Elections*, 2:406. "From James Wood, Jr., 17 February."
18. Freeman, *Washington*, 6:158 and 158 *fn*111. Patrick Henry cast his second vote for Anti–Federalist George Clinton. Ibid., *fn*111.
19. Meade, *Patrick Henry*, 386.
20. Hamilton, *Papers*, 5:265.
21. Spaulding, *Clinton*, 188–89.
22. Washington, *Writings*, 30:195. "To Samuel Powell. Mount Vernon, February 5, 1789."
23. *First Federal Elections*, 2:447.
24. Ibid., 2:474. The population in the State in 1790 was 53,000; census statistics did not break down the count by sex or by adults. *Statistical History of the United States from Colonial Times to the Present* (New York: Basic Books, 1976), 26.
25. Ibid., 1:254.
26. Meade, *Patrick Henry*, 385–86.
27. Brant, *Madison*, 242–43.
28. Ibid., 243.
29. Madison, *Papers*, 11:453.
30. Washington, *Writings*, 30:307–8.
31. *First Federal Elections*, 2:210–11. "George Washington to John E. Howard, Mount Vernon, 2 February."
32. Ibid., 2:123, 158.
33. Ibid., 2:218. "A.B." did not sign his name to this article or to an earlier one printed in the *Maryland Journal*, 3 February; he has not been identified in *First Federal Elections*.
34. Ibid., 2:234.
35. Ibid., 2:317. "George Washington Diary, 2 February."
36. Ibid., 2:346.
37. Ibid., 1:382.
38. Ibid., 1:570 *fn*3. Elections in Massachusetts were held on December 18, 1788. All returns from the Boston district alone were not yet in by December 31 due to "the badness of the roads."

Chapter 10

1. Madison, *Papers*, 12:3, "To George Washington. Baltimore March 5th. 1789."
2. *First Federal Congress*, 1:4.
3. Morris, *Encyclopedia*, 121.

4. Bickford, *Birth*, 10.
5. *First Federal Elections*, 4:208. "Paine Wingate to Timothy Pickering. New York. 25 March (excerpt)."
6. Bickford, *Birth*, 10–11. "*Morning Post and Daily Advertiser*, March 14, 1789."
7. Ibid., 10. When the Confederated Congress vacated on November 1, 1788, what is now called Federal Hall because of renovation, it lacked not only a formal meeting site but also a quorum to conduct business. Thus the United States ceased to have a national government for four months until the Federal Congress was called to order.
8. Ibid., 9. In the 1780s New York was still rebuilding after the great fires of 1776 and 1778 and recovering from the British occupation during the Revolutionary War. Both the Bowery and Greenwich Village were farming areas. Homes were estimated at 4,200 in this busy port city. Ibid.
9. *First Federal Congress*, 1:vii–viii.
10. Rakove, *Beginnings of National Politics*, 199.
11. Burnett, *Continental Congress*, 816–17. "Tench Coxe to James Madison. New York 27th Jany. 1789."
12. Madison, *Papers*, 12:38. "To Thomas Jefferson. New York. March 29, 1789."
13. *First Federal Elections*, 3:197.
14. Ibid., 3:436.
15. Ibid., 3:369. "Alexander Hamilton to Theodore Sedgewick, New York, 29 January 89 (excerpt)."
16. Ibid., 3:62.
17. Bickford, *Birth*, 51. The population of congressional districts throughout the newly formed Union was at best a guess, as was the number of apportioned seats in the first House. The first census was taken in 1790–91 (Art. I, Sec. 2, Par. 3 of the Constitution) and reapportionment was made, according to the more accurate figures, during the Third Congress. Ibid.
18. *First Federal Elections*, 3:144. "Abraham Clark to Jonathan Dayton. March."
19. Bickford, *Birth*, 16.
20. Rutland, *Ordeal*, 297.
21. Madison, *Papers* 12:14–15. "From Thomas Jefferson. Paris Mar. 15: 1789."
22. Schwartz, *Bill of Rights*, 2:983.
23. *First Federal Elections*, 2:16. "A Citizen of New Haven, *New Haven Gazette*, 18 December." James Madison identified Roger Sherman in a letter to John Randolph. Ibid., 2:17 *fn*1.
24. Madison, *Writings*, 43. "From John Fitch. Philadelphia April 2nd. 1789."
25. Van Doren, *Franklin*, 768–69.
26. Washington, *Writings*, 30:238. "To Samuel Vaughan. Mount Vernon, March 21, 1789."

27. Ibid., 30:239–40.
28. Flexner, *Washington*, 172–73.
29. Freeman, *Washington*, 6:159.
30. Madison, *Papers*, 12:41–43. "From George Washington. Mount Vernon March 30th. 1789."
31. Ibid., 12:42.
32. Washington, *Writings*, 30:268. "To the Acting Secretary at War. Mount Vernon, April 1. 1789."
33. Madison, *Papers*, 12:121. "Editorial Note."

Chapter 11

1. Bickford, *Birth*, 16.
2. *First Federal Elections*, 4:219. "William Smith to Otho Holland Williams, New York, 6 April (excerpt)."
3. Ibid., 4:218. "James Madison to George Washington, New York, 6 April (excerpt)." "The arrival of R.H. Lee yesterday has made up a Quorum of the Senate. A Quorum in the House was made on wednesday last." Also ibid., 4:224 *fn*2. Eleven States had ratified the Constitution. Thus, technically, of 22 Senators, 12 constituted a quorum, even though New York had not yet elected its two Senators.
4. The New York Legislature was still deadlocked and had not yet elected its Electors or Senators.
5. Ibid., 4:221.
6. Ibid.
7. Ibid., 4:224 *fn*4; 4:232.
8. Ibid., 4:255. "Charles Thomson's Report to John Langdon, New York, 24 April."
9. Ibid., 4:227. "Charles Thomson to Hannah Thomson, Bergen, New Jersey, 7 April." Charles's wife, Hannah Harrison Thomson, was an aunt of William Henry Harrison, who became ninth President of the United States. Ibid., *fn*1.
10. Bickford, *Birth*, 17. A political struggle over the Secretaryship took place during Thomson's absence. His supporters wanted to reward him for his long years of service as Secretary to the Confederate Congress, first as Secretary of State and then, when they lost that vote, as Secretary of the Senate. They lost that vote also. Ibid.
11. Ibid., 17. Mr. Otis conscientiously served for 25 years, preserving every scrap of paper delivered from or received by the Senate for the historical record. Ibid.
12. *First Federal Elections*, 4::222. "In Senate, April 6, 1789." Instructions to, respectively, Charles Thomson, Esq., and Mr. Sylvanus Bourne. Signed by John Langdon, President pro tem.
13. McDonald, *Washington*, 24.
14. Madison, *Papers*, 12:53–54. Editorial Notes by Rutland.
15. Brant, *Madison*, 248.
16. *First Federal Elections*, 4:234. "John Adams's Departure from Braintree, Massachusetts. 13 April."
17. Chinard, *Adams*, 225.

18. Smith, *Adams*, 2:235.
19. *First Federal Elections*, 4:235 *fn*1.
20. Ibid., 4:240. "John Adams's Arrival in New York, 20 April."
21. *First Federal Congress*, 1:23
22. Chinard, *Adams*, 224–26.
23. *First Federal Elections*, 4:286. "Senator William Maclay Diary, 22 June (excerpt)."
24. *First Federal Elections*, 4:243. "Benjamin Rush to John Adams, Philadelphia, 22 April."
25. Freeman, *Washington*, 6:235.
26. *First Federal Elections*, 4:219. "William Smith to Otho Holland Williams, New York, 6 April (excerpt)."
27. *First Federal Elections*, 4:225. "John Armstrong, Jr., to Horatio Gates, New York, 7 April (excerpt)."
28. Bickford, *Birth*, 25.
29. Kaminski, *Great... Man*, 100. "Elias Boudinot to George Washington, New York, 6 April 1789."
30. Ibid., 105–8. "Philadelphia *Federal Gazette*, 20 April 1789."

Chapter 12

1. Freeman, *Washington*, 6:180.
2. Flexner, *Washington*, 181.
3. Freeman, *Washington*, 6:180.
4. *First Federal Elections*, 4:245–46. "James Cogswell's Description." James Cogswell was a prominent New York physician and a surgeon in the Continental Army during the War.
5. Ibid., 4: 246. "Eliza S. M. Quincy's Reminiscence."
6. *First Federal Elections*, 4:240.
7. Harwell, *Washington*, 559.
8. Kaminski, *Great... Man*, 102.
9. Washington, *Writings*, 30:285. "To Charles Thomson [Mount Vernon April 14, 1789.]"
10. *First Federal Elections*, 4:239.
11. Washington, *Diaries*, 4:7.
12. *First Federal Elections*, 4:275 *fn*3.
13. Ibid., 4:286–87. "Martha Washington to Mercy Otis Warren, New York, 26 December 1789."
14. Washington, *Writings*, 30:286–87. "To The Mayor, Corporations, and Citizens of Alexandria. [Alexandria, April 16, 1789.]"
15. Flexner, *Washington*, 174.
16. Harwell, *Washington*, 561.
17. Ibid.
18. Lodge, *Washington*, 1:43–44.
19. Harwell, *Washington*, 561.
20. Kaminski, *Great... Man*, 114–15.
21. Flexner, *Washington*, 175.
22. Ibid.

23. Ibid. "The idea was that the hero, in his modesty, would have refused the wreath if offered in a more conventional manner." Peale family legend has it that he pushed off the wreath, but acknowledged the young lady, Peale's daughter, who had attracted his attention so that the machinery could be operated to drop the wreath. Kaminski, *Great... Man*, 114–15.
24. Bickford, *Birth*, 24.
25. Kaminski, *Great... Man*, 117.
26. Ibid., 119.
27. Ibid., 119–120.
28. Ibid., 121. *Gazette of the United States*, 25–29 April 1789. The entire account was reprinted, including the General's "card" to the Ladies, throughout the country.
29. Flexner, *Washington*, 178–79. Also Freeman, *Washington*, 6:178. Elias Boudinot was a member of the joint committee as a New Jersey Congressman.
30. *First Federal Elections*, 4:245–47. "James Cogswell's Description" and "Elias Boudinot to Hannah Boudinot, New York, 24 April."
31. Ibid., 4:247–48. "Elias Boudinot..."
32. Ibid. "*New York Daily Gazette*, 25 April."
33. Kaminski, *Great... Man*, 123. "*Gazette of the United States*, 23–25 April 1789."

Chapter 13

1. Flexner, *Washington*, 187.
2. Lodge, *Washington*, 46.
3. Freeman, *Washington*, 6:190–91.
4. Flexner, 186–87.
5. *First Federal Congress*, 1:29.
6. Freeman, *Washington*, 6:191.
7. Flexner, *Washington*, 187.
8. Freeman, *Washington*, 6:192.
9. Ibid., 193.
10. Flexner, *Washington*, 188.
11. *First Federal Congress*, 1:30–31.
12. Ibid., 1:32.
13. Ibid.
14. Ibid., 33.
15. Freeman, *Washington*, 6:196–97.
16. Bancroft, *Formation of the Constitution*, 363–64.
17. Flexner, *Washington*, 190.
18. Ibid., 182–83.
19. Lodge, *Washington*, 50.
20. Boatner, *Encyclopedia*, 1167.
21. Washington, *Writings*, 30:496.
22. Freeman, *Washington*, 6:197–98.
23. Bickford, *Birth*, 25.

24 *First Federal Elections*, 4:258–59. This was reprinted in many newspapers, from Massachusetts to South Carolina.

Chapter 14

1. Marshall, *Washington*, 5:179
2. Ibid., 5:179–80.
3. Washington, *Writings*, 30:326–37. "To Governor Beverley Randolph. New York, May 16, 1789."
4. Madison, *Papers*, 12:139. "From George Nicholas. Kentuckey May 8th. 1789."
5 Washington, *Writings*, 30:215. "To Harry Innes. Mount Vernon, March 2, 1789."
6. Madison, *Papers*, 12:59, 191 *fn*.
7. Brant, *Madison*, 264.
8. *First Federal Congress*, 3:48.
9. Madison, *Papers*, 12:57.
10. *First Federal Congress*, 3:50.
11. Madison, *Papers*, 12:120–21, Editorial Note by Rutland.
12. *First Federal Congress*, 3:46.
13. Brant, *Madison*, 256. Also McDonald, *Washington*, 30.
14. McDonald, *Washington*, 30.
15. *First Federal Congress*, 1:39.
16. Flexner, *Washington*, 190–94.
17. *First Federal Congress*, 1:49
18. McDonald, *Washington*, 30.
19. Smith, *Adams*, 754. Also Flexner, *Washington*, 183 *fn*. "The name George Washington rang more nobly in the fields of America and the capitals of Europe than any title the new nation could bestow, but luster would have been added to the name 'John Adams' by some elegant epithet. That Adams was not, however, completely wrong about an American yearning for titles is revealed by the extralegal habit... to call all government officials, from senators to sewer commissioners, 'the Honorable ——.'"
20. Brant, *Madison*, 256.
21. Madison, *Papers*, 12:183. "To Thomas Jefferson. New York May 23, 1789."
22. McDonald, *Washington*, 30–31.
23. Ibid.
24. *First Federal Elections*, 4:282. "John Adams to Benjamin Rush. New York, May 17."
25. Ibid., 4:283. "John Adams to Arnold Welles. New York, 21 May (excerpt)."

Chapter 15

1. Flexner, *Washington*, 212.
2. Freeman, *Washington*, 6:215. Anthrax, also called "wool sorters' disease," was an infectious disease transmissible to man through the

handling of infected products such as hair or sheep's wool. It is characterized by ulcerations of the skin and could be fatal.
3. Irving, *Washington*, 5:305.
4. Flexner, *Washington*, 212.
5. Madison, *Papers*, 12:258. "To Edmund Randolph. N. York June 24. 89."
6. Freeman, *Washington*, 6:215 *fn*81. Freeman: Historians of medicine conclude he may have had a carbuncle, not anthrax, since he had steady response after the incision.
7. Madison, *Papers*, 12:255–56.
8. Brant, *Madison*, 258–60.
9. Chadwick, *Federalist*, No. 77:415. "A. Hamilton."
10. Madison, *Papers*, 12:255.
11. Ibid., 12:56.
12. Flexner, *Washington*, 215.
13. McDonald, *Washington*, 35.
14. Schwartz, *Bill of Rights*, 2:1017–18.
15. Brant, *Bill of Rights*, 40.
16. Schwartz, *Bill of Rights*, 2:1019–20.
17. McDonald, *Washington*, 34.
18. William Wirt Henry, *Patrick Henry*, 442–44.
19. Meade, *Patrick Henry*, 392.
20. Miller, *Federalist Era*, 21–22.
21. Schwartz, *Bill of Rights*, 2:1024.
22. Brant, *Bill of Rights*, 43.
23. William Wirt Henry, *Patrick Henry*, 444.
24. Ibid.
25. Lee, *Letters*, 2:409. "To Charles Lee. New York Aug. 28, 1789."
26. *First Federal Congress*, 3:78–79.
27. Bickford, *Birth*, 21.
28. Madison, *Papers*, 268.
29. Seth Ames, *Fisher Ames*, 683–84. "To George Richards Minot. No 1 New York, July 8, 1789."

Chaper 16

1. Freeman, *Washington*, 6:217.
2. Ibid., 215–16.
3. Kohn, *Eagle and Sword*, 53.
4. Flexner, *Washington*, 64.
5. Freeman *Washington*, 6:217.
6. Hamilton, *Papers*, 5:345–46 *fn*1.
7. Boatner, *Encyclopedia*, 453–54.
8. Hamilton, *Papers*, 5:347. "Eulogy on Nathanael Greene. [New York, July 4, 1789]."
9. Miller, *Hamilton*, 225.
10. Ibid., 230–31.
11. McDonald, *Washington*, 36.
12. Ibid., 37.

13. Chinard, *Adams*, 228.
14. Adams, *Diary*, 3:219.
15. Smith, *Adams*, 2:775.
16. Ibid., 2:776. Also *First Federal Congress*, 1:86.
17. Chinard, *Adams*, 229.
18. William Wirt Henry, *Patrick Henry*, 2:443.
19. Rutland, *Bill of Rights*, 206–7.
20. Schwartz, *Bill of Rights*, 2:1057–58.
21. Ibid., 2:1050.
22. *First Federal Congress*, 3:27–30. "House Committee Report, July 28, 1789." The amendments here are extracts in a few cases of the complete wording approved by the Committee. Article 19 related to a renumbering of the amendments.
23. Rutland, *Bill of Rights*, 203.
24. Madison, *Papers*, 12:280. "To George Nicholas. New York July 5th. 1789."
25. Ibid., 12:311.
26. McDonald, *Washington*, 37, 41.
27. Washington, *Writings*, 30:356.

Chapter 17

1. *First Federal Congress*, 3:166.
2. Madison, *Papers*, 12:348. "To Edmund Pendleton. N.Y. Aug. 21. 89."
3. Ibid., 12:348–49. "To Edmund Randolph. N.Y. Aug. 21. 89."
4. Schwartz, *Bill of Rights*, 2:1051.
5. Ibid., 2:1066.
6. Ibid., 2:1066–67.
7. Ibid., 2:1068.
8. Rutland, *Bill of Rights*, 207–8.
9. Brant, *Madison*, 275.
10. Schwartz, *Bill of Rights*, 2:1098.
11. Ibid., 2:1104.
12. Rutland, *Bill of Rights*, 209.
13. Madison, *Papers*, 12:344.
14. Rutland, *Bill of Rights*, 209.
15. Schwartz, *Bill of Rights*, 2:1122–38. Also Rutland, *Bill of Rights*, 209. Madison knew that the amendments would be open to criticism, particularly in Virginia. But there was unexpected approval from George Mason, who had written Virginia's Declaration of Rights (1776), led the fight in Philadelphia for a bill of rights, refused to sign the Constitution because of this lack, and opposed ratification. He declared, "With two or three further Amendments... I could cheerfully put my Hand and Heart to the New Government." Rutland, *Bill of Rights*, 210.
16. Rutland, *Bill of Rights*, 211.
17. Schwartz, *Bill of Rights*, 2:1145. Also *First Federal Congress*, 1:145–46.

18. Schwartz, *Bill of Rights*, 2:1145. Senator Maclay of Pennsylvania kept a diary, but became ill and was not present during the Senate debates on the Bill of Rights. Although he discussed Senate business with visitors during his illness, Schwartz notes that "seemingly nothing was mentioned about the proposed constitutional amendments. This tends to confirm the curious point already noted, that the Congress was apparently much less concerned with the Bill of Rights issue than the country at large" as expressed during the State Ratifying Convention debates. See St. John, *A Child of Fortune*, for reports on the State Ratifying Convention debates and related newspaper coverage.

19. *First Federal Congress*, 1:114.

20. Washington, *Writings*, 30:372. "To the Senate and The House of Representatives. United States, August 7, 1789."

21. Bickford, *Birth*, 80–81.

22. Washington, *Writings*, 30:371–72.

23. Kohn, *Eagle and Sword*, 96.

24. *First Federal Congress*, 1:118. Also Bickford, *Birth*, 81.

25. Bickford, *Birth*, 81.

26. Washington, *Writings*, 30:385. "To The Senate. [August 22, 1789]."

27. Flexner, *Washington*, 217.

28. Smith, *Adams*, 776–77.

29. Ibid., 777.

30. Flexner, *Washington*, 217.

31. Ibid.

32. McDonald, *Washington*, 28.

Chapter 18

1. Washington, *Writings*, 30:496–97. "To Catherine Macaulay Graham. New York, January 9, 1790."

2. Ibid.

3. Freeman, *Washington*, 6:237.

4. Palmer, *French Revolution*, 58–59.

5. Madison, *Papers*, 12:305. "From Thomas Jefferson. Paris July 22. 1789."

6. Malone, *Jefferson*, 203.

7. Ibid., 243 *fn*3.

8. Morris, *Encyclopedia*, 122.

9. McDonald, *Washington*, 38.

10. Washington, *Writings*, 30:417. "To Robert Hanson Harrison. New York, September 28, 1789." Harrison, of Maryland, was one of Washington's appointees to the Supreme Court.

11. Lee, *Letters*, 2:502–3. "To Patrick Henry. New York Sep. 14th 1789."

12. Rutland, *Bill of Rights*, 212–14.

13. Ibid., 214–15.

14. Ibid., 213.

15. Ibid., 210.

16. Bickford, *Birth*, 62.
17. *First Federal Congress*, 3:220.
18. McDonald, *Washington*, 61.
19. Hamilton, *Papers*, 5:370 *fn*3.
20. Bickford, *Birth*, 80.
21. Ibid., 84.
22. Ibid., 84–85.
23. McMaster, *History*, 555.
24. Madison, *Papers*, 12:375. Also ibid., 378–82.
25. Ibid., 12:377. A Potomac location that met the conditions Madison presented to Congress "obviously lay to the Northwest of Georgetown, the ultimate location of the Federal capital." The editors suggest he may have been looking as far west as to where the boundaries of Virginia, Maryland, and Pennsylvania met. Ibid., 379 *fn*1.
26. Ibid., 12:381 *fn*, and 419. "To Edmund Pendleton. N.Y. Sepr. 23, 1789."
27. Ibid., 12:419.

Chapter 19

1. Lodge, *Washington*, 2:72. Also Irving, *Washington*, 318; Flexner, *Washington*, 208.
2. Washington, *Writings*, 30:436. "To Mrs. Elizabeth Washington Lewis. New York, October 12, 1789." Also Flexner, *Washington*, 228.
3. Washington, *Writings*, 30:442. "To Gouverneur Morris. New York, October 13, 1789."
4. Ibid., 30:427. "Thanksgiving Proclamation. City of New York, October 3, 1789."
5. Freeman, *Washington*, 6:239.
6. Flexner, *Washington*, 257.
7. Hamilton, *Papers*, 5:488. Beckwith served in the British army during the American Revolution. After the War he was in Quebec, and later in the United States for the purpose of observing events. In 1788 he again returned, this time to study the effects that the adoption of the Constitution might have on relations between America and Great Britain. In October 1789 he arrived in New York City "with instructions to inform American officials that his government was disturbed by the restrictions" that the new government was proposing to place on English commerce. Ibid., 5:482 *fn*.
8. Ibid., 483.
9. Ketcham, *Madison*, 305.
10. Hamilton, *Papers*, 5:484.
11. Ibid., 425. "To Marquis de Lafayette. New York October 6th. 1789."
12. Madison, *Papers*, 12:362. "From Thomas Jefferson. Paris Aug. 28, 1789."
13. Ibid.
14. Quoted in Irving, *Washington*, 5:315.

15. Washington, *Writings*, 30:449. "To Marquis de Lafayette. New York, October 14, 1789."
16. Ibid., 30:443. "To Gouverneur Morris. New York, October 13, 1789."
17. Madison, *Papers*, 12:363. "From Thomas Jefferson. Paris Aug. 28, 1789."
18. Rutland, *Bill of Rights*, 213.
19. Lee, *Letters*, 2:508. "[United States Senators from Virginia] to the Speaker of the House of Representatives of Virginia. Richard Henry Lee, Wm. Grayson. New York Sept 28: 1789."
20. William Wirt Henry, *Patrick Henry*, 2:449.
21. Reardon, *Edmund Randolph*, 180.
22. St. John, *Child of Fortune*, 242.
23. Ibid., 179.
24. Freeman, *Washington*, 6:237–38.
25. Madison, *Papers*, 12:200. "From Edmund Randolph. Wmsburg July 19, 1789."
26. Flexner, *Washington*, 230, and 230 *fn*.
27. Freeman, *Washington*, 6:244.
28. Lodge, *Washington*, 2:74.
29. Flexner, *Washington*, 230.
30. Lodge, *Washington*, 2:75.

Chapter 20

1. *First Federal Elections*, 3:303, 308.
2. Rutland, *Ordeal*, 302–3.
3. Ibid., 279.
4. Rutland, *Bill of Rights*, 216.
5. *First Federal Elections*, 3:393.
6. Ibid., 3:380.
7. Ibid., 5:380–81.
8. Risjord, *Chesapeake Politics*, 355–56.
9. Quoted in Conway, *Omitted Chapters of History*, 131.
10. William Wirt Henry, *Patrick Henry*, 449–51.
11. Reardon, *Edmund Randolph*, 182.
12. Risjord, *Chesapeake Politics*, 356–57.
13. Madison, *Papers*, 12:464.
14. Ibid.
15. Malone, *Jefferson*, 243–44.
16. Brodie, *Jefferson*, 247.
17. Malone, *Jefferson*, 245.
18. Meade, *Patrick Henry*, 292.
19. Flexner, *Washington*, 230.
20. Kaminski, *Great. . . Man*, 146.
21. Flexner, *Washington*, 229.
22. Kaminski, *Great. . . Man*, 155.
23. Washington, *Diaries*, 4:34–35.
24. Kaminski, *Great. . . Man*, 147.

25. Washington, *Diaries*, 4:47.
26. Freeman, *Washington*, 6:243.
27. Washington, *Diaries*, 4:48–49.
28. Ibid.
29. Washington, *Writings*, 30:455–56. "To Samuel Taft. Hartford, November 8, 1789."
30. Kaminski, *Great... Man*, 166–67. "*Massachusetts Centinel*, 25 November 1789." Braddock was mortally wounded, along with over half of his force, during the battle near Fort Duquesne. Ibid., *fn.*
31. Freeman, *Washington*, 6:246.
32. Madison, *Papers*, 12:451. "To George Washington. Orange Novr. 20. 1789."
33. Flexner, *Washington*, 231.
34. Freeman, *Washington*, 6:246. The Boston *Herald of Freedom*, quoted in the *New-York Journal*, complained that "The President can have nothing to do with the people, but through the governments of the federal states" and that he should have addressed himself to "the supreme executives of the several states and recommended it to them to appoint a thanksgiving upon one particular day...." Ibid., *fn*36.
35. Washington, *Writings*, 30:427–28.

Chapter 21

1. Irving, *Washington*, 321.
2. Ibid., 320.
3. Ibid., 321.
4. Palmer, *French Revolution*, 66–67.
5. Scott, *Robespierre*, 85–86.
6. Ibid., 86.
7. Palmer, *French Revolution*, 67.
8. Washington, *Writings*, 30:498. "To Catherine Macaulay Graham. New York, January 9, 1790."
9. Smith, *Adams*, 2:786.
10. Malone, *Jefferson*, 2:225, 227, 234.
11. Brodie, *Jefferson*, 248.
12. Ibid., 247.
13. Ketcham, *Madison*, 306.
14. Madison, *Papers*, 12:467. "To George Washington. George Town Jany. 4 1790."
15. Malone, *Jefferson*, 2:248.
16. Flexner, *Washington*, 241.
17. Bickford, *Birth*, 64–65.
18. Miller, *Hamilton*, 230–35.
19. Bickford, *Birth*, 82.
20. *First Federal Congress*, 1:216.
21. Washington, *Papers*, 30:501–2. "To Governor Charles Pinckney (Private). New York, January 11, 1790."

22. Ibid., 30:496. "To Catherine Macaulay Graham. New York, January 9, 1790."

Chapter 22

1. Warren, *Supreme Court*, 2:61. Chief Justice Jay's charge at the first of these Circuit Courts, held in New York on April 4, 1790, included his explanation of the necessity of a Federal judiciary: "We had become a Nation. As such we were responsible to others for the observance of the Laws of Nations; and as our National concerns were to be regulated by National laws, National tribunals became necessary for the interpretation and execution of them." State jurisprudence varied and "was accommodated to local...not National policy."
2. Franklin, *A Biography in His Own Words*, 403.

BIBLIOGRAPHY

★

The following list provides the complete titles of cited sources abbreviated in the Notes.

Adams, John. *Diary and Autobiography of John Adams.* Edited by L. H. Butterfield. Vol. 3, *Diary 1782–1804; Autobiography Part One to October 1776.* New York: Atheneum, 1964.

Ames, Seth. *Works of Fisher Ames.* Vol. 1. Boston: Little, Brown and Company, 1854. Reprint. Indianapolis: Liberty Fund, 1983.

Bancroft, George. *History of the Formation of the Constitution of the United States of America.* 2 vols. New York: D. Appleton and Company, 1882.

Bickford, Charlene Bangs, and Bowling, Kenneth R. *Birth of the Nation: The First Federal Congress 1789–1791.* Published for New York State Commission on the Bicentennial of the United States Constitution and United States Capitol Historical Society. Sponsored by the William Nelson Cromwell Foundation, 1989.

Boatner, Mark Mayo, III. *Encyclopedia of the American Revolution.* New York: David McKay Company, 1966.

Bowen, Catherine Drinker. *Miracle at Philadelphia.* London: Hamish Hamilton, 1966.

Brant, Irving. *The Bill of Rights: Its Origin and Meaning.* Indianapolis: Bobbs-Merrill Company, 1965.

————— *James Madison: Father of the Constitution—1787–1800.* Indianapolis: Bobbs-Merrill Company, 1950.

Brodie, Fawn M. *Thomas Jefferson: An Intimate History.* New York: W. W. Norton & Company, 1974.

Burnett, Edmund Cody. *The Continental Congress.* New York: Macmillan Company, 1941. Reprint. Westport, Conn.: Greenwood Press, a division of Williamhouse-Regency, 1975.

—————, ed. *Letters of Members of the Continental Congress.* Vol. 8, *January 1, 1785, to July 25, 1789, with Supplement 1783–1784.* Washington, D.C.: Carnegie Institution of Washington, 1936. Reprint. Gloucester, Mass.: Peter Smith, 1963.

Chinard, Gilbert. *Honest John Adams.* Boston: Little, Brown and Company, 1933.

Conway, Moncure Daniel. *Omitted Chapters of History Disclosed in the Life and Papers of Edmund Randolph.* New York: G. P. Putnam's Sons, 1888. Reprint. New York: Da Capo Press, 1971.

De Pauw, Linda Grant. *The Eleventh Pillar, New York State and the Federal Constitution.* Published for the American Historical Association. Ithaca, N.Y.: Cornell University Press, 1966.

Documentary History of the First Federal Congress of the United States of America, 4 vols. Edited by Linda Grant De Pauw, et al. Baltimore: Johns Hopkins University Press, 1972, 1974, 1977, 1986.

Documentary History of the First Federal Elections: 1788–1790. Vol. 1. Edited by Merrill Jensen and Robert A. Becker. Madison: University of Wisconsin Press, 1976.

—————. Vols. 2, 3, and 4. Edited by Gordon DenBoer, et al. Madison: University of Wisconsin Press, 1984, 1986, 1989.

The Federalist: A Collection of Essays, Written in Favor of the Constitution of the United States. . . . by Alexander Hamilton, John Jay, and James Madison. Edited by Michael Loyd Chadwick. Washington, D.C.: Global Affairs Publishing Company, 1987.

Flexner, James Thomas. *George Washington and the New Nation (1783–1793).* Boston: Little, Brown and Company, 1969.

Franklin, Benjamin. *Benjamin Franklin: A Biography in His Own Words.* Edited by Thomas Fleming. New York: Newsweek. Distributed by Harper & Row, 1972.

Freeman, Douglas Southall. *George Washington—A Biography.* Vol. 6, *Patriot and President.* New York: Charles Scribner's Sons, 1954.

Grigsby, Hugh Blair. *The History of the Virginia Federal Convention of 1788.* Vol. 1. Richmond: Virginia Historical Society, 1890.

Hamilton, Alexander. *The Papers of Alexander Hamilton.* Edited by Harold C. Syrett. Vol. 5, *June 1788–November 1789.* New York and London: Columbia University Press, 1962.

Harwell, Richard. *Washington: An Abridgment in One Volume of the Seven-Volume George Washington by Douglas Southall Freeman.* New York: Charles Scribner's Sons, 1968.

Henry, William Wirt. *Patrick Henry: Life, Correspondence and Speeches.* Vol. 2. New York: Charles Scribner's Sons, 1891.

Irving, Washington. *Life of George Washington.* Vols. 4 and 5. Edited by Allen Guttmann and James A. Sappenfield. Boston: Twayne Publishers, 1982.

Kaminski, John P., and McCaughan, Jill Adair, eds. *A Great and Good Man: George Washington in the Eyes of His Contemporaries.* Sponsored by the Center for the Study of the American Constitution, et al. Madison: Madison House, 1989.

Ketcham, Ralph. *James Madison: A Biography.* New York: Macmillan Company, 1971.

Kohn, Richard H. *Eagle and Sword: The Federalists and the Creation of the Military Establishment in America, 1783–1802.* New York: Free Press, 1975.

Lee, Richard Henry. *The Letters of Richard Henry Lee.* Edited by James Curtis Ballagh. Vol. 2, *1779–1794.* New York: Macmillan Company, 1914.

Lodge, Henry Cabot. *George Washington.* Vol. 2. Boston and New York: Houghton Mifflin Company, 1889.

Madison, James. *The Papers of James Madison*. Edited by Robert A. Rutland, Charles F. Hobson, et al. Vol. 11, *7 March 1788–1 March 1789*. Charlottesville: University Press of Virginia, 1977.

——————. *The Papers of James Madison*. Vol. 12, *2 March 1789–20 January 1790 with a Supplement, 24 October 1775–24 January 1789*. Edited by Charles F. Hobson, Robert A. Rutland, et al. Charlottesville: University Press of Virginia, 1979.

Malone, Dumas. *Jefferson and His Time*. Vol. 2, *Jefferson and the Rights of Man*. Boston: Little, Brown and Company, 1951.

Marshall, John. *The Life of George Washington, Commander of the American Forces. . . and President of the United States*. Vol. 5. Philadelphia: C. P. Wayne, 1807.

McDonald, Forrest. *The Presidency of George Washington*. Lawrence: University Press of Kansas, 1974.

McMaster, John Bach. *A History of the People of the United States: From the Revolution to the Civil War*. Vol. 1. New York: D. Appleton and Company, 1893.

Meade, Robert Douthat. *Patrick Henry: Practical Revolutionary*. Philadelphia: J.B. Lippincott Company, 1969.

Miller, John C. *Alexander Hamilton and the Growth of the New Nation*. New York: Harper & Row, 1959.

——————. *The Federalist Era: 1789–1801*. New York: Harper & Row, 1960.

Morris, Richard B., ed. *Encyclopedia of American History*. New York: Harper & Row, 1970.

Morse, John T., Jr., ed. *American Statesmen: John Adams*. Boston: Houghton Mifflin Company, 1884.

Palmer, R. R. *The World of the French Revolution*. New York: Harper & Row, 1967.

Rakove, Jack N. *The Beginnings of National Politics: An Interpretive History of the Continental Congress*. New York: Alfred A. Knopf, 1979.

Reardon, John J. *Edmund Randolph: A Biography*. New York: Macmillan Company, 1974.

Risjord, Norman K. *Chesapeake Politics: 1781–1800*. New York: Columbia University Press, 1978.

Rutland, Robert Allen. *The Birth of the Bill of Rights: 1776–1791*. Published for the Institute of Early American History and Culture. Chapel Hill: University of North Carolina Press, 1955.

——————. *The Ordeal of the Constitution: The Antifederalists and the Ratification Struggle of 1787–1788*. Norman: University of Oklahoma Press, 1966.

St. John, Jeffrey. *A Child of Fortune: A Correspondent's Report on the Ratification of the U.S. Constitution & the Battle for a Bill of Rights*. Ottawa, Ill.: Jameson Books, 1990.

Schwartz, Bernard. *The Bill of Rights: A Documentary History*. Vol. 2. New York: Chelsea House Publishers with McGraw-Hill Book Company, 1971.

Scott, Otto J. *Robespierre: The Voice of Virtue*. New York: Mason & Lipscomb, 1974.

Silverman, Kenneth. *A Cultural History of the American Revolution: Painting, Music, Literature, and the Theatre in the Colonies and the United States from the Treaty of Paris to the Inauguration of George Washington: 1763–1789*. New York: Thomas Y. Crowell Company, 1976.

Smith, Page. *John Adams*. Vol. 2, *1784–1826*. Garden City, N.Y.: Doubleday & Company, 1962.

Spaulding, E. Wilder. *His Excellency George Clinton: Critic of the Constitution*. New York: Macmillan Company, 1938.

Van Doren, Carl. *Benjamin Franklin*. New York: Viking Press, 1938.

————. *The Great Rehearsal*. New York: Viking Press, 1948.

Warren, Charles. *The Supreme Court in United States History*. Vol. 1, *1789–1835*. Boston: Little, Brown, 1947.

Washington, George. *The Diaries of George Washington: 1748–1799*. Vol. 4, *1789–1799*. Edited by John C. Fitzpatrick. Boston: Houghton Mifflin Company, 1925.

—————. *The Writings of George Washington from the Original Manuscript Sources*. Vol. 30, *June 20, 1788–Jan. 21, 1790*. Edited by John C. Fitzpatrick. Prepared under the direction of the United States George Washington Bicentennial Commission. Washington, D.C.: United States Government Printing Office, 1939.

INDEX

★

ABOUT THE AUTHOR

★

Jeffrey St. John is the winner of the Benjamin Franklin Award "for excellence in writing on the Constitution's import and the nation and people." The award was presented jointly by the National Press Foundation, Washington, D.C., and the Commission on the Bicentennial of the U.S. Constitution.

He has also received two Emmys, one for his work in translating historical subjects to television, and is the recipient of the George Washington Medal, Freedoms Foundation, Valley Forge, Pennsylvania, for his newspaper writings.

Forge of Union; Anvil of Liberty is the final volume of a trilogy on the creation, ratification, and implementation of the U.S. Constitution and the creation of the Bill of Rights, all of which required five years of research and writing, to mark the Bicentennial of these historical documents. The first volume, *Constitutional Journal*, was published in 1987, having appeared in part initially as a newspaper series in the *Christian Science Monitor* and in other newspapers nationwide through the Los Angeles Times Syndicate. The second volume, *Child of Fortune*, was published in 1990 and details the eleven-month political struggle in the original thirteen States to ratify the Constitution.

Mr. St. John is the author of five other works, including in 1990, with his wife Kathryn as co-author, *Landmarks 1760–1990: A Brief History of Mecklenburg County, Virginia*. He has written historical articles for the *Christian Science Monitor*, *Philadelphia Inquirer*, *Richmond Times-Dispatch*, *Chicago Tribune*, *Los Angeles Times*, and other newspapers, as well as contributed articles to the *New York Times*, *Newsday*, *Wall Street Journal*, *Barron's*, and other publications.

He conceived and wrote a weekly syndicated column, "Headlines & History," and narrated a radio version that was broadcast nation-wide on Mutual Broadcasting and overseas on the Voice of America in twenty-six foreign languages.

His career in broadcasting includes the NBC-TV "Today" Show; news commentator on the CBS-TV "Morning News," CBS Radio Network, and Mutual Radio Network; and moderator and producer of public affairs programs for television stations in New York City and Washington, D.C.

He is the scriptwriter for and associate producer of the feature film *A Republic If You Can Keep It*, produced for the American Studies Center, Washington, D.C., by Main Street Productions, Richmond, Virginia, and aired on the Arts & Entertainment cable network.

He was a State correspondent for the *Richmond News Leader* until it ceased publication in 1992, covering county government in historic Southside Virginia, where he and his wife, Kathryn, reside.